I Have My Doubts

I Have My Doubts

How to Become a Christian Without Being a Fundamentalist

H. M. Kuitert

SCM PRESS LTD
London
TRINITY PRESS INTERNATIONAL
Valley Forge, PA

Translated by John Bowden from the Dutch
Het Algemeen Betwijfeld Christelijk Geloof. Een
Herziening,
published 1992 by Uitgeverij Ten Have bv, Baarn, The
Netherlands

334 00746 1
1-56338-057-9
Library of Congress Cataloging-in-Publication
Data available

First British edition published 1993 by
SCM Press Ltd, 26-30 Tottenham Road, London N1 4BZ

Published in the United States by
Trinity Press International, P.O. Box 851,
Valley Forge, PA 19482

Phototypeset by Intype, London
and printed in Great Britain by
Mackays of Chatham PLC, Chatham, Kent

Contents

Introduction

There are good reasons for writing a book about the Christian faith which is slowly coming to be doubted everywhere. Here are some of them.

First comes confusion, the offer of concepts of faith, reconstructions and updatings on all sides, the collapse of the familiar unity with nothing new to take its place; in short, the Christian faith in the supermarket and, moreover, on special offer. That's more an occasion than a reason for writing this book.

Then there's the anxiety which afflicts those who say, 'I don't know any more', after living for years by the 'certainty of faith'. That's another occasion, this time more a reason.

And there's also irritation, irritation at the wretched fear of many Christians that they might burn their fingers over the faith, or their mouths: Christian faith's a hot potato which you don't swallow, but don't spit out either.

In this book I want to do something about this confusion, these anxieties and this fear, though I'm well aware that I can't live up to my aim. What am I going to do? I shall be presenting the tradition once again, that's what this book is about. Beyond the hot breath of topicality, beyond the adaptations, the pressure to be relevant or to make something useful of it.

Of course I'm not just ladling out answers: long years of conversations with others, experiences, interpretations made by others as well as myself, play their part. But what is the Christian tradition of faith? What do people imagine by it?

We want to see it differently from before, but what must the 'difference' be? Of course one needs to know if one's proposal isn't to be a castle in the air. The difference is a change of heart. Giving up the rush for adaptation and relevance. Perhaps the Christian faith isn't relevant at all, or is relevant to quite different things from what we would want.

Behind this book there's also a rash resolution to keep a promise. To make a personal statement. Not to ask 'What must I believe?', but 'What do I really believe?'. That's what this book is about. Of course it's written after much reflection (easy come and easy go proverbially belong together). Sometimes I would like to believe more than I in fact do. Nevertheless – what I really believe (but don't always trumpet from the housetops) is the result.

What seemed increasingly difficult as time went on was the form. Should I be extremely personal, in which case you would come across highly individual expressions of a highly individual emotion, and we've had enogh of that, or should I write a complete dogmatics, a doctrinal survey? I didn't want to do that either, it was too impersonal. So I've produced a compromise, in the sense of (a) what I believe, (b) why, (c) and what is to be done with it.

No theology. There could have been, but in theology theologians are (rightly) in dialogue with theologians, and this time I wanted to talk to others. Not a pep-talk, not a sermon, not an apologia (although there's something of that here), and certainly not modernization. Just talking. As though religious belief must be fascinating. Saying what Christian faith is all about.

To end with, a special note for readers of the English translation. I'm fully aware that my book isn't British or American, and in some cases you may find that I describe situations and views which are different from those with which you're familiar. It's a fresh look. But if you bear with it, I don't expect that you will have any real problems. You will probably find that we're looking at the same thing, but from a different perspective and background.

You might also like to ponder why the book received such a tremendous response in the Netherlands. I can see only one reason. This 'fresh look' gives an answer to the question how to become a Christian without being a fundamentalist.

You can skip the dull bits. The tradition of faith offers a means of expression, and you can express your faith better if you use it. That's all. It's not a matter of 'take it or leave it'; certainly you won't find everything important. Only a fanatic will be able to talk about everything. But some effort is required. This book doesn't suit the convenience of people who want to get to know about the Christian tradition of faith on the cheap.

Amstelveen, December 1991/November 1992

The Source of Knowledge: Tradition

I

The Christian Faith as Religious Tradition

'No one has dared to assert that religion is primarily the consequence of an intervention by or a contact with the Mystery in the human spirit. Researchers who take the phenomenon of religion seriously . . . have carefully avoided referring to any evidence of activity emanating from the Mystery itself' (*J. van Baal*)

1. The faith of the fathers: deterrent and incentive

The Christian faith was already there before we caught sight of it. On the one hand that makes things rather easier: Christians don't need to invent the wheel again. They often act as if they did, particularly when they get involved in new structures, reconstructions or providing 'new models of faith'. But that's just an impression. This sort of exercise presupposes the faith of the fathers, using it like a box of bricks; people shift the bricks around a bit here and there until they get a fairly satisfying pattern. There would be no new structure, alteration, review, revision or whatever had there not been a previous tradition.

The opposite is also the case: we don't come into contact with faith directly, but always at second hand. We get it from our parents, who in turn got it from their parents, who got it from theirs, and so on. That explains the ambiguity of tradition: we're attached to it or get at loggerheads with it. Moreover 'traditional' is an incentive or a dissuasive; sometimes both at the same time. The rocking chair and the recipes must come from granny, but with faith it's different. Here people just don't want to be traditional – if they still want anything! Why?

I think that happens because it's almost impossible to separate the tradition of faith and the church. If we dislike the church – and, of course, many people do – then we dislike the tradition of faith, since by definition this goes with the church. So in the religious context tradition easily acquires connotations of traditionalism, holding on to old recipes for life, to the ideas of people who, out of a fear of change, continue to swear by what was always the case and therefore must remain so. Such people exist, but they don't know what tradition is; they have nothing to do with it (so tradition has nothing to do with them either), but bury it in a napkin. It's dug up only when it has to be 'preserved' or 'defended'. Such action destroys tradition.

That's a pity, since the Christian tradition of faith isn't – first of all – a synonym for poverty but for riches. The history of art alone demonstrates that without question by showing us an inexhaustible source of motifs, images, inventions and ideas which inspire just as many new inventions and ideas.

Moreover the Christian tradition of faith isn't as alien to the world as is often suggested. Granted, it's alien to a world in which it's thought that everything is possible, but people hold that alien notion for only a limited period of their lives. To put it in a somewhat undiplomatic way – if the faith hadn't been pushed down their throats so firmly in their childhood years, they would find it rather easier to come through such a cultural rehabilitation than they usually do now.

What is this chapter – indeed this whole book – about? The word 'tradition' literally means handing down; it's a term we use in the twofold sense of what is handed down (i.e. as an independent noun) and the process of handing down (i.e. as a verb). We shall be looking at both sides of 'tradition', but I shall begin with tradition in the sense of what is handed down from one generation to another. Tradition always presupposes people who hand down the matter in question. How complicated the handing down is – a whole process – will come later.

Tradition, of course, includes more than just the tenets of faith in the Christian tradition. Christian customs and usages (or at least what passes for them) are handed down; a style of life (demonstrated by groups) is handed down; church rituals are handed down; and so on. There is an abundance of Christian tradition even outside the church. On another occasion I tried to make it clear that the whole of our Western culture derives from an inherent faith – a faith inherent in culture. Religion isn't just confessed but also lived, and often lived unconsciously.

I shan't be going into this side of the tradition. Not because it's unimportant, but because whether we become involved or switch off

4

depends above all on the credibility of the ideas which Christianity offers. So I shall be primarily concerned with the tradition of faith in the sense of doctrine: *what* Christians believe and hand down to the following generation. In this sense I myself am now part of the process of tradition.

2. *What developed in the past*

To hand down tradition is to pass on ideas about faith. They form the pictures in a great picture book which begs to be looked at. The pictures have to do their own work: either they're attractive and intriguing, or they aren't. Recommendations, summonses, etc., to use them in some way won't get very far. That's not how pictures work. The only significance pictures have is to help us to look.

Contrary to what people often think, the Christian tradition of faith isn't a monolithic whole. It's certainly turned into one, but I would call that a theological system. I shall come back to such systems shortly. The Christian tradition of faith isn't a system but something that's grown up in history. In the course of history, ideas have been attached to it and then peeled off again, so that today we have a whole, a doctrinal structure, which, while not heaped up like sand – that would be to go too far – is built up of elements which by no means always fit together. There are all sorts of things in it that we don't want to lose or can't be excluded. And conversely, over the centuries a good deal has been thrown out, some of which we regret.

So tradition isn't how it began but how it went on. It's more the stream than the source. Indeed that's its purpose: the source is there to form a stream. Hence the call to return to the source says less than we usually think. To return to the source involves swimming against the stream, and that's difficult, if not impossible. And it doesn't make sense to begin with the stream. Not everything that got into the stream came from the source, and – conversely – not everything that came from the source can still be found in the stream.

To change to another image, over the last few centuries colossal breaches have been made in the structure of the Christian tradition. Christian doctrine isn't in favour; the church which hands it on has lost respect and influence (although we mustn't underestimate the number of people who still belong to it): one popular way of describing Christianity is even to say that it's become a 'cognitive minority', just a strange element in the mix.

Hence there is certainly some panic in the church and theology:

5

they're teeming with schemes to make the faith more useful. These go so far that the fossilization against which the plans were directed is turning into confusion. What is a form of renewal for some is called apostasy by others, and vice versa. As a result many Christians are becoming uncertain about the purpose of faith and then filling in for themselves just how much of it they want to keep. There's nothing against this, indeed it has always happened: believing is never collective, but personal. But before people fill in personally what tradition means for them, they have to know what it offers. It may well be that the Christian faith is generally doubted, but of course you have to know *what* you doubt before you begin doubting.

3. *A total view: the decay of tradition*

It's certainly possible to turn the Christian tradition into a doctrinal system, but if we do that we've moved into the sphere of theology. There's even an established term for this, systematic theology, a discipline in which the Christian tradition is ordered by specific principles, gaps are filled in, and shaky notions are strengthened. This is an occupation which is both exciting and necessary, but it has clear limits (schools discuss with schools, theologians with theologians) and there are great differences between systems.

There's nothing against systematic thought in theology, but there is something to be said against theological systems, and everything to be said against systems which seek to provide total views of God and God's work. I don't think that we're in a position to do this, and it can only harm the church and Christianity. I'm deliberately bringing the church in here, because I think that the Christian church and its teaching (which is indispensable) have gone much too far in the direction of a total view, and have saddled one generation after another with a religious upbringing which has simply been counter-productive. What do I have against tradition or doctrine in the form of a total view? Those concerned to achieve a total view by definition seek power by the perfecting of Christian doctrine. But however important 'doctrine' may be, it isn't there for its own sake, but serves another purpose. As we shall see, 'doctrine' is a kind of puzzle picture; and we have to find the One who is portrayed in it. Of course the picture must be a good one, otherwise it will lead us astray. But there's a limit to the usefulness of doctrine, of its structure and perfection, and that lies in its function. Anything beyond it isn't out of bounds; you can speculative in theology just as you can sing to

6

God's praise. But that no longer has anything to do with the puzzle picture of God, which is the aim of the tradition.

So it's too much of a good thing to develop the Christian tradition into a total view. We simply know too little of God to be able to make such a rounded structure. A total view disguises the gaps, fills them in, suggests that we never need to stand tongue-tied and never need to pray 'we know not what'. But the gaps are there, indeed there are a great many of them, and they can't be removed. If we take no account of them, we remain stuck in 'doctrine about doctrine'. That may be good for 'questions' and doctrinal differences, but it's no good for searching and finding God.

The greatest objection to a doctrinal system is in fact the claim that a total view of God and his salvation is *possible*. That's not only too much of a good thing; seeing the whole picture is something that only God can do. For such a view you must as it were adopt God's standpoint. The remarkable thing is that more than one theologian quite innocently does this. Thus I read somewhere that human existence presents a confusing picture, but looks quite different 'if one adopts the standpoint of God'. That's not a slip of the pen; the author thinks in all seriousness that he's adopting such a standpoint. 'Is he then so stupid or so arrogant?' we might ask. No, but he's presenting a total view and has no problem in stating that to achieve it one must adopt God's standpoint.

Of course we don't have God's standpoint. Those who present themselves to society like this damage faith in at least two ways.

A church which talks about human beings and the world 'from above', as it were from God, ultimately makes church doctrine seem very alienating. Ordinary people don't look at things from God's perspective; the real way is from below upwards, from the question to the answer, from people who seek to the God who is found. If doctrine were no longer constructed from above but 'from below', it would look very different: much more human. Now it's a deterrent. It even robs those who adhere to it of what the great nineteenth-century German theologian Schleiermacher called 'a sense and taste of the infinite', and in this way blocks the approach to Christian tradition for new generations.

The second consequence is on the same lines as the first. If the church makes the tradition a total view, then it has to present itself to men and women as the authority which has the truth in pledge, if not in its own possession. 'Let's present Christian doctrine in a way that people can understand,' I recently heard a bishop say. That's plain speaking: the church understands doctrine already, understands it so well that it can even present doctrine simply when it has to. This is certainly well meant, but if church doctrine is regarded as a total view, it doesn't just begin 'from above', with God; another 'from above' also comes into play: a knowledgeable church which talks down to ignorant people. The one 'from above' conjures up the other.

Faith can't be presented like that. It must remain what it is: the account of an accumulation of experiences over the generations. And – I would firmly add – it is meant to attract experiences by its experience.

4. The Christian faith as one religion among others

Moreover, the Christian faith is one religion among others. There's no point in denying that, for example by claiming revelation for Christianity and thinking that other religions don't have it. Nor does it help to say that Christians live by 'faith' and that the other religions are just 'religions'. These are very questionable definitions, but quite apart from that, this whole approach derives from a particular view of Christian religion as being revealed by God and therefore unassailably right. Quite apart from its pretentiousness, it's too simplistic to be true. In this way we deprive ourselves of aspects of the Christian faith which become clear only if we're ready to see Christianity as one religion among others.

So we first turn to the religions that our world knows. We can best understand religions as networks of myths, ideas of belief, rituals and codes of behaviour which are kept in being by a community and in turn keep this community in being. In talking of 'networks' I want to indicate that religions have a history behind them. Millions of people have shared in the process of making them. In the formation of democratic opinion (which isn't the issue in religion, but never mind), the tradition always has more votes than the best of popular innovators. In other words, history explains the power that these religious traditions have, and also makes it clear that traditions have undergone a process of incrustation and erosion (and still do, in so far as they still exist) which has led to a system of elements that can't be unravelled and whose origin is beyond reach. Here I'm talking about the outsider's perspective. For the committed who live with their faith day by day, it looks like a familiar complex.

8

I see such a network as a specific answer to the constantly recurring questions which our humanity poses to us and to all people. Thus the religions present us with human experiences that all people share, which 1. also prompt all people to reach out for a sense of God, but 2. have filled in that sense of God in different ways by religious tradition and developed it into an image of God. I shall be coming back to that in detail, so here I shall limit myself to essentials. What are these universal experiences?

Let's say that all people tend to laugh and cry at the same things. Prosperity, healthy children, vitality – all cultures or peoples rejoice over these. Death, sickness, pain, suffering and a bad conscience – to make just a small list – cause sorrow everywhere. And then there are further uncertainties: chance, inexplicable reverses, the dark future which harbours no one knows what in its bosom. There are universal joys, and universal sorrow and anxiety. There is no culture in which people don't connect these basic experiences with the sense of God, and they have given that sense its specific colouring. In other words, the different religions are different representations of God, and the differences are connected with the way in which the communities or cultures have seen God as an answer to these basic experiences.

That answer is in turn based on prior experiences. The life of generations has shown that God is a power who can or cannot be moved, is or is not to be feared, has both frightening and friendly aspects, or yet others which are divided between several gods – aspects which aren't compatible. I mention only some possibilities in order to indicate the great differences in the way in which religious traditions react to one and the same problematical situation.

The Christian tradition is one of these religious traditions. So Christian faith 1. goes back to the same basic experiences of human existence that we find all over the world, and 2. in working them out connects them, as everywhere, with the sense of God, but does so in a distinctive, specific way, so that the word 'God' takes on a distinctive content specific to Christianity.

5. The many traditions of faith

Religious traditions presuppose questions about existence which are universal, and specific answers to them (shared by a particular community) given with reference to God. What do people make of these answers?

The answers offer a basis by establishing or defining who we are,

9

what our world is and what powers ultimately determine us and our world. So religious notions call for faith. The answers to the 'eternal questions' which they give aren't self-evident, and are reassuring only if one trusts them.

Some people certainly find believing – in the sense of living by notions of faith – a very easy way out of the 'eternal questions'. But that convenience could prove disappointing. Why have people – who are usually keen on their own convenience – stopped believing? Moreover, it seems to me a mistake to think human existence so simple that you can get by without faith. No one gets by without faith.

The shakiness of the traditions of faith cannot be disguised; nothing can be done about it. It's an integral part of them. Religious traditions don't come out of thin air or fall from heaven: they're human work. Everything that we say about what is above comes from below.

That's most intriguing. It means that we ourselves are also involved in religious belief. We construct an idea of God for ourselves (shortly I shall go deeper into the question whether there is such a thing as a power which we can call God, but I shall take that for granted here), but of course we do so in such a way that at the same time we introduce into it an idea of ourselves and our world, with all the questions which that entails. Are we creating an idea of God to match the image that we have of ourselves and our world, or does the image that we develop of God determine our idea of what human beings and the world mean?

For the moment, I go for the former alternative. We create an idea of God. We can't do otherwise. But this results in the latter alternative: remarkably enough, the whole phenomenon of religion is to be found here. That can only happen if our approach 'from below' doesn't go astray; how that can be I shall discuss in the chapter on God.

Religious belief also gives a definite answer to how people experience themselves: as doers, as immortal souls, as disposable articles or as sinners. Religious belief always implies an explanation of ourselves. That doesn't mean that religious belief is to be reduced to anthropology, to holding a normative view of humanity and no more (everything about God is really superfluous). If that were the case, why is there such a thing as religious belief at all, and why does it continue? Religion clearly meets a universal human need (to put it as provocatively as possible). That doesn't mean that God exists *as portrayed*. The question is, given the multiplicity of religious traditions, whether there is any answer to this need.

That doesn't make the phenomenon of religion any simpler. Nor does it make the definition of the truth-value of Christianity as one of the religions any simpler. It's understandable that people should want to avoid all uncertainty and to appeal to revelation. I shan't do that in this book because I think that we can and may establish the truth-value of religion without any appeal to revelation – an appeal which of course excludes non-believers from forming an opinion.

6. Affinity and difference

What this view has to offer us is a relationship between Christianity and the other religions which is one at the same time of both affinity and difference. The affinity is the prior given sense of God, the universal basic experiences of human existence, and the fact that the assimilation of these experiences gives closer content to the (vague) sense of God. This content, then, is provided in terms of a religious tradition which in turn lives by the experience that God corresponds to its idea of God.

So the affinity consists in the undeniable fact that all ideas of faith in God and his salvation, even the Christian idea, are 'from below'. ✗
The difference, not only between Christianity and the other religions, but also among the other religious traditions themselves, lies in the way in which the content is filled in. We mustn't envisage that difference (or better, these differences) too simplistically. They can even go so far as to give different content to the basic problem of human existence to which religious belief must give an answer.

This isn't the place to go further into the difference between Christian faith and the other religions. I simply want to prevent a few misunderstandings.

I begin with a truth which in my view can't be repeated enough. If religion is nonsense, then so too is Christianity. That follows from all that I've said above. We can only avoid this conclusion by giving Christianity a special position aimed at securing its own truth. I have already shown above that there is no possible basis for this notion. I would add here that inter-religious dialogue is ruled out if we begin like that. Dialogue involves partners dealing with each other on an equal footing. Difficult though that may be to achieve, it must happen. Otherwise we have nothing but testimony, and that's too little for a dialogue.

We can't resolve the tension between Christianity and the other religions by the notion that other religions are saying the same thing as Christianity. That's well meant, but wrong (all religions don't say the same thing) and counter-productive. Those who do that deprive Christianity and other religions of their distinctiveness for the sake of dialogue, and at the same time frustrate this dialogue further, because they aren't taking the other seriously (nor is the other taking them seriously). Strictly speaking, the need for a dialogue has disappeared. Why dialogue, if it all comes to the same thing? Moreover, are the differences really so innocent? That's implausible in the light of religious practice.

Far less must we adopt the approach that the God of revelation and so-called natural knowlege of God are different things. That means claiming revelation for Christian truth and denying it to the other religions. And as I've just commented, it removes the basis for a dialogue, this time from a pre-existing sense of superiority.

In what direction do we go, then? Can one be a convinced believer and at the same time relativize one's own faith? That doesn't seem to me to be an easy matter, but nevertheless we can't avoid a degree of relativization, if only because we have no other approach to God than through the tradition in which we grew up. But there are more traditions. I'm thinking only of the 130 million Japanese of whom not even one per cent have accepted the Christian faith. Are they all wrong? The best that we can say is that traditions of faith have the same credentials, and give content to the sense of God against the background of their own experience. Are these credentials valid? We must talk about them again, once we have seen how Christianity came to its knowledge of God in the same way as everyone else.

II

Tradition and Faith

'You can't say that we have no faith. Simply from the fact that our life is inexhaustible in its value of faith.'
'Is a value of faith at issue here? Can't a person not-live?'
'That very "can't" rebukes the sick power of faith; it takes form in this denial' (*Franz Kafka*)

1. *Faith is not a playback of tradition*

A tradition of faith is there to be believed. The very term already says it. Let's see what this can and cannot mean.

To begin with I shall clarify the word 'believe'. On the whole we use it with two meanings. In a statement like 'I believe, help my unbelief', 'believe' amounts to performing an act, an act of trust, the acceptance of a challenge or an offer. 'Belief' in this sense always contains an element of commitment, committing something of your-self to the 'good cause'. When the 'good cause' is formulated above all in terms of social criticism, faith in this sense is also above all 'critical commitment'. But originally that needn't be the case.

The other meaning in which we use 'belief' relates to what is believed. In that case we have in view the content, the set of ideas in which Christianity believes (for example, the Apostles' Creed). In this context 'believe' quite simply means 'hold true'. Belief that God rescues the oppressed makes sense only if we hold it to be true that God exists and acts in the way in which Christian tradition defines God. 'Holding true' is as indispensable an ingredient of 'belief' as commitment. I won't go into the finer points here. Of course the two meanings are connected. What is belief (as commitment) if there is nothing to commit oneself to? And vice versa, to hold a set of ideas about faith means nothing if no commitment is involved.

This makes something else clear. Through faith as commitment we can show that we believe authentically, but what we believe in doesn't become more or less by our commitment. 'True or untrue?' is a separate question which requires a separate answer. You can also believe in views of or about people which are untrue, not worth believing in, and so on. So the question of the truth of ideas of faith (do they relate to anything, and if so what?) is and remains an inescapable one.

What do we mean by 'believe in the tradition of faith'? Not that we have to accept all the ideas presented by Christian faith without any further problem. That would be a matter of 'take it or leave it', something quite different from belief as commitment.

The most obvious thing to do is to go through the ideas of faith (the pictures it presents) and ask ourselves whether we can make anything of them, and if so what. This isn't being irreverent or uncommitted; on the contrary, it's the only way in which we can deal with them. Where does it end up? That differs from one person to another. For some people, believing has become something like embracing doctrinal views. What is there against that? Nothing, as long as we aren't compelled to believe in this way. Others stop at carefully considering whether 'there's anything to it'. That's also a way. There are many possible approaches. One could sum it up by saying that faith makes us think. Things only become acute at times of need or delight – in particular situations, but not permanently.

Why this emphasis? Because believing must remain believing, a voluntary acceptance of ideas of faith based on insight and conviction. The German theologian and resistance fighter Dietrich Bonhoeffer promised himself that when he got out of prison he would write a book about what Christians must believe. All at once he then remarks: 'What *must* we believe? The wrong question. What do we really believe!' Certainly I shan't say that we can't or may not spur ourselves on to hold ideas from the Christian tradition of faith, but anything more than that makes belief a playback, an imitation, and not a personal voice. That can't be. Clearly the tradition is ready-made. It consists of words, images, ideas from generations before us. But to believe is to assent – literally. I can't assent to every idea, and if I could, I couldn't do so indefinitely. Is that bad? Should I have a bad conscience about it? Sometimes people suffer from this kind of obsession. Anyone who doesn't believe doesn't live in love with God. But that's a distortion of faith, a very bad one. Acceptance becomes a condition, and the possession of the faith a reward for perseverance. That's nonsense; in that way we debase believing so that it becomes a kind of obligation which belongs in the framework of 'one good turn deserves another'. But nothing is more free – or more voluntary – than to believe. It's a way of living in which we find ourselves, not hanging on to views out of a sense of obligation or anxiety about being punished.

So in the church we need to be able and to be allowed to say, 'I can't go along with that'. Or even, 'I'm going through a period in which I just can't make anything of, say, the resurrection of Jesus.' There can even be times when people can't make sense of anything. That's a problem for them and the group to which they belong, but in my experience it's quite normal. The Christian tradition of faith doesn't alter that in any way, even if we come along with new interpretations. There must be experiments, otherwise what I shall shortly be calling 'the process of appropriating and handing down' stagnates. As the Dutch poet Jan Eijkelboom put it, 'What remains, never returns'. That's the case with the Christian tradition.

2. *The knowledge of faith as a pledge*

It's clear that, like any other tradition of faith, the Christian tradition of faith is 'from below'. There are people who have piled experience on experience and – schematically speaking – used these experiences to give content to the word 'God'. The knowledge of God provided by the Christian tradition here has the character of a sketch; it's knowledge of *faith*. That doesn't mean that it's a lesser kind of knowledge; it's knowledge of a particular kind. All the knowledge we have begins with an expectation, a hypothesis which we hope will be confirmed in practice. If this confirmation always takes place without exception, we no longer talk of a hypothesis but of knowledge. All knowledge began modestly like this, as a hypothesis, as the acceptance of an pledge prior to confirmation. It's not at all silly to keep that in mind in connection with statements about faith. Faith is a form of knowledge, but it's outline knowledge. It's personal by nature; I would compare it with finding someone attractive. That's an expectation, a hypothesis from which we begin and which has to be confirmed on closer acquaintance. But we accepted a pledge prior to confirmation when we said, 'I find her attractive'. As a pledge, this kind of knowledge is itself a venture. Will anything come of it or not?

So there is knowledge of God and knowledge of God. Knowledge

15

in terms of accepting a pledge that something will come of it; that's the knowledge that is stored in the tradition of faith, 'religious knowledge' (which we must increase, as I read in a church porch). It's the fruit of the cumulative experience of previous generations and depends on confirmation in practice: in other words, on confirmation by our own experience. That's knowledge in terms of the outcome, real knowledge. It's mystical by nature, the kiss of the Eternal. If there is no confirmation, never any hint of confirmation nor anything that can be explained as such, then the faith dies like a plant which is no longer getting any water. There can be no faith without experience.

To sum up: the knowledge of faith goes back to cumulative experience; it has the character of an outline and awaits its ultimate confirmation from God himself. The person who believes accepts a pledge of the ultimate outcome.

3. Tradition and revelation

Does that mean that the Christian tradition isn't firmly based on revelation? Indeed, as is emphasized by the view I expressed in the previous section, I see no salvation in making use of that term, at least to serve as an indication of a supernatural source of knowledge of God. Its purpose was clear: it gives our knowledge of God an unassailable position. But that only seems to be the case. First, others (Islam, for example) also refer to a revelation, so we are back where we were. Revelation isn't a distinctive term. Moreover, secondly, when it comes to dialogue with outsiders we price ourselves out of the market if we not only begin with our own view but also make it immune to any attack. Revelation is always right by definition.

At this point I also have objections to making Christian faith begin with a 'leap'. That's too much like saying, 'You must believe before we talk further'. It makes Christian faith a kind of circle that you can only get into by jumping – though not with your eyes closed. Apart from the objection I've already mentioned, Christian tradition doesn't need such a leap because it holds that every human being is already in relation to God the Creator and doesn't need any feat of strength to establish that relationship.

So is it nonsense to talk about revelation? Certainly not. It just depends what you want to use the term for. The God of the Christian faith is a God who reveals himself: that seems to me to lie at the heart of the Christian tradition. We shall come back to this in the chapter about God. God is no silent primal ground, no deep ocean, although these images have their uses, but an active God who does not leave himself without a witness. According to the Christian faith people learn to know God because God makes himself known to them. But God doesn't do this by revealing truths about himself in a supernatural way which people need to accept if they are to be called Christians. There are indeed Christian truths about God, and I myself accept them. But they haven't fallen from heaven; they're descriptions of God and God's salvation which derive from human beings and are formulated in human language, based on the experience of generations and generations of people before us. They are in no way guaranteed, bear no divine stamp or seal to tell you 'this is well founded'. Even the fact that they occur in the Bible doesn't make them authoritative, for the fact that the Bible could give them authority is in turn a view of faith which has no guarantees. They have no other claim than to contain what Christianity believes to be God's work in human beings and the world. There is nothing against anyone wanting to call that God's revelation, but in that case we aren't talking about a supernatural source of knowledge but, for example, a value judgment of Christians on their own tradition of faith.

So I shall drop revelation as a foundation for the Christian tradition of faith; I prefer to give it a quite different substructure. A substructure! Religious faith, including Christian faith, has been described by a number of scholars of religion and anthropologists as a universe of symbols by means of which people acquire an orientation in life. God, Jesus, the cross, the hereafter – they are all symbols which show us our place, like a national flag or banner.

I've no objection to this way of talking about faith. It fits; it sticks in our heads (and in our hearts). But how did it get there? The argument doesn't answer this question, essentially because it isn't interested in it. But I find the question important, and in this chapter I'm trying to give an answer to it - in my own way. How did God and his salvation get into our heads (and our hearts)?

4. Tradition as a chart

Why did the Christian tradition hand down its sketch of God? Because its function is to be a chart, a picture or sign set up by previous generations to help new generations to find their way to God. Without a sign or a picture you don't know where to direct your search. Everything can be God, so to speak, or nothing. And even if we *are* armed with a plan or chart, we can get terribly confused. The picture can have errors in it, be wrongly drawn and invite us to regard as experiences of God what cannot be an experience of God. Those are complications in religious traditions – including the Christian tradition – as a chart, but I shall leave them aside for the moment.

As I showed in the previous section, this chart is the fruit of experience and depends on experience – the experience of subsequent generations – for its ongoing existence. I'm convinced that in saying this I've put the whole structure of Christian teaching on another basis, and for some people disturbed its foundations. But that's nothing to be afraid of; on the contrary, it's reassuring, because it's characteristic of an exploration. If we regard the Christian tradition that we learned earlier as a chart, we can deal with it in a much more relaxed way. The tradition isn't just there to be 'swallowed'; it's there to be followed. Christian truth isn't absolute truth; it's capable of improvement. It can come up against telling opposition, fail to find confirmatory experiences, or find that experiences turn into counter-experiences, and so on. At all events, Christians can no longer be fundamentalists.

Not only are all people of good will involved in this exploration, as the philosopher Aratus said (and the apostle Paul agreed with him), but those who search will be in a community which believes a good deal. Those who seek will find.

And the finding itself? The finding is the test which we may apply to any chart, including the Christian one. We can't think of a better test; it fits in with our normal way of checking. If anyone makes an assertion and we want to discover whether it's true, we must test it; and all tests, even the most complicated, go back to their most simple demonstration: experience. We must deal with the Christian tradition in the same way. As a tradition of faith it claims to convey information; it confronts us with statements about God which it expects us to regard as true. Now what is more natural than to put these statements to the test that I've just called experience? This can consist in only one thing: finding the One who is indicated to us in the chart. Of course, anyone can join in the testing, indeed all are even invited to do so; to put it more strongly, they're needed. The more people join in, the firmer will be the final result of the test. You can do so for a lifetime, and the Christian church has been involved for centuries. The procedure will only be completed in eternity.

This last consideration is one that makes many searchers sceptical and sometimes even prevents them from joining in the testing. But that's how it has to be. People only decide whether they're right, really and finally right (or wrong!), at the end, not before. Today, to quote the apostle Paul, our knowledge is still like 'seeing through a glass darkly', but in the end we shall see 'face to face'. Now we know in part, but then I shall 'know even as I myself am known'.

5. The language of tradition

Tradition and communication belong together. First of all, in a vertical direction, tradition is there for communication with God. In the previous paragraph I called that 'finding'.

At the same time the tradition serves to communicate horizontally; it's the way in which people understand one another when they talk about God. Views about religion are always shared views; we get the language in which they are expressed free, from the tradition. It forms the means of expression; with the help of this language we can talk about God. If we don't get it from the beginning, then we have to learn it or we're struck dumb. People who for one reason or another (e.g. out of perplexity) stop talking of God are ultimately unable to do so. Indeed, the same is true of people who have spoken too much about God.

Means of expression are the precondition for communication. Sin, grace, reconciliation, creation, God – these are words, not definitions, far less dogmas which you can sell over the counter like hot cakes. When I call them means of expression I'm leaving the content open. That isn't a matter for regret; on the contrary, it creates the conditions for an ongoing discussion of tradition, for example in terms of 'What do you mean by it?'

Doesn't that end up in 'the language of Canaan'? Sometimes. There are people who have no other language at their disposal than the stereotyped language of tradition. Why should we speak disparagingly about them? Because this language consists of clichés? But what is a cliché for some people is living language for others. Listen to young people talking about pop music and you keep hearing the same thing. But surely they must mean something by it?

As I've already said often, it's all right as long as we aren't forced to accept this terminology as a hallmark of the truth. Of course it isn't that; on the contrary, it is and remains clumsy language, the sign of a lack of integration of faith into life as it is lived.

Two more things. The means of expression that the language of tradition gives us establishes communication not only between people living today but also between us and the past, the generations before us, and the future, the generations still to come. Tradition is a heritage; we are blessed by it and can in our turn bless those who come after us with it. I see that as an extraordinarily formative aspect of the Christian tradition.

So one last word about tradition as 'doctrine'. That's a somewhat narrower term, with a different accent. In Christian doctrine God and his work are so to speak expressed in more or less fixed formulae. This is a risky but indispensable form of transmission from one generation to another. Doctrine transmutes the gold of tradition into currency. So the Christian church can begin a catechism, give instruction, provoke theological reflection, enter into discussion about the content of the Christian chart and other things. Nor is that all. 'Doctrine' also contains something of a view of life, of the self-interpretation of a community, even of a world-view. Doctrine is an orientation for life streamlined for daily use, relative but indispensable.

III

Tradition and Interpretation

'One can judge a metaphor only when one achieves insight' (*J.J.van Ess*)

1. Appropriating and handing on

As happens with traditions, the Christian tradition of faith is appropriated and handed on. With these words I am describing a complicated process which determines the form in which we meet it. If there were no tradition of faith, faith wouldn't need to be so complicated. For although faith has to be formulated if one is to talk about it, faith isn't a formula which we get into our heads, but a message of salvation which we appropriate. It provokes emotions and calls for assent which affects us to the very ground of our existence. Moreover, we always receive the tradition of faith in the form in which previous generations have appropriated it and – if it is good – hand it on to subsequent generations in the form in which we have appropriated it. Of course there can be handing on without appropriation (you can hear that from parrots), but in that case the faith becomes a formula, and formulas don't grab people. A good deal of the speechlessness of people who are perplexed over their faith arises from this. Their faith has remained something alien. In turn, to use a phrase of the Dutch writer Godfried Bomans, they hand on the box unopened. In this way the handing on dies its own, gentle, death.

As I've said, the form in which the Christian faith is received is that of appropriation. The fingerprints of previous generations are on it, and when our grandchildren come into contact with it, our fingerprints will be on it too. That explains why the Christian tradition of faith – like all religious traditions – depends on explanation and interpretation, today perhaps even more than before. The appropriation and handing down is much less collective in our day than in previous centuries, and has much more of an individualistic colouring. That's all right. As I showed earlier, the Christian tradition can take all kinds of personal interpretations. Sometimes they're so interesting that they're worth handing down further. Then a theology comes to be called a 'theology of peace', a 'theology of work', 'feminist theology', and so on, and that in turn can be given a further, personal label (Mary Daly offers a different feminist theology from that of Rosemary Radford Ruether). All too many of these 'theologies' then become mayflies, or rather they seem to be. You can think all too quickly that your personal discovery has world stature. At all events we mustn't confuse personal interpretation with the tradition, even if it comes from a theologian of stature.

With tradition it was only too simple to say: here is the real message, and there you have the fingerprints of those who handed it down. Interpretation would then amount to taking the message out of the packing. But that's the problem: what is the message and what is the packing? And what instrument can you use to separate the two? These questions become acute when we get to the first witnesses, the New Testament. The New Testament speaks to us in terms of a culture and a time which is a long way away. What does it seek to say to us? What are we to call the fingerprints and what the message? We need to solve this question if we're to appropriate the message and hand it on. How? The appropriation and the handing down are themselves the solution. We appropriate a message when we 'understand' it, and to 'understand' it means that we've brought it into our own world of life and thought. Only when that has happened can we hand it down further.

2. Exposition and interpretation

So interpretation, in terms of 'what it says to me' and 'what it does to me', is necessary; tradition presupposes insight into the significance of the expressions that are handed down. 'We're in it too' (and not just our ancestors) is thus not a brutal observation but an inescapable link in the chain of those engaged in handing down. Without us, our generation, the process comes to a halt. We aren't the criterion; no single generation is. For the tradition transcends us. But our exposition and interpretation are indispensable.

Expound and interpret, two words. I use 'expound' more as a bridging of the historical distance, for example the distance between a culture of farmers and their agricultural language and the culture of the high-tech industry in which we find ourselves. I use 'interpret' to denote searching for the meaning of the tradition of faith. Do we provide this meaning or do we discover it? Both, but in the following order: we provide because we discover. That is – again – to do justice to the priority of the tradition over those who appropriate it and hand it on.

The interpretation of the tradition can have a great many sides, but not all sides. One criterion for distinguishing between acceptable and unacceptable exposition can sometimes be the question 'what did the author mean?'. However, that becomes difficult when there has been more than one hand in a work. Much is possible, except what cannot be right because the exegete isn't reading what is there. For example, to say that resurrection is a call to rebellion doesn't seem to me to be the intent of the evangelists and apostles (although rebellion is sometimes necessary). The English words are similar, but the metaphor of resurrection which we find in the New Testament has nothing to do with rebellion.

In the appropriating and handing down (and thus in the interpreting) we must learn from trial and error. This book, too, is 'trial', and least of all a word that mustn't be contradicted. Trial and error isn't a disturbing way. The Christian tradition of faith doesn't just need structures of plausibility; it also creates its own plausibility. At least, it does so if it offers something and doesn't end up in folklore. That's where tradition differs. We have to maintain folklore if it is to continue to exist; it lives by traditionalism. But it is thanks to tradition that we continue to exist.

3. Transferred use of ideas: metaphor

Next a section with an insight which in my view is essential for understanding the Christian tradition of faith well, and above all for dealing with it fruitfully. To talk about God and his work, religious faith, including the Christian version of it, makes use of language in a transferred way. For the sake of brevity I shall call this metaphor.

A metaphor is a form of pictorial language which people regularly make use of, but it's of a particular kind. To 'cross on the zebra' is a metaphor. A zebra is an animal with black and white stripes and at a particular moment someone thought that pedestrian crossings resembled a zebra. However, that piece of the street isn't a real zebra; we use something of this zebra (the striped skin) to describe the crossing.

Now this is simply a matter of terminology in a particular

expression. Metaphors can extend further, and in this chapter at any rate – and elsewhere in this book – by metaphor I shall mean above all the transferred use of ideas and even whole complexes of ideas. Here's an example. A local weekly said that the mayor had been able to pilot his proposal safely through the council. That's a metaphor in which the mayor is seen as a pilot, and the council as a dangerous stretch of water. However, he isn't a pilot and his council aren't of course a stretch of sea; rather, the journalist who wanted to describe the mayor seized on the idea because it gave what he at any rate thought was good information about him.

Thus metaphors involve 1. transferred use of facts known to us which 2. are applied to something or someone else, in order 3. to give characteristic information about this someone or that something, 4. on the basis of an accord which speakers think they can see between such a known fact and the people or things about which they want to give information.

In this sense all language about God, all religious use of language, has the character of metaphor. No one has ever seen God, so we can't express ourselves other than in terms that we derive from the reality known to us. I say 'terms', but that isn't enough. I must say 'ideas'; there is no idea about God and his world which doesn't have a metaphorical character. A metaphor isn't the same thing as a simile. We also need similes in our talk about God and his salvation. 'As a father pities his children, so the Lord has pity on those who fear him' is a simile. Like all similes it makes use of the word 'as'. With that word speakers or writers already make it clear that their statements must be understood in a transferred sense. Moreover, they indicate what they have in mind with their simile. Neither of these is the case with metaphors. 'I believe in God the Father, the almighty Creator of heaven and earth' is a metaphor; we have to find that out for ourselves, and then feel the point of agreement which inspired the speaker to illuminate God's goodness by means of fatherhood as we know it.

4. How far does metaphor go?

Here I've reached the problem which metaphorical language poses to us. It doesn't lie in the fact that metaphors aren't 'authentic', in the sense of giving inauthentic information about God. That's an idea which gets nowhere. You can give just as good information with pictorial language as with formulae; indeed, to put it more strongly, formulae say very little and pictorial language says much more, both about things and people and about God. Of course we're forced to speak about God in metaphorical terms; we can't do otherwise. But in itself that doesn't tell against the character of metaphors as information. Nor is the problem that metaphors in pious language are often so mixed up that intelligent people simply shake their heads. Thus I once heard a minister pray that we should all be made 'children of the Lord Jesus'. 'Children of God' is all right, that's a stereotyped metaphor/idea; but 'children of Jesus'? There's no rhyme or reason in ideas of faith.

But we can survive that. The real problem lies elsewhere: what point of agreement does the speaker have in mind in, for instance, calling God Father or terming Jesus' death on the cross a sacrifice? In this case I am talking about the speaker as though we could track down such a 'first speaker'. But of course that isn't the case. Metaphors pass from hand to hand; they become part of the vocabulary of a tradition of faith and begin a life of their own as a source of knowlege: they prompt the transference of as many features of the idea as possible and in so doing even suggest an increase in our knowledge of God. Is that the case? I think that we can't be too restrained here. Metaphors can be overburdened, taken to absurd extremes, by the transference of elements for which the idea wasn't intended. In this way a metaphor gets stuck, and worse. First the reality (of God) conjures up a picture and now the picture conjures up a reality, as it were constructs reality instead of informing us about it. So the first problem is: where does what a particular concept of faith seeks to transfer to God and his work begin, and where does it end? It's said of Jesus that he will give his life as a ransom for many. What does that mean? If you take the idea too far the question arises: to whom must the ransom be paid? To God? Does God then want to see blood? But 'to the devil' is no better. Can the devil – whatever he may be – require that sort of sacrifice? On what basis? All the disputes over these questions can be traced back to an overloaded metaphor, taken to absurd extremes.

Another example: Jesus is presented to us as our 'advocate' with the Father. Does that mean that there are two in heaven? And didn't they originally agree? An absurd view of things, of course, but that's what you get when you allow a metaphor to say more than it is capable of.

But what isn't it capable of? Who defines where the metaphor is stretched too far, what is absurd, and what criteria are available here? Indeed, here we land up in disputes which can't be resolved except with a word of authority. If we don't want that (and we needn't do so), then there's nothing for it but to recognize that on this point great differences exist and may exist between Christians.

All conceptions of faith have this question-mark over them. I find it a good thing and a bad thing. We needn't adopt every interpretation. What must/may be transferred to God and what not is sometimes very clear, sometimes disputed and sometimes accepted by some and not by others. When that happens, we are neither less nor more Christian.

The recognition that the idea of faith is a metaphor thus frees us from a compulsion to stick to the letter. We see better that conceptions are there to prompt thought, not to be swallowed. Moreover, under the illusion that everything has to be accepted, people have often departed from the ideas and thus from the emotions from which they began. That needn't be the case any longer. We needn't allow the emotions which lie behind the ideas of faith to be taken away by these ideas themselves.

God the Creator

IV

What Belongs to God

'As man is, so is his God,
that is why God is so often mocked' (*J.W. Goethe*)

1. *Do we know anything about God?*

For believers God is a key word, a code which opens or closes the
door to another world. For this reasons it is also the most used, not
to say misused, word in the religious vocabulary. Ministers and
priests use it too much or, in reaction, stop using it. And those who
aren't professional believers are too confused to talk of God.

Between much-used and confused comes the question of what we
really know. Can we know anything about God? Isn't the notion of
'God' already highly remarkable, literally 'plucked out of thin air'?
And isn't the infinite variety of meanings that people have given to
this notion a clear sign that illusions which we ourselves have created
have led us astray and that we're at the mercy of any fashionable
whim or idea? Who tells me that God exists and does so in the form
described by Christianity?

That's a modern question. In Luther's time, believers asked anxi-
ously whether God was a gracious God, and there was no doubt as
to God's existence. But we doubt, with all the guilt feelings which
that involves, not to mention the anxieties which arise as a result.
Some Christians break out in a sweat when they see that even believers
can be overcome by fundamental doubt.

So an answer must be given. If it isn't, or if we can't investigate the
question in at least a satisfactory way, the reader can forget the rest
of this book. For down to the last page it is a closer description of
what Christians mean by 'God', who God is and what God does. To
pick just one issue: the assessment of an individual called Jesus of
Nazareth depends on this. Jesus is important only because and to the

extent that God is important. If nothing can be said about God, then Jesus goes, and not only Jesus but the whole of the Christian tradition.

So back to the question whether God exists. Is there an answer to it? Certainly, and not just the prevarication that 'existing' doesn't apply to God. God is said to be too great to exist: only creatures exist. That seems to me to be a dead end. Everything exists in its own way. A stone doesn't exist as a human being exists, and love doesn't exist as a language does. So, too, God doesn't exist (if God exists) in the manner of a creature. But that doesn't mean that God doesn't exist or that we must be content with saying that God 'exists' in quotation marks (because God doesn't really exist). In that case we get in a muddle with language, because while you can write quotation marks, you can't hear them. So that's no help, and people no longer understand if they're told that they may say that God 'exists' in quotation marks, but not that God exists. Another thing that can help is that doubt is a typically Western phenomenon, entirely bound up with our culture, with its relativizing and self-confidence. If we look at the religions of countries like India or at the religion of the Islamic world, we get quite a different picture. In the light of the world religions, to say 'God does not exist' is greater nonsense than to say 'God exists'.

The most appropriate answer – an answer in which we ourselves become involved by putting the matter to the test – is to ask the question with which I began this passage: who told me that God exists? In the literal sense it was my grandfather and my grandmother. Or more broadly (for they too heard it from someone), the Christian tradition of faith says that. So the real question is: how did our forebears acquire this knowledge, and how can we know that it's right (if it is right)? I shall devote the present chapter to answering these (and related) questions.

I don't start from the presupposition that a rational answer to this question will help anyone to faith. Few people will abandon their doubts on the basis of rational arguments. But they might come to doubt their doubt.

2. God didn't begin with Christianity

All believers begin with their own belief: it can't be otherwise. That doesn't, however, exclude the need to give a reason for it. When we add an acquaintance with other religions, this need becomes a necessity. Where does Christianity come from, and why do so many other religious traditions exist alongside Christianity?

The historical course of events can give us some answer here. Christianity is inconceivable without the faith of Israel, which preceded it. I would simply point to the compilation of the Bible, in which the Christian church took up not only the story of Jesus (and the interpretation of it), but also the Jewish Holy Scriptures – as the so-called Old Testament. I would note in passing that Islam, too, is a post-Jewish, even a post-Christian, religion. And Israel in turn stands on the shoulders of Semitic religion, which in turn is inconceivable without its predecessors. I leave aside the question whether we have to see this course of events as a rising line (although I think that this view has good credentials) and simply state that all kinds of schemes of God and his salvation preceded Christianity. According to the famous phenomenologist G. van der Leeuw, the Christian God is a latecomer in the pantheon of the gods.

That brings me to the word 'God'. Originally it was an adjectival noun: God = godly. An event, a happening, a power which people sensed was given a label: it was of a different order, an order which exceeds human measure. Classical Greek mythology is constructed on the adjectival use of the word 'God', and the gods which Israel encountered in the Semitic world are of the same kind. They are more or less personified powers which represented a 'surplus value' for the community, for example fertility for farmers and vital physical power for conquerors.

Greek philosophy taught Western culture not to depend on a multiplicity of gods. Plato finally dismissed them: to accept many gods means accepting conflict in God (Homer's gods go around fighting), and that's incompatible with the term God. But a glimmer of that additional use of the term (God = divine) remains in his writing. From Israel we've learned not only that there is only one God (monotheism), but also and at the same time that God isn't an adjectival noun (godly), but a being with a personal colouring, characterized by power and will (theism). I shall come back to that, but first of all we must pause over the history (and the use) of the word God.

An adjectival noun thus first became an independent noun, a concept, and later, when all its rivals had been shaken off, a term for the God of Christian faith who at the same time was the only God. This is a confusing outcome, since only a name is unique (consequently, earlier, the gods had names). If we make the word

31

'God' a name by reserving it for the God of Christianity, then it lies in a kind of no man's land between name and concept. It has something of both about it, and that causes problems. If we understand the word God as a name, then the theologians who argue that God cannot be a concept are right. If the word is a concept, then it becomes clear why there are a number of gods. A concept is always open, and can be applied to more than one thing. For example, the concept 'table' is open, and we can use it for a top on one leg or four legs, for square and round tops, high and low – all these are still tables as long as they display at least one or two essential characteristics of the term table. So, too, there are candidates for the term God. The history of religion is eloquent testimony to this.

Must we choose between name and concept? No, there is more than one reason why it is better to keep this ambiguity. I can demonstrate that by a famous story from the Old Testament, contained in I Kings 18.20-46. According to this story, the prophet Elijah arranges a kind of test on Mount Carmel to show who the true God is: Baal, the name of one of the fertility gods (very popular with the farmers!), or the LORD, the classic translation for the name of Israel's God. Leaving aside the finer points, the test amounts to giving an answer by fire from heaven which has to set light to the sacrifice which has been prepared: will it come from Baal or from the LORD? The challenge is thus in terms of 'Will the true God stand up?'

After the priests of Baal have called on the name of their God ('but there was no voice; no one answered, no one heeded'), it is Elijah's turn to call on the name of the LORD. And then it happens: fire shoots from heaven and consumes the whole sacrifice.

'And when all the people saw it, they fell on their faces and said: "The LORD, he is God; the LORD, he is God" ' (v.39).

What gives the story its tension is this test: who now is really God, Baal or the LORD? But this again presupposes that God is a concept. Only the LORD is God. It follows from this that in order to call the LORD God, the word God must already have been known (and comprehensible). What about that?

3. Where does the sense of God come from?

We use words to indicate concepts, or if the term 'concept' already presupposes too much reflection, we can also speak of 'sensing'. One

32

of the most enigmatic facts about our culture is the sense of God. How do we arrive at it?

On the basis of the story of the prophet Elijah (see the previous section) we noted that the word God 1. has to go back to a shared sense and 2. moreover to a sense which must have had a recognizable content, otherwise the invocation wouldn't make sense. So logically in the statement 'the LORD is God' some sort of God precedes knowledge of the LORD as God.

That's a remarkable fact, because we usually begin from the notion that God is the result of particular, deep, human experiences: it's from such experiences that the word 'God' so to speak emerges. I've even claimed that myself, but it isn't accurate enough. Certainly, people identify particular experiences with the help of the words God and godly, but the sense itself doesn't come from the experience; on the contrary, it's because of the presence of this sense that experiences are explained as experience of God. This last entails – and I shall come back to this later – that the sense of God clearly can't play a meaningful role without being adapted to particular situations, events, experiences or whatever. But where does it come from?

The Christian tradition has called it 'natural knowledge of God'. The term causes misunderstandings; its presupposition is the distinction between a 'natural' and a 'supernatural' source of knowledge, and that's something that we can no longer make anything of. If we have to choose between the two, then I can only say that all knowledge is 'natural'.

However, 'natural knowledge of God' can also mean knowledge of God which doesn't come from the Christian tradition of faith but rather precedes it, and is even the necessary condition for it. Without natural knowledge of God there can be no Christian knowledge of God, as the story of the prophet Elijah shows in such exemplary fashion. But what does that mean? The church father Tertullian says that human beings are by nature Christian. That says a very great deal, indeed too much. But do they have a sense of God by nature, a religious sense? That sounds more modest and more in keeping with perceptions in the religious sphere. But what do we then mean by 'by nature'? The Christian tradition enlarges on this by saying that the sense is created in us. Because we are creatures of God, human beings know about God. That sounds quite vague, but perhaps that's inevitable. The only thing is that we shouldn't understand by inborn (or innate) an inner fund of knowledge which comes automatically, but rather a human capacity to react to the known presence of God the Creator in our lives. Not through a special organ, but through our normal human endowments. As creatures of God human beings are made in such a way as to be able to have a relationship with God.

4. Religious traditions of faith as sketches of God

A sense of God, even (according to the Christian tradition) a sense created in us: if that is the case, where does this plurality of religions come from, and how do we explain the differences between them?

'No one has ever seen God': that is the first background factor that has to be mentioned. Everything that human beings do and have done in religions down the centuries amounts to sketching a picture of God. Not in the literal sense, although tangible images played a role in some religions, and for this reason Israel was forbidden to make any 'graven' or 'molten' images. But human beings can't talk about God without images: giving God names, titles, outlines, characteristics and so on. Even if we say (as Paul Tillich does) that we take back our conception the very moment we frame it, it becomes a name, a characteristic or a description of God.

Now the word 'sketch' is an off-putting term. Believers don't like to call the idea of God offered to them by their tradition of faith a sketch. But I've chosen this term because it shows how precarious faith is. All we can do is to make sketches. Here's an indication of how that could happen.

Religious traditions of faith are collective ways of filling in the sense of God in terms of community, in terms of an image of God, a sketch of God. The difference between them isn't arbitrary. It presupposes universal problems of existence recurring in all cultures which bring about religious assimilation; we could follow the English theologian John Bowker in calling them 'religion-making character-istics' of human existence. The reason why this assimilation turns out so differently is that the different cultures ultimately don't associate the same events, circumstances, expressions of power – I could also say unequal events in an unequal way – with the sense of God.

First this universal problem of existence, the 'ever-recurring prob-lems' of humanity. These are the quite recognizable basic human experiences of all times and all cultures. To refer back to the chapter on tradition: there are a number of things at which all people in all cultures laugh and other things at which all people everywhere always weep – i.e. constants. People are happy if they have healthy children; they weep when they mourn their dead. Uncertainty is also a constant: people everywhere and always encounter it as a result of what happens to them. What happens in religious belief is that these experiences are explained in terms of the sense of God. Death – to give one example of a universal problem of existence – isn't real death, but a 'transit' (brought about by specific rites) to another world. Or – another possibility – it's a state of being kept in the kingdom of shadows, the realm of the dead, where the Ruler of the underworld has us in his grasp. Guilt isn't real guilt but pollution, to be removed by rites of purification or to be atoned for by sacrifices. Or it's also a tragic mistake; tragic because innocent people must atone for it.

People try to cope with these never-ending problems of existence by interpreting them in terms of the sense of God. Sometimes their attempts overlap, but usually they don't. Often we don't even understand the answer given by other religions. But they all have one thing in common, or rather two: they are always attempts 1. to cope with the problems of existence, 2. by connecting them with the sense of God.

Cultures go their own way in making this connection depending on the experiences of power or powerlessness in which they have experienced God (bringing either salvation or disaster). Thus they give content to the sense of God in different ways. Is God the one who overcomes death? Is God the helping hand when nothing else will succeed? Is God the power that one can manipulate when embarking on a great enterprise? I mention only some of the possibilities.

This isn't the place to go further into the religious traditions. In this digression I wanted to stress three things. First, that Christian faith, too, arrived at its specific form in this way. It's a sketch of God, from below, by people who have never seen God, made through dealing with the problems of existence in the Christian way (i.e. by giving the word God a Christian content). I went into the question in detail in the chapter on tradition and I won't be returning to it here.

But there's something else. The primal questions have been given a Christian answer in the Christian tradition. The best way of understanding what the Christian religion means – it means something other than holding a doctrine – is to see it as its own (Christian) way of dealing with the problems of existence. Think, for example, of a question like 'Why am I here?'. In the Christian tradition this gets a Christian answer: we are here to the glory of God. Suffering and death get also get a place of their own in the Christian faith: they aren't denied or smoothed out of the way, but overtrumped by eternal security with God. Indeed, this universal problem of existence can even be reformulated in the light of the Christian content of God: the primal problem is not mortality nor even suffering, but the alienation of people from their Creator. The Christian tradition (from Adam to Christ) can be understood properly only if we hold it up to the light of questions to which it seeks out to be the redeeming answer.

5. Religious faith as a need

In all cultures, the sense of God seems to work by people developing their experiences into a more or less mature sketch of God. As is well known, religious faith presents itself as a need. Even more, the existence of such a need seems to me to be an unassailable truth. It can be clarified in more than one way.

A first fact is the ineradicable need of human beings to devote themselves to something higher than themselves. Human beings aren't just open to this; they actually seek something or someone to whom they can surrender themselves. Is this irrational? Certainly, but that doesn't meant that it's to be despised. The German philosopher Theodor Adorno remarks somewhere that if we had only recognized this need better, not so many people would have stupidly thrown themselves away on Führer, Volk and Fatherland. In this way they miss the One who is really worth their devotion and loyalty: God. Usually they discover that too late and become the slaves of harsh lords and strict ideologies. That's tragic. Religious need can also create its own tragedy.

So far I haven't got further than the psychological side of need. But we can also approach it from the religious side. Martin Luther does that, for example in his Catechism. People seek a firm ground for their existence; they seek something or someone that they can trust. Luther goes on to say that where you finally entrust yourself to someone, where you put your heart, is your God. It's rather like the formula with which the philosopher Paul Tillich describes religion as our 'ultimate concern'.

These are adequate descriptions, but we must reflect that they haven't yet said anything about the true God, i.e. the truth about

God. As we know, people can make anything their ultimate concern. So we're back to the same ambiguity we encountered above. Need very easily creates its own firm ground. Isn't that suspect? Can hunger make bread?

In fact many Christians find the side of religious belief that relates to need narrow, if not suspect. Doesn't God necessarily become the product of projection if we begin from religious need? That's certainly a lurking suspicion. But first of all, I don't see how Christians can speak about God other than by saying that such talk (still) meets human needs generally. And secondly, we can't get anywhere without projections.

That brings me to another question: what are all these sketches of God good for? For the answer I shall quote another classic remark, in this case from Calvin. In his view the history of religion – i.e. all these gods – proves that human beings are colossal 'fabricators' of gods. I would want to follow Calvin here and would even venture to universalize him in order to emphasize the scope of his statement. Calvin in fact made himself and his own tradition of faith an exception: God isn't a 'fabricated' idol. But that gets out of it rather too easily. The making of gods, on the basis of the sense of God, also applies to Calvin himself and his Christian tradition. No one has ever seen God. Even the Christian content is a sketch, and time – if not eternity – must tell us whether it indeed led us to God or only to our own reflections. So we project, like everyone else. There is nothing against recognizing that in an adult way. The question is not whether or not there is projection, but whether we believe that reality corresponds to our projections. Did we see ghosts when we had these ideas, or did we come up against God who provoked us to such projections?

In philosophical anthropology, what I'm describing here is termed 'being directed towards'. People are directed for their humanity to what goes beyond them, a point of transcendence, which puts them in a position to take 'sure steps'. That's a formal characteristic which as yet has no content. Whether what they direct themselves towards really transcends human criteria or offers firm ground is a question which can't be decided 'from below'. For that we are directed to what is 'from above', to no less than 'Will the true God stand up?'.

6. Not everything can be called God: a first sieving

Not everything can be called God. The least that we can ask is for the God in whom a person trusts to last down the ages as God, constantly to transcend human beings and human criteria in order to be able to be the power on which we build. Otherwise we end up with 'the God that failed'.

Here I've already mentioned a factor which brings about a first sieving of the sketches of God which is both obvious and sufficient: history, regarded as a never-ending waterfall of historical changes. History in this sense functions as the criterion for religious movements and religious traditions. Gods who produce nothing leave the historical stage prematurely and thus at best get a place in a museum. The standard examples of these are the fertility gods who were in vogue among agricultural peoples. It was very natural to associate fertility with God, since it was vital to farmers: their survival depended on it. But as survival can involve different factors, for example because society goes over to industrial production or because artificial fertilizer appears, the gods and goddeses of fertility have lost their power of attraction. They are not in a position to survive cultural changes, but perish with the culture in which they came to life.

Thus many religious traditions have perished, and more will follow. Not a single tradition escapes the test, even Christianity. Should that cause anxiety? On the contrary, if Christianity is 'from God', it will survive, and if no one still follows the Christian version of God, that version will clearly have rested on a mistake. Of course this test also applies to our more personal gods. Love, sex, business or a career – you can make a god of them. But if they don't bring you what you seek – and they certainly won't – they're like a reed that pierces the hand which rests on it.

However, this form of religious criticism needs time (if not eternity). We need to do something before then. Experiences which are incompatible with the sense of God, in other words incapable of passing for experiences of God's power or God's will, are experiences in which God doesn't remain God but is declassed to become a part of us and/or of our world. Water, fire, air and earth can never be God, however much the Ionian natural philosophers saw them as 'what holds the world together'. Classical philosophy, both Greek and Christian, saw this clearly and associated God with properties like invisible, immaterial, incomprehensible, eternal, omnipresent and almighty. A concept of God which does not meet these demands does away with itself. That happens to all concepts of God in which the word God derives its content from putting labels on things which a particular society experienced as a surplus value – as for example the farmers did fertility.

Here we have a first sieving of the multiplicity of religious traditions. Of course the basis is philosophical, but it was adopted by the Christian tradition. I quote as an example the beginning of the Netherlands Confession of Faith, a work from 1561. It's a Protestant confession (its author was hanged in 1567 for producing it), but in a compact way it sums up the whole of the previous Christian tradition on this point.

'We believe with our hearts and confess with our lips that there is one sole and simple spiritual being whom we call God: eternal, incomprehensible, invisible, unchanging, infinite, almighty, perfectly wise, just, good, and an overflowing fountain of all good things.' At first hearing, this terminology won't attract many people. Has that to be the Christian picture of God? It utterly lacks the warmth of a confession of faith. It's a wonder that such lines have come down to the present day.

Indeed, but a fortunate wonder. The terminology is abstract and needs further interpretation, yet it is indispensable. That becomes clear when we return to 'the LORD is God'. If we don't know what God stands for, we also lose 'the LORD'. Of course anyone may choose other and better terminology. But first, that's not so simple, and second, it must be able to perform the same function as this abstract language: give a description of God's transcendence. The God of the Christian faith is at all events God; no matter what else we say about God, God is qualitatively different from God's creatures. Human beings aren't eternal, immortal, omnipotent and so on. They aren't even – or at least most of them aren't – wise, just and good. So God is at least other, other than people are, and to express that the Christian tradition makes use of these abstract concepts. Moreover in tradition they are known as the 'incommunicable properties' of God.

There are even some people – including theologians – who find God such a great mystery that they reject any attempt to name God as being a sort of betrayal of God's divinity. That seems to me to be a misunderstanding. Even the statement that God cannot be named is a statement about how God is (indeed a crude one). It resembles another misunderstanding, namely that we can't speak logically about God, because God doesn't fit into the laws of our logic. That might well be the case, but it doesn't in the least mean that we can't speak logically about God in this way. You can have a very logical conversation even about someone (God or a human being) who doesn't act or speak logically. One last remark is worth making here. Isn't it pedantic or even impossible for human beings to establish criteria for God? Certainly, if the issue was in fact establishing criteria for God. But these are criteria for testing the ideas of God that we form. Not to form any picture at all is also a criterion. We shall be bound to criteria as long as we don't want to be reduced to silence in talking about God.

7. At least like a person

Philosophical definitions of God may be necessary for the Christian concept of God, but they aren't enough. 'God is love' sounds much better: it expresses something personal, and that is in fact basic for the God of Christian faith. How did Christianity come to dare to call God 'personal'?

To answer that question I must anticipate the chapter about God the Creator of human beings and the world. The meaning of creation will be explained at length in due course, but at this point I shall already emphasize one fundamental fact: if God is to be God, God must at least be God's creation; God must at least be able to do what we do. God is more, infinitely more; God is eternal, invisible, incomprehensible and all the other things that the previous section showed us (now the philosophical terms prove their worth). But God is at least ourselves. This perspective has an extremely practical consequence for the Christian image of God. What is characteristic of human beings is that they are equipped to communicate. They can think, feel, will, make plans, react, both to other people and to other situations or events, express themselves in words and actions or keep silent and withdraw into themselves. All this together I call the personal aspect of human beings. It is what distinguishes human beings from other living beings; for us only human beings are persons.

Now it would be strange if God, the creator of human beings as persons, was not also at least personal, in a position to will, to have plans, to react to situations and events as creatures can, to be able to intervene at will, and so on. Should he who planted the ear not hear? And he who created the eye not see?

I'm not using the word person, since this term seems to me to be too precarious. Rudolf Otto's judgment on it ('God is too great for such boxes') is by no means nonsense. God isn't a human being writ large, although the metaphors with which we talk of God are inspired by human action and experiences. But this last fact, too, isn't fortuitous, and not just because things can't be otherwise. Things could very well be otherwise; there are religions in which God is imagined in animal form rather than human form. To meet Rudolf Otto's objection I'm saying that God is like a person, but that's also essential for God as described by the chart of the Christian faith.

In the Old Testament (and also, of course, in the New), God speaks as persons do. Hundreds of times we can read there: 'Then the LORD spoke and said . . .' The intention isn't that we should rack our brains as to how that speaking could work (God speaks by way of speaking), but that we should see God as a being with personal features. Therefore God also has a name, as persons have a name.

The personal aspect in turn has a practical consequence which in my view is the focal point at which the whole Christian tradition of faith ultimately comes together. According to Christian faith, God is a God who can be called on. 'Anyone who calls on God in need finds his favour infinitely great' is the line of a psalm which in passing shows how the Christian God was originally a saviour from need and is of little use if humans have no more needs.

The whole network of the Christian tradition of faith, all Christian theology and any response of faith that we can think of, only serves to explain how God is a God who can be called on. So I'm not very keen on paraphrases which see God as another word for solidarity between human beings. I can certainly appeal to that, but I can't call upon it as I call upon God, and it was for that that the Christian image of God was sketched out. Behind it is the unexpressed idea that human beings can also find life in God.

8. Power and will

The move from abstract terms like 'sole and eternal Being' to God as personal is a fundamental step which characterizes the Christian tradition of faith. But this in turn needs to be given content. Or better, there is need for an explication, an unfolding, of the personal, so that we see clearly what is special about the Christian sketch of God in comparison to other sketches.

I shall attempt this with the help of the terms 'power' and 'will'. Granted, these too are quite vague concepts, but they perceptibly take on substance if we realize that they are usually read out of the earliest Christian tradition, the Bible. The God who is thought of there as the true God becomes manifest as a being characterized by 'power and will'. These are terms which make their own contribution alongside 'personal' and therefore can serve as a further explication of that term.

In the first place, 'power and will' is capable of communicating precisely that flicker of mystery that must above all be connected with the personal character of God. Even 'person' is too smooth, provokes misundertandings, and makes God all too recognizable.

But that's not all. Read off the oldest tradition, this means that 'power and will' isn't a bit of theology or a response of faith to a sketch of God, but God as experienced. With the 'oldest tradition' I have in mind above all the Old Testament, but that was Holy Scripture for the writers of the New Testament and therefore isn't in any way restricting. Moreover the reference to the Old Testament again shows us how close the Christian sketch of God is to Israel's. It's a version of it, a variant.

To what experience(s) does 'power and will' relate? To the most normal and at the same time the deepest in our life: to what happens to us, to events which change the course of things. Sometimes they bring us happiness and sometimes sorrow, but we have no mastery over what they bring us. There is a power and a will behind them, a formidable power which can make or break us. And a will, certainly, but what does this power want? Is it a good power, a power which is well-disposed towards us? I imagine that this is the way in which belief in God as a personal being unfolded. Events become experiences of God whose purposes are or aren't to be trusted. A simple idea? That may be, but it's of far-reaching significance.

I can demonstrate that by an opposed belief. Over against God as 'power and will' (in the history of religion called the theistic conception of God) stands God as 'the unmoved mover', the opposite of 'power and will' and the idol of classical philosophy: God as power but not as partner. This idea, too, is of course a conclusion from an experience: God does nothing. Of course all the things happen by which people and the world change, but what happens doesn't point to God, so you mustn't seek God in that sphere. God is far exalted above the flurry of existence. God can't be described in terms of action and reaction, of 'will and power'. Immutability, immovability in the midst of all that comes and goes (and happens to us) are God's sure characteristics.

I grant that sometimes the two experiences – and images of God – run over into each other. But again, they don't do so so crudely that the difference between God as 'power and will' and God as 'unmoved Mover' disappears. That difference is fundamental. It's a nice illustration of the far-reaching difference (in practice!) between two charts: the theistic chart (power and will) and the deistic chart (God remains unmoved). Do we come upon God in the changes of our life, in what happens to us, or must we call that the tumult in which God isn't present? The currency of theism has declined in value in recent years. Many Christians find it impossible to maintain that God has anything to do with events. I shall return to that in connection with the Christian tradition of belief in God's providential ordering of things. Here I shall say only that while we can dismiss 'power and will', if we do, we need to know what we're doing. It's an essential datum for the Christian tradition of faith.

9. What does God want?

A power which can make us and break us – what does that mean? As an answer to this question I would have to quote the whole of the Christian tradition of faith. It's one long endless litany of assurances – sometimes against all appearances – that God's will is not to break us but to make us. That begins with God's name as Creator and ends with God as Redeemer. It's the essence of the Christian faith. It presupposes God as a power, and on the basis of that everything, story after story, image after image, text after text, phrase after phrase, serves to impress on us that God's power, formidable though it may be, is to be trusted. God wills to have and keep us whole.

To cite just one such striking phrase from Christian terminology: with the appositions in the form of sentences beginning 'who', step by step we can portray the face of God. If we reflect that all these sentences reproduce experiences which people have had of God, we can say that precisely these appositions disclose what people with a living faith imagined by the word God.

Here is just an arbitrary selection: 'God who comforts the sorrowful', 'God who rescues the poor', 'God who helps in need', 'God who wills that all people should be saved', 'God who is ready to forgive', 'God who is faithful for ever and does not forsake the works of his hands', 'God who in no way holds the guilty to be innocent' – this is a fixed terminology drawn from prayers, forms of address and encouragements.

God wants companionship. That is perhaps the boldest, almost incredible, summary of all these phrases. God attaches importance to human beings, to every person, to the individual. 'Who am I that he thinks of me?' We've understood the Christian tradition properly only when we've dared to affirm that, with all the diffidence that goes with it.

Of course it can also be summed up in a more systematic way. The Christian tradition of faith can express God's purpose in the great basic themes of Christian belief: God the Father and creation, Jesus Christ and redemption, the kingdom of God and the consummation – the whole Christian tradition as an unfolding of God's will. And this book can in turn be seen as an unfolding of this unfolding. Creation says that God doesn't want to be alone. God wants company. We live with God, it is said, but the converse is just as true: God lives with us. That is typically Christian.

Reconciliation is that God continues to want our company, that God accepts us with all our faults (and acceptance is more than toleration), because God is so concerned for our company.

Furthermore, Christianity says that God gives us a place in eternity; God takes us back 'as new' after all our wanderings.

I must add a note here. Apparently the three themes follow from one another, but in reality they can't be fitted together quite so easily. They clash, as so many parts of the tradition – indeed of any tradition of faith – clash. That leaves the way open for different accents on the handing down of the tradition. We can keep everything under the heading of the Creator, but also regroup it from the perspective of Jesus Christ. I shall come back to that in a separate chapter. For the moment it's enough to leave all three themes as they are. Anyone who speaks about creation is also speaking about ordinary life (but only if it's worth living). Reconciliation brings us to the church as the 'odd one out' and consummation in the future for human beings and the world.

10. God is love/God can do everything/God sees everything

A firm datum from Christian tradition is the chapter on the so-called attributes of God. Is this abhorrent terminology, a reason for dropping one's faith? Certainly, but it makes much more sense than we usually realize. The so-called properties spell out what according to Christian faith we should expect of God. Sometimes we have no difficulty here; sometimes these properties cause us problems; and sometimes – as experience shows – they even get between us and God. That's why I shall go more closely into some of them.

1. God is love – this is the virtue attributed to God by Christianity that is most used and therefore says least. The formulation (taken from the New Testament) makes God even coincide with this property. It can cause misunderstanding when reversed: love is God. That's going too far and would be a lapse into the adjectival use of the word God which would rob God of precisely what an exodus from polytheism signified: God is a someone, a personal being, the bearer of power and will. But God and loving do come very close together in the Christian tradition. Where love is, God is.

But is God love? We can understand the woman who says, 'I believe it, but I've never seen anything of it'. We have to stretch the word 'love' a very long way if we're to be able to express by it what God keeps doing to us. We come up against what has been a nagging problem for Christianity all down the centuries. I won't go into it here, but only refer to it, and come back to it at length in the chapter on God's providence.

2. The problems surrounding God's omnipotence are of a similar kind. The Christian tradition leaves no doubt that God is almighty. God would cease to be God were it otherwise. Nevertheless, especially in theological circles, there is great resistance to talking of God's omnipotence. What lies behind it? Certainly it's also a question of definition. Is omnipotence meant as a kind of irrational dumb force? Of course not. Nor is it meant as a concept which leads to logical contradiction: God who can make a stone which God himself cannot lift. We can best envisage God's omnipotence as 'What his love wills to do, his capacity does not deny him'. In this sense God's omnipotence is power over all things. There is nothing abstract or contradictory about it.

So we mustn't understand omnipotence as irrational force or power, nor as 'superior power' which deprives human beings of freedom and free-will. Here omnipotence would be another word for empowering, spiritual empowering. The Christian tradition has never meant that by it. Even if it made God's omnipotence a kind of pan-causality, it would be setting up this omnipotence as a kind of rival to human freedom and free-will.

The deepest objection to assenting to God's omnipotence doesn't lie in the sphere of philosophy but stems from everyday practice. If God is power is over all, why doesn't God do anything about the misery in the world? Why doesn't God at least act against the worst things? This is indeed a great problem for people who believe in God as 'power and will'. I shall come back to all the issues I've stirred up here in the chapter on God's providential order.

3. God sees everything. This is the bogey-man idea, which is handed on with remarkable pertinacity, both inside and outside the Christian church. Should we, to quote Jan Eijkelboom, have a secret anxiety about 'the one who sees everything, even if he does not exist'?

It's time to do away with this misunderstanding. God's eye isn't the perfect means for the schoolmistress to use to compensate for her failing control of her class or for priests and ministers to use to keep their flocks in order even in the private sphere.

According to the Christian tradition, God is different. God isn't niggardly or narrow-minded, doesn't get cross if you don't look him in the eye. God's eye isn't the evil eye, but rather a look-out. It's not fixed on us. So it's be better to be delivered over to God's eye than to what the Czech writer Milan Kundera calls its substitute: the television camera. Moreover there are situations in which the notion that God sees everything is our last resort. I remember the end of a dissertation on Latin American liberation theology. When the dictatorship in Argentina was over and the prisons were opened, people found a cell with writing on the wall: 'Alone with all my sorrow, Ana.' Fortunately, God sees everything.

11. *The heavenly Father*

In both the Jewish and the Christian traditions God is addressed as 'Father'. A much-used variant of this – on the same lines as 'Our Father, who art in heaven' – is 'Heavenly Father'. For a great many Christians this sort of terminology has fallen into discredit, partly because it opened the gate to a sugary kind of piety or even a familiarity which I personally can't take, and partly because it can be understood in patriarchal or even sexist terms.

Before accepting uncritically what the Christian tradition offers us, or – conversely – approving just as uncritically the criticism of the tradition, we would do well to remember the metaphorical character of this language. It's a form of transferred language, and in this case means transferring to God the characteristics of a human father. But what characteristics?

Not all of them, of course, for in that case we run the risk of taking the metaphor so far that it becomes ridiculous. The important thing is to bring out that feature of fatherhood which has been the occasion for calling God, too, Father.

One thing is clear: this characteristic can't be masculinity in the biological sense of the word. So to replace father by mother makes no sense, unless the concern is really for a form of sexism. Nowhere in the Christian tradition are there any allusions to sexual attributes of God; on the contrary, opposition to the idea that God coincides with one of the two sexes is already characteristic of the oldest tradition. God is quite clearly not a mother goddess nor is God the father god. Moreover it's impossible to draw sexist or patriarchal conclusions from the fatherhood of God. To the degree that this has in fact happened in the course of history (or still happens), the metaphor is used for purposes for which it was never intended.

I would in no way deny that the Christian tradition – from the Bible to Barth – betrays a male-centred culture. That's undeniable, just as much as it also presupposes a pre-industrial world. Anyone who doesn't see that can't understand its images and terminology.

But just as that latter aspect doesn't mean that we have to go back behind industry to agricultural conditions, so the former doesn't mean that we are bound to a culture with patriarchal masculine behaviour. It's undeniable that Jesus and his twelve apostles were men, undeniable that the emphasis on sons is the order of the day. 'You are all sons.' The apostle Paul, whom I'm quoting here, says nothing about daughters. But does that oblige us to do just the same? Where that does happen and people for example want to entrust church offices only to men, they are doing precisely what people resent in feminists. It seems to me even a cultural mistake and not just the overburdening of the metaphor 'Father'.

What the address 'Father' seeks to transfer to God from the earthly father is, it seems to me, the care, the loyalty and the trustworthiness which a good *paterfamilias* extends to his family. God is called Father: God is as faithful as a father, and cares for human beings and the world as a father; we can count on God. If we take more out of the title, want to use it for other ends, then we get irrevocably stuck.

Even with the qualifications which I am making here, there is something else to look out for. Does it follow from this that we have to see the relationship between God and human beings as a kind of father-child relationship? That would make good sense, as long as we think of the 'child' as an adult. In families in antiquity the children were the adult children, the sons and the daughters. However pious that may seem, it goes much too far if we make the relationship into

47

the adult (God) and the child (human being). That would be to make the faith childish, and we can't have that. We aren't children, even before God, but responsible, adult beings.

But what if you've never been able to get on with your father, if you only know a father who kept you in your place rather than giving you room? I don't think that in that case it makes much sense to say Father when we mean God. Although the prayer which Jesus taught us begins 'Our Father', there's no obligation to stick to it. There are countless other metaphors, and they're just as good.

12. God is great/Allahu akbar. Worship

God is great/*Allahu akbar* can degenerate into an expletive. However, originally the call was part of the living language of worship. If we are full of someone, out of love, admiration or respect, we say, 'I worship her'. In fact this is transferred language, a metaphor. Human beings don't worship other human beings. Only God is worthy of our total dedication, so worship is a religious term. In this section, which serves as a conclusion to the chapter on God, I shall emphasize two ways in which worship is practised among Christians. First, worship in the liturgy: I put that under the heading 'etiquette'. Then worship in terms of 'fingers on lips'. By that I mean God's incomprehensibility.

1. The Christian picture of God contains many features which we also encounter in other religions and which were taken from the social conditions of more primitive societies: God is king, rules for ever, God's power stands firm (read the Psalms), and people are described as God's subjects. These are all metaphors from a king-subject model. Hence the terms in which worship is expressed: serve God, worship God, sing God's praise, appear before God's throne (think of the term worship), all referring to the subject who, whether diffident, jubilant or ashamed, appears at court to prostrate himself before his exalted king. Religious piety is as it were etiquette: to know how to approach God properly. Those who know no etiquette don't know how to behave before the Most High, indeed don't even know that they're in search of the Most High. So what is such a person really doing here? For us these terms are less obvious. Praise, honour, bow down, serve – these are terms which we don't like using among ourselves. They seem somewhat servile. And even for God they are unusable, if not abhorrent, unless we see their origin and reserve them for religious terminology. When the minister says 'the

Lord' from the pulpit, we mustn't think of the master/servant relationship, however solemnly he speaks the word. For it no longer means that. It must take on its own religious connotations; it gives the one involved a special position. That's the aim, not the degradation of human beings so that they become slaves.

In the Christian tradition these metaphors have become part of the liturgy, the homage performed by Christians. In the liturgy we can go outside ourselves, to God. The Reformed part of Christianity finds more difficulty in relaxing than the Anglican and Roman Catholic wing of the church. Except when it comes to singing the psalms: that's what the Reformed do best.

Worship can also take a different course from that of liturgy and homage. God is great/*Allahu akbar* is also an invitation to put our fingers on our lips and stop chattering. 'God is great' means 'We don't understand God'.

Here I'm touching on what the tradition calls God's incomprehensibility. It's a confession and not a forced admission. Those who honour God must see to it that they're honouring *God* and not their own construction of God (however dependent we may be on our constructions). So the incomprehensibility of God means letting God be God, a Being who far transcends our knowledge and understanding in all that can be said. All words point to God, yet all words fall short of doing God honour. So the Dutch theologian Herman Ridderbos's idea of the 'empty middle' isn't as crazy as all that: the spokes of a wheel are indispensable if the wheel is to revolve, but in the middle there's a gap: the spokes don't go that far.

Here I'm touching on the function which God's incomprehensibility had and still must have in the Christian tradition. It must certainly prevent us from thinking that we know better. But even more, it must keep us from a God whom we have so modelled in accordance with our desires and views as to eat out of our hand. For some people, if God doesn't seem to do that, and ultimately doesn't fit into our framework of thought, that God is sent packing.

But a comprehensible God isn't the true God; a comprehensible God is a made-to-measure God, and we can't worship a comprehensible God. I maintain that the confession of God's incomprehensibility must be emphasized even more than before. The Reformed theologian Herman Bavinck began the chapter that he devoted to God in his book on Christian doctrine with a section on God's incomprehensibility. I can agree with that. We must be rescued from a good deal of knowledge if we want to worship properly.

V

The Creator of Human Beings and the World

'I recognize the statement "nature is God", coming from a believing disposition – as a Christian statement' (*Calvin*)

1. *Why am I, rather than not?*

Human experience underlies belief in God as Creator of heaven and earth, as it does all conceptions of faith: experience in the sense of putting into words (and thus giving meaning to) what happens to us. What makes human beings begin to speak of God as Creator in order to express their experience? Let me sum it up in a proverb, a question really: 'Why am I, rather than not?' The formulation sounds enigmatic, and indeed that's the intention: we're reflecting on a riddle. But it stems from a feeling which can go through a person like a flash: I am, but also I mightn't have been. This is a perplexing feeling which has at least two sides.

First of all it can issue in grateful wonder at my existence. Who am I that I may be? What power has called me into being? I quote Ossip Mandelstam as rendered by Paul Celan.

They gave me a body – who can
tell me, why? It is only mine, it alone.

Quiet joy: being allowed to breathe and live.
Whom do I thank for that?

The other side: it's also creepy to note that we could just as well not have been. The world wobbles when we think of it. We find ourselves in the hands of a power which – as daily experience shows us – can make us or break us. What kind of a power is that? Can it be trusted or not? Here we face the most crucial question of human existence.

Religious traditions have given names to this power, names which aim to give us more information about what this power imagines and what we can expect from it. The Christian tradition has also done that and called this power God the Creator of human beings and the world. The whole of Christian teaching is simply a further exposition of what Christians mean by 'God the Creator', ending up in the belief that this power is to be trusted.

How did the Christian tradition arrive at this answer? For that I have to refer to Israel, from whom Christianity took it over. And it, too, in turn stands on the shoulders of others, especially the agricultural peoples who were aware of their dependence on nature and its cycle and readily made a divine power of it. The fertility religions – as they are called – are not so incomprehensible or stupid as was once imagined. Nature with its inexhaustible capacity to begin again each spring evokes an almost religious awe in us to the present day.

Almost, I say. Jews and Christians haven't equated nature with the power which can make and break people. Above nature stands God, to whom people – so to speak – can appeal against nature. We might say that nature is *from* God, an instrument of God, a garment of God. But according to the Christian tradition of faith God doesn't coincide with his garment. Is belief in God the Creator the easiest way into Christian faith? It seems to be: don't you meet the Creator everywhere? That's true, as we shall see, but at the same time it could well also be the greatest frustration for belief in God. Luther, one of the Protestant church fathers from the sixteenth century, liked to say that it's much easier to believe in God as Redeemer: who doesn't want to be redeemed when in distress! But in his view, to believe in God as Creator was a real work of art, for in that case you had to connect daily experience with God: your work (or your unemployment), your handicaps, the personal and collective disasters as well as all the joys of existence. In short, God then comes closest to this power that we cannot fathom. Or – another possibility – we must deny that God has anything to do with everyday experience. But in that case what becomes of the Creator? I shall return to this at length; for the moment it's enough to note that belief in God as Creator isn't as simple as it is often made out to be.

What are the implications of believing in God as Creator? For many people, in the first place the notion of the construction of the world with all the problems that that involves. These problems are certainly also involved, but they don't come first, nor are they the main issue. Construction points to the origin of human beings and the world, but for information about that we have to turn to scientific research. Rightly, no one reads the creation stories any longer as the account of a process of coming to be. Far less do we rack our brains over the question how to describe this action which is called creating. For the most part the chapter about creation isn't insight into the construction work of the Most High. We know nothing about this, and the creation stories aren't told to enlighten us about it.

We read the accounts properly only when we see them as a kind of confession of faith that 'the earth is the Lord's and all the fullness thereof'. The words I've quoted are a line from Psalm 24 and are engraved on the façade of the Bank of England in London. The same amazement is echoed in them as in the creation story from Genesis 1. The author of this indefatigably sums up absolutely everything that was known to him (and the world of the time) and says: we owe it to the work of God the Creator. Genesis 1 is a very sunny and positive story, a song of praise to God as Creator. There is nothing terrifying about the varied cavalcade of human beings, animals and things of which reality is made up: it is the work of God's hands, and therefore we can feel at home in it.

But the notion of the 'power which can make us and break us' hasn't disappeared. It recurs in the picture of God who makes human beings out of clay (Genesis 2), and above all in the image of God as potter. I stress that here because only against this background – let us say over against this sense that we are clay in the hands of the potter – does it become clear that Christian doctrine about God the Creator offers a liberating faith. Must we be happy that the earth is the LORD's? Yes, that's the intention. It also could have hung in a void; it could also be in the power of capital or subjected to the right of the strongest. But no, it's the LORD's.

And if we now also knew who the LORD was, we would be completely reassured. In fact the whole Christian tradition also does its best to tell us who the LORD is. The climax, the gospel of Jesus, is in fact no more than further information about who willed us and created us.

The question what the power which reaches to the depths of our existence really wants is thus answered by belief in God as Creator. It wills us; it isn't a jealous, alien power whom we should fear, but God, who saw that what he had made was good. That means that we not only are, but also believe that it is good to be. The world isn't just there; we believe that it is embraced by God, who strengthens it daily; that it is pregnant with the promises of God the Creator; that it is a quite special world. It gives Christianity courage to be there.

3. God is at least God's creation: familiarity

Nor is that all. Alongside the bond of trust stands the familiarity between the Creator and his creatures. The Creator is familiar with us, as the author of one of the Psalms says:

Before a word escapes our tongue, he knows all our thoughts.

How can that be? In a book by Piet Schoonenberg, a Roman Catholic theologian, I read a riddle which is an eye-opener: 'What is the border if only one land borders?' At first sight this sentence is nonsense, but appearances are deceptive. Two lands border on each other in such a way that only one land has a border when one land encloses the other, just as a tyre encloses a wheel or an ocean a drop of water. We can imagine that God and human beings border on each other in this way. God embraces us, but we don't embrace God; our border is that we aren't, nor shall we be, God, but God has no bounds, God embraces us. God is at least his creation, at least what we are.

That is explicitly more than: God *can* do at least what we can do. That's what the present chapter is about. The Creator who planted the ear also hears. How strange it would be were it otherwise! But now I shall go further and argue that God also *embraces* us. God *is* at least God's creation. It is not that we exist from God, but that we exist in God. Our life, our joy, our suffering and dying come about within God. At the same time God is much more than we are; God is not limited to what we are and can be. Little would be left of God's government of all things if God were only God's creation.

But that 'at least God's creation' remains. God knows of us because God embraces us, with all our ups and downs. God also embraces us in our suffering, our mortality and our death. All that falls within God. That is the reason why the Creator is much more familiar with us than we think. Everything needn't be said; really nothing need be said, since everything is already known. I can't think of a more comforting faith in the wilderness of our world. No matter what riddles existence may saddle us with – and it does that, as experience shows – we are embraced by the Creator.

So it isn't the case, I would add, that God knows only the suffering and death of people and takes it up into the person of Jesus. The Christian tradition can certainly talk of death as punishment, the death penalty. But this idea of things also fails to do justice to God as Creator, out of a need to give something extra to the person of Jesus. Here we distort the Christian tradition in the same way as the Greek church fathers did when they preferred to see God as impassive eternity, a remnant of the unmoved Mover. God the Creator isn't without passion: God suffers and dies with God's creatures. And that's not all. At the same time God is above all that we are and do and suffer. God doesn't go under with us, nor fail. God doesn't need to be helped or rescued by us, as our moving Jewish martyr Etty Hillesum thought and many New Age philosophers assert after her. From the perspective of the Christian tradition that's a mistake. God is at least ourselves, at least his world, but at the same time infinitely more than that.

4. What are we here for?

Unless I'm mistaken, the first question in the Roman Catholic Catechism was, 'What are you on earth for?' A classical question, which reminds me of a mediaeval rhyme which goes:

> Don't know whence, don't know whither,
> surprising that I'm still so cheerful.

Now fortunately we don't ask ourselves every day where we come from or where we're going. But of course that's certainly a question. What are we really doing here? Who can tell us that? Is life just a matter of eating, drinking, surviving – as good and as bad as that?

This is the question of the reason for our existence. But no one knows this reason. Our existence is without necessity, without justification in terms of higher interests, contingent: an event or happening that takes place only once. What it's good for – God only knows. And indeed that's all that's left: we know only that we are there to the glory of God. That's a classic piece of wisdom from the

Christian tradition – mocked, well-worn, but in the end the only answer that survives.

In the first place, it also says that I don't know, nor do I need to know, but God knows and that is enough. 'To the glory of God' rescues us from a pile of headaches.

We're part of a purpose, of a game – if the word doesn't seem too superficial in this connection – which is played before God's face. 'To the glory of God' means that Christians say that they needn't grasp all the game to have trust in it. It's God's game; God is the Creator who plays with his creatures, and those who have learned to trust the Creator perhaps don't always enjoy this; however, they do experience peace.

What I've emphasized here – and this is my second comment – is the joyful side of existence. To be active, to do what people do (need to do), to engage in science, to use technology, to reflect on things and so on – all that is to be busy in the Creator's garden. God is glorified by the development of knowledge and ability, by industry, trade, nuclear energy, by dominating the forces of nature and putting them to human use. Ordinary life – not primarily church life – is life to the glory of God.

Thirdly, the game is a rough game; so rough, even, that the word game now dies on my lips. It has a dark side, which isn't so cheerful. To mention just one thing: we may to our surprise be alive and find it worthwhile, but we can leave it only through the narrow gate of death. To say nothing of what can come before that: sickness, decrepitude, exhaustion and pain. Abhorrent things, of which we find it hard to say that God is in them, whether we can oppose them or not. To say nothing of the blows that we human beings inflict and have inflicted on our own lives and the lives of others, and which can unsettle and sour people just as much as sickness and decrepitude.

Fourthly, the game can be so rough that trust in the one who put us in it collapses. I myself think that this is inevitable: no one can persist in believing in the goodness of the Creator. Unless someone could convince us that God – despite everything – is to be trusted. That's the purpose of the Christian sketch of faith. In a sense one can regard all the Christian proclamation which follows the doctrine of the Creator (e.g. the whole of the New Testament, Paul, the Gospels) as one enormous sermon about trusting the Creator. However, that doesn't always work out. There's something ambiguous about creation: life is delightful, but on occasion also atrocious. I shall be coming back to that shortly, more than once.

5. Creation in terms of a view of life and the world

So far I've kept personal relations – trust and familiarity – to the fore. But belief in God the Creator also deeply influences our view of human beings and the world. Much of this influence has become so much a common possession of European culture that we've almost ceased to be aware that it comes from Christianity.

For example, there is a secularized echo in the American constitution of the view that all human beings have equal dignity as creatures of God and therefore need to be treated with equal respect: 'All men are born equal.' That is Christianity which has become a view of life. One needn't be a Christian to accept this social rule, although Christians in particular will certainly subscribe to it and practise it – on the basis of their belief in God as Creator.

That's not the only thing. Belief in God the Creator also entails that human beings and the world stand on the side of createdness, which in any case means that they aren't God or divine, but creatures. There, too, is something which determines all our thought and actions: Christians shouldn't elevate a piece of created reality (sexuality, fertility, the flame of life, politics or weapons) in such a way that it seems to be getting near to God.

What we do much better to say is that Christians – I keep assuming that, but in good faith – are concerned with the creation as what has been made, i.e. all our reality, because it's God's creation. Still human beings most – it's not for nothing that in the Christian tradition they are said to be in the image of God. But among Christians, if this doesn't sound too pretentious, the creation is in good hands. Love is conservative; it keeps what is worth preserving.

Creation in the sense of createdness isn't the same as nature, not to mention nature in the sense in which the natural sciences speak of it. For the characteristic of the natural sciences is that God doesn't occur in them. That's been called methodological atheism, and anyone can be happy with it. But what if it becomes more than a methodological approach? What if this abstract concept of nature in the natural sciences becomes a view of life? This question brings me to yet another more far-reaching ideological element. Belief in God the Creator isn't only *opposed* to a view of life which leaves God out of reality; it's also the opposite of it. To believe in God as Creator is to begin from a connection between reality and God and to see this connection as a necessary ingredient, an element which can't be dispensed with. That changes the character of reality. Let me briefly explain why.

First I stress the 'whole of reality'. The Christian tradition doesn't use the word creation as another word for virgin nature, far less as an indication of the sphere in which we must be sparing. These things too are part of creation and therefore we must conserve them, in accordance with the nature of love. But the same goes for our cities and the industrial production by which human beings keep themselves alive. Creation isn't a term which is meant to bathe the world in a romantic aura. For reality to change character means that it changes status. It's the same world, but it's different. Here's an example to show what I mean. Anyone who sees my wife going down the street will see a woman and no more. I myself know better; I know that she's my wife. That doesn't mean that there's another person in the street: it's the same woman. But I know her relationship and others don't. To see the world as a relationship is to see the relationship in which God has placed us and which helps us through as an essential aspect of our reality. People are free to see this as an interpretation by a group of dilettantes. But that doesn't tell us anything. On that basis, to see the world without God is equally an interpretation by dilettantes. Which interpretation does justice to the complex reality of human beings and the world? That's the important question. The answer stems from the outcome of our history, and thus brings us to eternity. As long as we haven't got that far, belief in creation remains a piece of Christian knowledge, as honourable as it is challenged.

6. Creation, fall, redemption

'Createdness', as 'all there is', is summed up by the author of Genesis in terms of the knowledge of the time. All there is comes from God. This summary is then defined more closely: God saw that it was good. Remarkable! Is all that is, good? That seems too much of a good thing. In that case, what about evil?

It seems to me inconceivable – to answer this question – that the author of the creation narrative knew nothing of natural disasters, of diseases which bring us down or of defects and deformities in human beings and animals. 'The good creation' cannot possibly mean that everything that is, is good. Rather, the conclusion must be that 'all that is' doesn't coincide with creation in the sense of 'createdness'. So one could explain the fact that God saw that it was good like this. Human beings and the world are created good by God, and to the degree that there is also evil, this comes about through us human beings: we have infected the creation. Moreover that's the classic interpretation of the creation stories: it turns them into a historical sequence. First there was the good creation: human beings and the world were in the 'state of righteousness'. Then came the fall of us human beings, and as a reaction God began on the redemption of fallen humankind.

Today we can no longer find such historical steps in the creation story. There was no time when everything was good, a period which was replaced by a time which began with the Fall. Such a historical sequence certainly provides an easily manageable scheme, but you can't make more than a 'teaching model' out of it. So we must give other content to creation, fall and redemption. Creation doesn't denote an earlier event but describes a characteristic of our reality. What we find in it is first and foremost God's creative effort to be human and world, as it were God's intervention in history. And the Fall? We must also see that story as a description of reality and not something from former times. It's a characterization of *our* contribution. In order to describe the reality of human beings and the world, we also need the dark tint of evil, the evil done by human beings, caught up in the nets of their own wickedness. But that's not the whole picture. The third characteristic of human beings and the world is that their Creator is also their Redeemer. To hear that we must go to the church, where the gospel of the Redeemer, Jesus Christ, is preached. We shall come back to this later. So to sum up: we can best regard creation, sin and redemption – the three classical headings under which Christian tradition has been summed up from antiquity – as three descriptions of our reality, three powers which are active. As far as that goes, creation is a battlefield. But we must keep all these three separate if we want to express where, according to faith, we're at with our world.

At this moment we're interested in the contribution of God the Creator, with which I began this section. What comes from him is good. That's unmistakable: God is good. We also read *ad nauseam* in the creation story that 'God saw that it was good.' But in that case the inescapable question is, 'Where does evil comes from?'

As I've already indicated, the Christian tradition has sought the answer above all in human wickedness. And indeed there's no mistaking the fact that our contribution to creation has damaged and still continues to damage all that God has created good. It's a good Christian view, in accord with Christian tradition, to maintain that. But there's more to be said.

Does a tidal wave which hits Bangladesh and causes hundreds of thousands of deaths come about through human wickedness? Pious Christians see nothing against this conclusion. Nature has been put out of joint by sin, and Bangladesh too is our fault. If a volcano begins to be active somewhere and engulfs some villages under a rain of fire and ash, the background is the same. It has to do with human wickedness and is a kind of punishment, if not for the people who live there then, for humankind in general.

I don't believe anything of the sort: those are easy debating tricks which demonstrate nothing except the pharisaic heart of people who have such attitudes about the world and think that others are greater sinners than they are. There must be more than that. What?

7. The bitter riddle of the good creation

Creation can't mean that 'all that is, is good'. And people also knew that earlier. Already in the creation narrative, for example, death is made an exception here: it's imagined as a kind of punishment for human disobedience, and thus doesn't belong with the 'good'. Paul later adds that not only death but also sin, the malice of people and the way in which they are held captive by it, isn't good. And today we would add even more things to that: not only sin and death but also disease, deformities and natural disasters aren't 'good'. Cancer isn't something in which God can be involved as Creator, and yet there is cancer.

So as far as we're concerned, not everything that is, is 'good'. We encounter the 'good creation' only in conjunction with what with the best will in the world we cannot call good.

Must it be like that, then? I think that there's a mistake here. No one, not even God, asks us to call 'good' what we cannot possibly find good. That would condemn us to a daily display of dishonesty, and that can't be intended. So it is we ourselves – if I may put it that way – who may say (even must say) what is good in the sense of whether or not it belongs to the good creation. There's no alternative.

Here we encounter problems. First of all, there's the mere fact that it's a very risky undertaking to state what is good and what isn't. Would all people at all times and in all cultures agree on that? Is the cup of goodness ever unalloyed? Can't we be mistaken in our definitions of what is good and what isn't? These are all questions which arise very quickly and aren't easy to answer. But the author of the creation narratives also had the courage to distinguish between what is good and what isn't. So why shouldn't we do the same?

Thus, as we saw, he didn't say that death was part of the 'good creation'. For him, death stood on the other side of the line. A bold and understandable decision. But is it true? What would happen to the world if there were no death? Untimely death is no part of the 'good', but mortality is part of our humanity; we are created by God as finite beings. So both life and death belong with God. Endless life could be very boring and, given the organisms that we are, not at all pleasant. If we accept being human as a fact of the 'good' creation, then we also accept dying. It's a very different matter just to stop there – we can argue against it! Sinners can't do that, says the apostle Paul; they think that they abide in death and see it as a punishment from God. But that comes later.

Moreover, although we ourselves may say whether something belongs to the good creation, this is no answer to the painful question with which it all began: where does what is 'not good', the evil in creation, come from? The previous section helped us a little by attributing evil to us: dirty hands can't do good work. But that didn't take into account *all* the evil that is around in our world, where the rest comes from: like the tsetse fly which produces fatal sleeping-sickness. We don't think that that's good. Nor is the earthquake which destroys half a province, but it happens. Where does it come from, if not from our dirty hands?

There is no other answer than what has been called 'the bitter riddle of the good creation'. In the world created by God there is also evil, bitterness, cruelty without parallel. We cannot call this good, nor need we do so. I hope that I've been clear enough about that. Of course something can also come from God which isn't good. A contribution from God, but one which we don't think good. That – and not human sin – makes creation an ambiguous event. Does it really come from God? Yes, I would want to maintain that. The alternative, that it comes from nowhere or from another power that we don't know, tells us nothing. On the contrary, it makes things even worse. So does evil come from nature itself? But that would be to go round in a circle, for surely nature in turn comes from the Creator.

To sum up: the 'good creation' doesn't mean that all that is, is good. Far less, as we shall see, does it mean that everything that happens in it is good. We ourselves must evidently say whether or not something belongs in the good creation. If we think that it doesn't, then the possibility is open to us, 1. to put the evil down to human misbehaviour or 2. to include it in the bitter riddle of the good creation. In the first instance we don't cover all evil, so there must be a portion left over which can't bear any other name than 'not good' and yet comes from God. It's part of the freedom and independence of human beings as creatures of God that they can also say that to the Most High.

8. Problems of construction: evolution

Nevertheless, in one respect we can't avoid the questions of the construction of our world. The creation story may be a characterization, an interpretation given to our world in Christian faith, but if we want to have interpretations, they must fit in with our reality, be capable of making themselves understandable in terms of our reality. The question which we must at least answer is: where then is God to be found in our reality? If we think that creation doesn't denote an event from the past but is a description of our reality, how do we imagine the presence of the Creator in his creation?

In answering this question it's impossible for us to ignore the theory of evolution as a scientific explanation of the origin of human beings and the world. This theory has caused difficulties for many Christians and still does today. In my view that rests on a misunderstanding.

In the past an underlying intent behind the theory of evolution was to show that God was a superfluous hypothesis and thus to be rejected. That's understandable if we remember that the classic doctrine of creation held firm to the idea that we must read Genesis as an account of the formation of human beings and the world. The militant experts on evolution held the same view and therefore would have nothing to do with Christian belief in God as Creator. But the theory of evolution has long since lost its ideological overtones. It aims to provide a scientific reconstruction of the origin of human beings and the world which in no way makes the problems which we have with the ups and downs of our world greater than they already were. The scientific explanation which we have in the theory of evolution is an explanation after the event, or at least a forecast. That's the attractive thing about it: it emphasizes the unpredictable character of development. It explains how it could come about (and not how it had to come about) that a simple amoeba could develop into infinitely higher forms of organized life. The process has already taken place: the theory of evolution as it were follows its tracks and discovers the mechanisms by which the development happened. But these mechanisms, too, only say by what 'method' the development took place and still takes place, not what way it follows or what the result will be. In short, evolution is an unpredictable process: it has no purpose, and can only be described after the event.

Is such an explanatory theory in conflict with belief in God as Creator? For many people that's a direct consequence. Once you begin from evolution, God no longer has a place. Anyone who sees things this way holds a view of God and God's work which may be popular but is untenable, and isn't endorsed by the Christian tradition. God can't be recognized in supernatural interventions, nor is God present only where we can imagine supernatural interventions.

The story of the two riders shows what I mean. 'I had a scary adventure; my horse was terrified, stopped and threw me to the ground. I see it as God's hand that I didn't break my neck.' His friend replies: 'I see it as God's hand that I could ride on quietly and my horse didn't stumble.'

Evolution and supernatural space for God are difficult to combine. But is God present only where we experience something miraculous or supernatural?

Christian faith has nothing to do with 'supernatural intervention' or with the denial of scientific facts (facts of natural science). Knowledge is knowledge, and we can be happy that it is there.

9. Where do we find God?

If God isn't present in a supernatural way, then how is God present? Where can we encounter God in reality? Where is the famous hand of God, the 'finger of God' in history? This question already half brings me to the chapter on God's support and rule of our world, but that comes later. Creating runs over into sustaining, into God's providential order. Those who say A must also say B. And those who no longer want to say B (providential order) should look out, because they've also disposed of A (the creation).

Let's begin with God's hand in the very process of becoming or, in a rather limited way, in nature, the cycle of the seasons. Is that a good beginning, given the horror in Israel and Christianity of nature worship? Yet no less a figure than Calvin in an unguarded moment (though did Calvin have any unguarded moments?) was bold enough to say that if one's intentions were good one could call the whole of reality God. In the language in which he wrote his textbook (Latin): *pie dici potest naturam esse deum.*

However, that doesn't mean 'all that happens is God'. Calvin was very careful in what he said, and his statement amounts to more than this. What? Let's go back to the formulations of one of the earlier sections of this chapter. God is at least all events (all that happens), but all events don't amount to God. In and under the event God remains hidden as power and will. That is the hidden way, for us often the unrecognizable way, in which God dwells in creation. Let me give three indications of this.

'Where is God, then?' That's a well-known question, with equally well-known answers, like 'high in heaven' or 'deep down' in our innermost being. That's mythological language, to which no one can object, but it's also no more than that. Where is God? If God isn't on earth, hiding himself as power and will in all that happens, God is nowhere. Secondly, that means that in everything that challenges us, determines us, delights us, unsettles us, makes us sick, or whatever, we encounter not just the working of our genes, the politics of Pol Pot or sudden death, but in the end – in all these events – God himself. So do we also encounter God in the cycles of nature, where according to many Christians we may not seek God? Perhaps. It wasn't for nothing that prophets like Isaiah remarked, 'Look at the stars if you want to come under the impact of God.' And why shouldn't we be able to say, 'Experience the spring, if you want to see an incomprehensible miracle of creation'?

But in that case – and this is the third comment – we encounter God as a 'someone', as at least a 'someone' with a purpose and the power to accomplish this purpose. This last, the purpose, is the great crux for humankind. What is the purpose of existence? The religious traditions may venture to give content to the purpose behind God and the world, nor is Christianity afraid of doing so: we live to live; life itself is the meaning of living. That's not superficial: that's grateful and committed belief in God the Creator.

Unfortunately it isn't always true and, as we shall see, people get very perplexed about this belief. But Christian faith can't do with less than faith in the God whom we encounter in our human existence as power and will. At least not if we don't want to end up in an 'empty world'.

63

10. Creation is wider than human beings

The human being as creation occupies a special place in Christian creation faith. I shall go into this more deeply in the next chapter. But we mustn't understand this to mean that everything revolves around human beings and 'the rest' is just there, either as the background against which the drama of God and human beings is played out, or as something which is given for human beings to get their teeth into freely.

First of all, this already clashes with our experience. If we keep a sense of proportion, then compared to the universe in which we are embedded we are the least of nature. In weight human beings are a particle on the scales, latecomers in time, who appear on the scene about five minutes before midnight. Not without power – it is not for nothing that the creation story says, 'Fill the earth and subdue it'. This is the confirmation of an experience and at the same time an encouragement, although nowadays that's perhaps rather too much of a good thing. According to some people we've already gone much too far in this 'dominating' and 'subduing'.

That doesn't alter the fact that we aren't here alone. According to Christian faith, God isn't just concerned with human beings, animals and plants, but also with the whole ecological system which is also his creation. Why shouldn't all that be significant for God? It seems to me a very real possibility that we can harm the Creator by attacking his work.

A second comment. To take account only of human beings and of God, and of God and human beings, and to regard the rest as scenery, introduces an impossible mysticism. Augustine was very charmed by it. 'To know God and the soul. Do we need anything more? Not at all.' But I would disagree with Augustine. There's nothing against mysticism (though it depends a bit on the definition), but this must be a mysticism which goes beyond creation as createdness. That amounts to saying that we must dispense with the creation in order to experience a relationship with God, and that seems a pity to me (it's the wretchedness of dying), an insult to the Creator (in that case, what is our world there for), and contrary to the way towards encounter with God. This way goes through created reality (all that happens).

So we must take a step back from what is nowadays a favourite way of looking at things. God as liberator, God as redeemer, God who makes our cause his own – all that was a trump card in the churches a decade ago, but it easily turns into our making our cause God's cause. And that comes all too close to the God who is there to fulfil our wishes – and if God doesn't do that, then either God isn't God or we're mistaken in our belief. It seems to me that our aim must be more modest. It's for us to know that our living, working, sufferings and loving are *one* of the things which according to Christian tradition are close to God's heart. But God has, so to speak, more concerns: a whole creation. To the degree that people voluntarily damage themselves and consequently become a plague to themselves, their fellow human beings and the whole creation, the human cause is indeed God's cause. God straightens out what is crooked.

Christianity thus offers a somewhat less egocentric conception of faith. In this way the environment gets a chance as an essential ingredient of God's creation – and not just as an indispensable ingredient for our own survival.

11. *The Creator and everyday life*

The Christian church today doesn't say much about creation. People reluctantly pick up the theme here and there, but it doesn't take off. Why is that? In the background is the influence of the theology of Karl Barth. Barth was an acute critic and reconstructer of the Christian tradition. In his view, we may no longer say that God reveals himself in nature, history or a fact of creation, and then also in Jesus. No, there is only one Word of God, and that one Word is the Word that God speaks to us in Jesus Christ. Moreover, all that God has to say, God's gospel and God's commandment, must be read off the person and the work of Jesus.

I don't want to ignore the good intentions of this reconstruction of the Christian tradition: the person and work of Jesus are central factors in Christian faith. But if we make them the only factors – there is only one word of God – then this concern becomes counter-productive. God as Creator disappears behind God as Liberator or Redeemer, and in this way the whole of ordinary life disappears behind life in the church.

And doesn't human existence play a role there, too? The factors which determine our existence lie outside the church, in ordinary life (which is so extraordinary). They begin with biological equipment which we ourselves have not chosen and end with the fellow human beings who determine the world in which we live (personally, or through society). Of course, in most cases we haven't chosen these either. In this world we in turn are affected by the life of others, whether we want to be or not: in work, in the festivals, in personal, social and political dilemmas, in the joy, the sorrow and the suffering that we experience from all these things. All this (I've mentioned only a few key words) is what I call ordinary life, in which we have a family, run a business, have or lose a job, have to play housewife (whether we want to or not) and often retire, disintegrate and are buried.

Now for Christian faith it's incomprehensible that God should stand outside all that. That's my attitude, and I end this chapter with it. We encounter God as the one who governs our portion and lot (which doesn't exclude our controlling what we can) and as the limit of what we can and may do (which doesn't exclude our going as far as we can). It is God's primary way of dealing with us. Life is a matter of accepting these dealings, preferably deliberately. How that must happen and what problems it can cause will come later, but what I said at the beginning of this chapter has simply been confirmed: belief in God the Creator isn't the easiest but rather the most difficult part of the Christian tradition.

I know that there's more, the church and the forgiveness of sins (which we've come across in ordinary life), but to receive the forgiveness of sins is rather different from bearing a child, and reconciliation isn't the same thing as seeing the tulip fields in flower.

I would venture to say that anyone who doesn't encounter God in ordinary life will end up not finding God in the church either.

VI

Human Beings as Creation

'Some people have discovered a strange land,
but none know themselves' (*Anonymous*)

1. *Is there a Christian picture of humanity?*

Those who talk about human beings and human ideas are talking
about themselves. That's why people never have an unpartisan image
of humanity. We have an interest in how we're portrayed; we don't
want to be all that others make of us. And to start from the other
side, sometimes views of humanity turn into what we find very
important at a particular moment.

It's clear that the Christian tradition also has a particular view of
humanity. But the deeper we go into it, the sooner we find that there
isn't one picture of humanity but many, and that the dispute over
them will probably never end. So we would do well to be modest
about ourselves. Certainly the Christian tradition has something to
say about humanity, but I would prefer not to talk in terms of a
complete picture. There are particular features in human nature
which the Christian faith emphasizes, illuminates, brings out or
interprets in its own way. I don't want to go further than that.

A Christian interpretation – that seems to me to be acceptable
terminology. As long as we don't think of interpretation as subjective
(in the sense of arbitrary) views which anyone may weave out of so-
called hard facts. If interpretations don't go further than that, they
don't achieve anything. It's all very well arguing that facts are facts;
that human beings remain human beings, whether you regard them
as an image of God or as four-legged animals on two legs but without
a fleece. But it isn't like that: there are no hard facts. Factual details
always stand in a context from which they derive their significance.
Even to make events 'hard facts' is to give them a meaning.

So there's nothing intrinsically alien in a Christian interpretation of being human, nor is it 'more subjective' than any other interpretation. The only thing that can and must be asked of any interpretation – and thus of any Christian interpretation – is that it shouldn't do violence to the data of humanity as we've learned to know them.

But we haven't yet arrived at this minimum condition. How should we proceed if, let us say, ten pictures of humanity begin to compete with one another as so many interpretations of being human? Is there any conceivable criterion, apart from the demand that we mustn't falsify things, any criterion which can be helpful to us in regarding one another in a more or less acceptable way?

There certainly is. The prize goes to the image of human beings which can still most satisfactorily bring together into their mutual context the characteristics of humanity that we have at our disposal without disguising anything, without overshadowing certain aspects. We must see whether the picture of human beings offered by Christians (I'm deliberately not saying the Christian view of humanity) meets these conditions.

2. The human phenomenon: (i) biological existence

What is characteristic of human beings? The question needs to be clarified. Human beings come in an infinite number of varieties: one person isn't another; men aren't women; one woman isn't of course another woman, and so on. I don't want to ignore these differences, so hitherto I haven't spoken about 'the human being'. That's a term which levels people out, because it treats everyone alike. So let's begin by emphasizing that each human being is a unique example of its kind. Unique means not exchangeable or interchangeable with other examples. But there are also features which all human beings have in common, both physical and psychological. I would sum them up in the term 'characteristics of being human', and from this I derive the freedom to talk in the context of this chapter about 'the human being'.

All human beings have in common the fact that they are biological organisms. This form of existence has limitations which determine human conduct. We don't choose our own genetic equipment; we get it from our parents. This genetic equipment meanwhile determines our physical constitutions and in a rather broader sense even our dispositions, our vulnerability to particular diseases and deviations, and so on. It's also part of this existence as organisms that we're in a position to procreate, to have children, to become older and finally to die. People are finite. They die. That's not a disaster, a shipwreck of existence, but is given with the mode of our existence. I shall explain elsewhere why we have so much difficulty here: the sinner can't oppose it.

It's also the case that people have needs which must be fulfilled if they are to be able to live: physical needs, but also psychological needs. So is a human being to be characterized as a bundle of needs? Certainly, that fact is very important for all the relationships in which human beings are involved, from their relationship with God to their relationship with their loved ones. But of course it also depends on *what* needs we fill. For example, the need to take responsibility also belongs here.

Are human beings determined by their biological constitutions? That doesn't follow, but people do have their limits, in body and mind. Anyone who doesn't take account of that and asks people, for example, to exert themselves unsparingly for God and their neighbours will note that at a certain point physical and mental weariness appears. To illustrate this, Freud tells the story of a penny-pinching farmer who wanted to show that his horse could do anything, even work without being fed. Every day he gave his horse a little bit less, and just at the moment when he had the proof – that for the first time the animal had eaten nothing at all – the animal died.

Human beings can't do everything they want to; certainly not everything that others want them to do. But that's not the same as being determined by biological laws. People don't coincide with their biological organisms. The mere fact that I can write this sentence and distinguish myself from my organism is evidence of this. Within certain limits (see above), people can say yes when their organism says no and vice versa. So they have some freedom over the material of which they are made. But if we keep talking about determination, on the basis of their physical constitution they are determined not to coincide with their organisms, as other living beings are. That's their weakness and their strength. Human beings don't have a fixed repertoire that they go through, but have to think out afresh what they have to do in each situation, if only to think out a repertoire.

I said 'think out'. 'People have to think out their conduct' means that they act 'meaningfully'; that there is meaning behind their actions. They can't do otherwise; that's what they're human for. The question is, where do they get this meaning from?

3. *The human phenomenon: (ii) human beings as social and cultural beings*

Human beings are also social beings, in the sense that they're dependent on others. First of all, merely for their existence: at least two other people are needed for them to come to life, a procreator and a mother. But human beings also can't survive without others: they depend on help, on some benevolence, on co-operation. Robinson Crusoe is an attractive invention, but he's a fictitious character. Loners don't survive. Daniel Defoe also knew this, so in the end he added a second person, Friday.

The picture isn't yet finished. A human being depends on others not only to survive but also to be someone, a person with his or her own characteristics. The simple fact that a person needs a name by which he or she can distinguish themselves from others already makes that clear. Who gives him or her their name? The others. What makes a person more than a living being interchangable with other living beings? The fact of being recognized as John, as a shopkeeper, as a model or as Michael's mother. To be recognized is to have a name and to get a place among others *through* the others. Society, or whatever else we like to call 'the others', thus gives people their social identity.

Karl Marx concluded from this that we mustn't make human beings more than they are: 'a social ensemble', beings composed of social ingredients. People receive their identity from the society of which they're a part, and have no other identity.

But that's to take things one step too far. That we cannot be human without other human beings, without the society of which we are a part, doesn't mean that we're dissolved without remainder into this society. That would be the end of us as human beings. Where this view of humanity has been put into practice, it has also been the downfall of human beings: this is precisely the way in which we lose our identity.

Human beings can keep their human identities, as persons, as those with names, only if they still have a relationship which goes beyond social relationships. As social beings, men and women are dependent on more than merely society, if they don't want to be caught up in society and thus submerged.

Men and women aren't just social beings, nor do they exist without a minimum of 'world', culture which they have wrested from chaos. By culture I mean what people make of their surroundings: a place to live in, to work in, to enjoy, to play in, to die in and be buried in. As soon as people rise even a millimetre above naked survival there is room for the miracle of creativity, and culture begins. That is so characteristic of human beings that it's seen as a milestone of evolution: where a place to live in is made, where the dead are buried, there for the first time we come upon human beings.

Because we find ourselves in the midst of culture – even highly developed culture – we are no longer struck by how special this is. At most we think that we're better than so many other, more primitive, cultures. But that rests on a misunderstanding. Better? That's the question. Different. But with the same inexhaustible curiosity and creativity.

Religion goes with culture and is in fact a cultural phenomenon. It needs imagination, creativity, the capacity to project (in the sense of forming an image of), a sense of God and of infinity, and challenges to associate that sense with events and circumstances which have a 'surplus value'. Without culture there is no religious faith and its tradition.

So much for the human phenomenon. What do these three characteristics add up to? They're facts which must form part of any picture of human beings, including a picture which brings God into it. This last doesn't seem to me to be difficult; rather, I see problems for a picture of human beings which tries to leave God out. From the characteristics which I've indicated, it becomes clear that human beings (if I may put it that way) are dependent for their humanity on what goes beyond them, on real transcendence. They take it into account, work with it, unconsciously or consciously (in their religion).

4. Incurably religious

It's one thing to say that human beings are dependent for their humanity on what goes beyond them, on transcendence. In the chapter about God we saw how this fact results in a quest which ends up in a multiplicity of religious traditions of faith. All this is the description (to some degree interpretative, of course) of how things are. But how do we explain the fact that human beings are so dependent for their humanity on God that – as I have said – they are incurably religious? The apostle Paul refers to the Greek philosopher

Aratus for the idea of 'being dependent on God'. Paul takes over Aratus's bold statement that 'we are of his (= God's) offspring' and makes it the background to the human quest. 'Offspring' is a somewhat wooden translation of a word which usually means 'sort' or, rather more scientifically, 'genus'. So the apostle is saying that there is a certain affinity, something of a 'like seeks like'. That sounds good to his contemporaries; they had always asserted this. Moreover, some of the apostle's interpreters claim that he's going beyond his brief. But I have some sympathy for his explanation, and although it may be going too far, the fact that an apostle can be drawn so far out of his tent says a great deal.

How does it come about that human beings seek God and do so stubbornly? Because they have something of God in them. Some Greek church fathers called this a splinter, a spark of God, as a result of which people are homesick for their original home. The theme recurs in mysticism down to the present day. But it goes one stage too far, since then you have to locate that splinter. Is it our reason? Is, as Meister Eckardt assures us, the soul 'God's vineyard'? Is our spirit akin to God? If we wanted to look in this direction we would be forced to explain what soul, spirit or reason are. But there has already been so much speculation about that in Christian views of humanity that I see no future in this undertaking. There is another reason why we mustn't take that splinter or 'spark' literally: within a very short time we would find ourselves back at the view that human beings consist of two components, a higher part (soul or spirit) and a lower part (the body). The Christian church has fallen into this trap – for that is what it is – more than once, with consequential damage to its own physical existence.

We always do better to keep to 'indwelling' as an image: we seek God because he dwells in us. 'Whom I found in myself to be the ground of my ground', as Jan Luyken put it, seems to me to be a splendid summary of this. It can keep alive the sense that the Christian tradition of faith doesn't just give us firm ground outside ourselves. The mystical trace is also there. 'Were Christ born a thousand times in Bethlehem and not in your heart, it would be of no use to you.'

That brings us back to the question with which we were concerned: how do we explain the fact that human beings are dependent on God? The disadvantage of the mystical line is that we no longer need the external world for our quest. As Augustine, and Calvin after him, remarked, it's enough to know God and the soul. As has been said many times, mysticism makes people unworldly. We know without experience who or what God is; he is what is most inwardly ours.

So I myself opt for what I've called in a previous chapter 'the sense of God'. People seek God because they're stimulated by God, provoked to communicate with him, as their Creator. That's an idea of things which connects the sense of God with the experience of human beings and the world, and doesn't let the world be the world.

6. *Right away from God? Human beings as sinners*

Human beings may be a unique phenomenon, but at the same time they're full of contradictions. That, too, is obvious. All the conditions are present for a society with a human face, and yet such a society can get off the ground only here and there, and then only with the utmost difficulty. Good intentions unexpectedly run up against individual and collective violence. As individuals we are moral, but put us together and the result is an immoral collective in which with much skill a rock-hard group egotism helps the right of the strongest into the saddle. How does that come about, and why is it such a stubborn phenomenon?

'There's a worm in our apple,' as Annie Schmidt said, that's certain. But what kind of a worm, where does it come from and what have we to do with it? The Christian tradition of faith seeks the explanation of the riddle in something that concerns all human beings equally – as we might say, 'something in humanity'. Human beings aren't incorrigible sinners, habitual offenders.

Other explanations are given. A mistake by the Creator which the Creator later makes good? That could be. A risk taken deliberately when God created free human beings, since to be free means that you can choose the wrong side? That could also be. But the Christian view of humanity doesn't say that; it calls human beings wilful sinners and claims that all the misery begins there.

What is sin? The word – to begin there – is indispensable, so I'm not one of those who look for or use another one. There is nothing wrong with it. We use it many times a day, and the term 'sinner' is also a natural one in our vocabulary. What we need to do is to free it from the caricatures with which religious upbringing has saddled so many people.

The church father Celestius said that sin is 'something you can give up'. A fine definition (which is what of course it was meant to be), but one-sided and superficial. Celestius is right that sin is a collective term: the word covers a great many attitudes and actions of a moral kind. It mustn't be robbed of that connotation, since in that case it loses its usefulness. But to limit sin to failure brings you to 'something you can give up', which has been far too simple a definition for the Christian tradition and moreover, as Goethe well saw, is in conflict with all experience. 'It is always the curse of the evil deed that evil must always bring forth evil.' These failures have a root; they emerge from a basic attitude which – I would remark in passing – we can at the same time use as a test as to whether we're talking about sin or about something else.

Selfishness – that seems to me to go some way towards helping to describe the basic attitude. Luther put it very precisely: to be turned in on yourself. But why should people be like that? For fear that they will go short. Behind selfishness lurks anxiety as the source of the behaviour that the Christian tradition calls 'sin'. Thus selfishness is not the only phenomenon. Anxiety can also lead to aggression, hostility, hatred and deception.

With this content we still find ourselves at a moral level. Why sin is a word from the religious vocabulary will become clear as we go deeper into this anxiety. People are anxious about going without (without love or food) because of their isolation from their Creator. The primal evil for human beings is, almost literally, their forgetfulness of God; they are not completely detached from God but a long way away. That's the reason why they easily exchange trust in life for anxiety. With this content we've gone some way from 'something you can help'. But the picture isn't yet complete. Sin also has the enigmatic aspect of helplessness.

6. Original sin?

The church father Augustine experienced a deep sense of helplessness in the face of evil and sketched out a background to it: we cannot remove sin from the world because sin is original sin. That was a misconception, in both content and terminology (although the term had already been coined before Augustine appeared on the scene). Sin isn't hereditary, a matter of genetics, and therefore 'original sin' is nonsense. It's all the more enigmatic – which was what Augustine meant in any case – that we can't stop it.

We have Augustine and his private life to thank(?) for the way in which in large areas of the Christian church sin was primarily connected with sexuality. For a long time Augustine had problems here; he experienced sexuality as a power to which human beings are delivered up, to their shame. For him this was the power of desire or, as church Latin put it, concupiscence. The proof that you were delivered over to this, whether you wanted or not, was in his view proved (as we read in *The City of God*) by erections, since men get these without being able to do anything about them. Of course this is nonsense – even three mistakes in one argument. First, Augustine was clearly thinking only of men when he wrote that. Secondly, sex isn't something you must oppose as much as possible, or engage in as little as possible. Hence this strange rule that sex may serve only for procreation and for nothing else.

But above all, sin isn't the same thing as sex – unfortunately for all those people for whom sex can only be exciting if it is sin. Sex isn't like aggression, an animal remnant in humanity, but a normal function with which human beings are equipped. You can get into trouble with it, but that also applies to other vital emotions, and usually these are more devastating than transgressions of sexual morality.

Guilt is attached to sin, and according to the Christian tradition, the ambiguity of culture is the fault of us human beings. Sin is a dangerous word, which clever people, inside and outside the church, like to use as a means of dominating others. In this sense sin is the guilt-feeling that we accumulate about parents, schoolteachers and our own unassimilated drives. We have to go to a pscyhiatrist for it, since it's a kind of poison. It destroys a good deal of pleasure, and creeps where it can't walk.

Nevertheless (or precisely for that reason), sin can't be removed from the vocabulary of Christian faith: our humanity depends on it. Animals cannot be guilty. The trials of animals which people held in the Middle Ages weren't a joke (there was a good deal of anxiety and guilt-feelings behind them), but it's impossible for us to take them seriously. Guilt can arise only where there are people, free people, who could have acted against an other (even then without a capital O) differently from the way which they had chosen. Why then didn't they choose otherwise? This is the riddle: guilt is a riddle which can't be explained. Any explanation is an excuse. Anyone who says, 'Yes, but it came from . . .' is well on the way to excusing their guilt. But that cannot be; or rather, if we succeed, we indicate our own bankruptcy. We clearly don't want to be accountable.

I rediscovered this at the end of *Room at the Top*. Joe Lampton, the main character, tells Alice he no longer loves her; she goes out and gets drunk and drives her car into a wall, killing herself. Joe takes it very badly and his friends try to comfort him: 'Nobody blames you!'. To that he has no other answer than, 'That's the trouble.'

Sin, guilt and helplessness are facts of experience. Why do people change so little? Why doesn't the world change? Why (from Antony's sermon to the fishes) do pikes stay thieves and eels lechers, although they all say that 'the sermon was a good one'? The Christian tradition doesn't have any answer either; it simply confirms the experince by calling evil a power and sin an imprisonment which people involutarily enter and in which they involuntarily stay. That seems to me to be a better formulation than 'original sin'.

7. Human beings as the image of God

Hitherto I've been able to base my description of the human phenomenon on the facts of experience. People don't coincide with their biological 'nature'; they're religious, and an enigmatic mixture of grandeur and misery. What appears in the last sections of this chapter is more difficult to base on experience, and in any case isn't a conclusion from it. According to Christian faith, God is concerned with human beings not only as Creator but also as Redeemer. People have to get out of the morass in which they're stuck, so that they become what they are: human.

That sounds somewhat ambiguous (become what you are!), but I can express myself like this because we can use the word 'human' in two ways: descriptively (what a person actually is) and normatively (what we need to be). I gave the description under the title 'the human phenomenon'. In this section I'm investigating the human as a normative concept, i.e. the humanity to which we must correspond if we are really to be human. I'm doing that under the heading 'human beings as the image of God'.

The expression comes from the creation narrative and has preoccupied Christian tradition down the centuries. It isn't my purpose to give a kind of biblical exegesis of this kind of terminology. It has seemed open to a variety of more or less speculative interrpretations. I shall just give a summary of reflection on it, point by point.

1. The classical church tradition couldn't help looking for the image of God in the creaturely human constitution – after all, it was in the creation story. There had to be something in or of human beings that got them this title, something that distinguished them –

to mention something important – from animals. Understanding? Self-awareness? Walking upright? Many theologians have even ventured to connect this image with masculinity, excluding women from it. Such ideas occurred earlier in the best circles and weren't specifically Christian. But they're nonsense. Human beings are human as man or as woman, and according to the creation story in this capacity any person – man or woman – is created in God's image.

I don't think it helps to look for specific human characteristics in which we could find the image of God. It's better not to do that. If we want to seek the image of God in a quality, then we must allow it to be in everything that makes human beings human, in their whole endowment.

2. There is more unanimity over the interpretation that the image of God relates to a function: 'image of God' denotes a task. Doesn't the same creation story say that human beings must rule over animals and subdue the earth to themselves? What is more obvious than to think that the image of God suggests the lord of creation, the call of human beings to be God's plenipotentiaries, stewards or whatever.

This is a possible interpretation, but like any other interpretation it's questionable – and has been questioned.

3. What is certain is the special position which this expression gives to human beings in the midst of other creatures. God is in the definition of what it is to be human. This also indicates the honour and dignity of human beings (any human beings, regardless of what else this may mean), and therefore also their need to be protected. Why must human beings be treated with care? The Christian tradition says, 'Because they're created in God's image and likeness'.

The expression had this protective function right from the beginning (in the Old Testament and in Judaism). Christians can't allow human beings to be ill-treated. Even more strongly, anyone who violates a human being violates God.

4. The Christian tradition has always wrestled with the question whether the image of God was lost at the Fall and has to be impressed on human beings again, or whether it has still been preserved (at least to some degree). The question stands or falls with the Fall as a historical event. If this idea isn't true (a position which I have defended earlier), we needn't choose. People are not to be written off, yet they must be changed.

So, in later Christian terminology, the image of God can be used as a fixed term for human determination: we must become what we are. What is our task? To show God's image, to act as God, to be followers of God. To be merciful and gracious, long-suffering, ready to forgive, and not remain angry for ever – to quote some classic characteristics of God. Being human isn't just a gift, an honour, but also a task.

5. Some church fathers were ahead of their time, and made this definition the endpoint of a kind of evolution. We haven't progressed as human beings so far as to reflect God: we're only on the way, but one day all human beings together will form the image of God. An attractive idea, but no more than that. Others take a much more individualistic, but still optimistic, view. To become the image of God is a matter of personal growth: during our lifetime we slowly change in the direction of our determination. The apostle Paul also says that, but true to his radical belief in another world, at the same time he preaches the need for a transformation: we don't just change; we are also changed. Here we begin with answers to our determination (he can call it bearing the image of God), but an intervention from eternity is necessary for the definitive change.

8. Humanity as a fact, as a gift and a determination

Human beings are phenomena in our reality which are studied by biologists, psychologists, philosophers and anthropologists in order separately and together to acquire as much knowledge about them as possible. I call that the knowledge of human beings as a fact. A Christian view of humanity, if there is such a thing, counts for nothing unless it's based on the most normal facts about human beings and their world, which experience and science give us. It mustn't argue away these facts, as if they were unwelcome or didn't fit into tradition. Christianity will have its own ideas about what people need to be or do, but these must remain in the realm of what a human being – seen as a phenomenon – is and can do. You can't get blood out of a stone, and for most people celibacy is an impossible task and therefore an improper demand (quite apart from the superstition that sex makes people impure and thus unsuitable for performing a ministry in the church).

Nor need the Christian view of humanity be gratuitously identified with what is laid down as a 'fact'. We ourselves are involved, unavoidably, in what is claimed to be knowledge of human beings. That puts us on the look-out. For these reasons, too, today's knowledge is always accurate knowledge of yesterday. If a Christian view of humanity incorporates too specific facts, it later has to reject them or they will bring it down. There's nothing against this, except that the word Christian is again being used once too often.

So what is it that is Christian? We mustn't seek this in all kinds of specialities which have been represented as typically Christian down the ages. Like 'masturbating make you deaf', sex before marriage is bad, homosexuality is contrary to nature, and other clichés of that kind which are based on so-called human nature (which in turn is then reduced further to biological nature). Such a nature is far too vague a term for us to be able to work with. The Roman Catholic church certainly does that, but any investigation shows that the term 'nature' doesn't seem to go further than what people in the twelfth century (like Thomas Aquinas) found natural. So to teach this to people of today leads to absurdities and to sheer extortion.

Thus the appeal to human nature doesn't work; it isn't 'nature', and if it was, nature doesn't give us any pointers. Surely the fact that women are by nature equipped with a womb doesn't mean that they need to give birth?

According to some Protestants, the mistake lies somewhere else: we needn't go so quickly to so-called nature, but must go to grace, and thus derive the essence of humanity from the person of Jesus Christ. So is Jesus the true man and therefore normative for us? But that too doesn't help. Jesus was unmarried, at least as far as we know, since his life story tells us nothing of any man-woman relationship. He didn't know from experience what being a father means (we hear nothing of children); he lived as a Jewish male in an agricultural culture, in a world in which slaves were a regular phenomenon, and so on. I don't see how we could construct a normative picture of humanity from his life and work. And I would add that that makes sense. Jesus is one of us; he bears our human marks and characteristics. If we know how *we* are constructed, we also know this of Jesus, and not vice versa.

So is the children's song 'I want to be like Jesus' nonsense? Not at all, but here we're talking about an ideal that we want to follow, and ideals are given content from the demands of the time. 'So humble and so good' children sang in the nineteenth century, and in the twentieth they sing 'so challenging and revolutionary', and yet other contents will follow. These are ideals, not norms that we derive from the humanity of Jesus. We find norms in what Jesus does and suffers, especially in the exemplary way in which he loved God and his neighbour to the death. But even of these I have to say that they are so closely connected with his calling that it's impossible for us to make them a general model.

9. Know yourself

So does faith add anything else to human beings as facts, and if so, what? My answer would be that it puts humanity in a framework which serves us as a guide, tells us where we are. A human being is a creation of God; human existence is granted us from above as a gift to bring us joy.

That doesn't always seem to be the case, as the Christian church knows very well. Things can go wrong with the gift, though it comes from God. People can be condemned to a life with physical or mental handicaps or even both at the same time. Others are tried by illnesses which tear them to pieces – and so I could go on. Sometimes people can accept such an existence, and sometimes they no longer have a spark of delight, let alone being able to experience life as a gift. Moreover the somewhat lofty language of faith comes to grief on the wretched situation in which they sometimes find themselves. God no longer gives them any dignity. That may be said. We may hand back our ticket, like Ivan Karamazov, if we think that we've good reason to do so.

Christian faith doesn't just evaluate existence as a gift, but also sees a promise in life. Human beings *qua* human beings are on the way to their destiny and will reach it, here or in the hereafter. So it's worth fighting for it, making what we can of it and letting the individual (the last indivisible entity) be what the Creator had in mind in calling us into being: 1. as man or woman; 2. as social beings, directed to seek the company of other human beings; 3. as makers of culture or developers of the world in which they find themselves.

I would sum up what the Christian tradition has to say about people as being a contribution to knowledge about themselves. 'Know yourself' stood above the entrance to an ancient Greek temple. The Christian tradition not only approves of the invitation but also claims to make its own contribution by calling human beings creatures of God, a sketch of God's concern. If you know who or what God is, then you also know better who you yourself are. 'Know God, then you know yourself better' wouldn't be out of place as a summons above the door of the Christian church.

So can anyone know themselves? A friend who had to take leave of life found it a bitter experience that during his lifetime he hadn't become clear enough to those he was leaving behind. 'If only someone understood me, could explain me to myself and to the others!' I remember that I then read him the first lines of Psalm 139:

Lord, you have searched me and known me.
You know when I sit down and when I rise up;
you discern my thoughts from afar.
You search out my path and my lying down,
and are acquainted with all my ways.
Even before a word is on my tongue,
you, Lord, know it altogether.

In the cauldron of existence, with all the competing relationships and loyalties of which a human life is built up, there is always One who knows what I wanted, although I wasn't able to explain it to others.

VII

God's Providential Order. On the Sustaining and Governing of All Things

'Of the two hundred children in my school, one hundred and ninety three were gassed. It's a strange notion that the Father must have had a hand in that. And if he didn't have a hand in that, what did he have a hand in?' (*György Konrad*)

1. Everyday life as a place of encounter with God

When I was a small boy, I used to like going to church, because exciting things happened there: the organ playing, the singing, a collecting bag that you could hold. Later, when I grew up, that stopped, or rather, it changed: then I found things more exciting outside the church than in. And I was right!

A person's real life takes place outside the church. You go to school, you work, you start dating, you lose your heart to a person or a job, you make plans which occupy your thoughts and actions, you get due recognition (or fail to get it), and you finally encounter decrepitude and death. A varied, sometimes bewildering series of ordinary and extraordinary things one after another – that's what our life looks like. It would be quite remarkable if we had to think that God stood outside our ordinary life or that our life – to put it the other way round – stood outside God. The most important thing, the clue, real existence, would fall outside faith. How irrelevant God would be were that the case! And how few chances we would have of encountering God!

With this introduction I'm picking up the chapter on creation, almost in the form of a repetition of its last section. But there is a more important reason for this: creation and what was once called God's providential order – God's preservation and rule of all things

– overlap. The classical tradition already had difficulty with this: when are we still in creation and when do we move into sustaining and ruling? It couldn't yet as it were tie up the ends because it could think of creation only as a well-circumscribed, definite act of God finished on the seventh day, in other words an act in the past. We can no longer do that. As I've shown, creation takes the course of a process. Since we human beings appeared on the scene, the word process is no longer appropriate and I would prefer to speak of 'history'. Creating and sustaining don't just overlap: the difference between them has lost its compelling character.

I shall mark that by beginning this section with the words with which I ended the chapter on creation: ordinary life is the place where we encounter God. If we don't encounter God there, an encounter in church is of no help.

Before my account goes astray, I need to remove a misunderstanding. By 'God in ordinary life' I don't mean (at least not primarily) the presence of God as the one who imposes tasks. It's true that God also becomes present – according to Christian faith – in the task of practising justice and love of neighbour. It may not be simple to determine what 'treat justly' involves, but that doesn't mean that it's not a task in which we encounter God and that therefore it isn't worth while trying to do well.

But does God only impose tasks? That would make God another word for commandment, and in any case limit God to that. The Christian tradition has never done this, and where it did begin to do so it made Christianity a tense, hard-fought religion of doing. God isn't just command but also companion.

Nevertheless, there are many Christians who can't think of 'God in ordinary life' in any other way. It seems to me that this is because they're perplexed by the Christian tradition of God's providential order. They can't imagine that it's God who directs their lives. That's a pity, because it's a solution of perplexity which is catastrophic for faith. If we cannot or may not any longer interpret the daily things which dominate our life, the events which change its course, as an encounter with this God who sustains and governs not only human beings and the world but also our life, God can no longer be thanked, indeed no longer desired, and faith loses its significance for human existence.

It's clear what the problem is: if God shows his face by means of what he does and allows to happen to both human beings and the world (and thus also to us), what sort of a face does he have? Does he indeed still have a face, or has he lost it?

2. Providence and what we encounter in it

The classical idea of God's providential order is that the Creator does not let his world out of his hands but 'sustains and rules all things as with his hand'. God is in one way or another behind everything that happens in the world, and thus behind what happens to us in our personal life. This already follows from the description of God as Creator which I've given in the chapter on creation.

Honesty requires me to say that this idea is particularly unpopular among Christians and that resistance to it is much greater than it used to be. I think that's right, and can't be otherwise. Before I explain this comment, though, I want to remove a few objections which rest on a misunderstanding. Then I can be all the clearer about the real resistance.

Providence or providential ordering are terms which cause problems. They come from classical philosophy and were taken over by the church fathers, after which they never disappeared from Christian terminology. What's wrong with them? Nothing, as long as you define them properly. But that tends not to happen, or happens in terms of a closer exposition of the word 'providence' itself. The term suggests 'see in advance': unlike human beings, God sees everything in advance, which is why God can govern everything so well. Or can God? Of course God doesn't always govern things well in the eyes of those concerned, but God certainly does so in God's own eyes. Everything comes out as God wills, and everything that happens is thus by definition what God wants. This explanation, generally speaking, gets rid of three approaches, each of which makes God's providential order a caricature. They seek to make it:

1. A justification. Here I have in mind references to God's providential ordering of someone like Adolf Hitler. We are asked to see the fact that he was the Führer of the Great German Reich as a disposition of Providence. What's wrong with that claim? It has to serve as justification for his actions, but faith in providence cannot do that. If it could, anything could can be justified; the reference to Hitler shows that as clearly as one could wish.

2. Reassurance. Providence lends itself equally easily to reassurance. Everything happens as it has to, and as it has to, it happens. We make no difference, so there is no point in opposition and

resistance. But in this way God becomes fate, and that's not what Christianity meant by 'providential order'.

3. Confirmation. God's providential order is sheer wisdom; it can be confirmed splendidly by nature and history. An anthill bears witness to God's reason, and anyone who sees a rainbow over the thirsty earth praises providence, 'above all' – added a witty theologian from the eighteenth century – 'if he's standing in the dry'. Karl Barth tells this joke and adds that the next toothache will drive all other thoughts from your mind. Indeed, if that's what providence has to be, little else can come out of it than a confirmation of bourgeois prejudices.

Justification, reassurance and confirmation – at all events those are three purposes which faith in God's providential order cannot serve. They're misunderstandings. The God who rules and governs is different. This God isn't blind faith; this God isn't the God who will make 'everything come out right'; this God isn't the support behind us which we can make use of when we want. He is power and will, and as such a much more risky reality than we think. God's providence or God's providential ordering or whatever term we want to give to God's 'power and will' isn't the particle of belief in God that everyone can share in; on the contrary, it's the last thing that succeeds, the culmination of Christian faith.

3. How can God allow it?

God's providential order becomes a real stumbling block not because of misunderstandings but when it is properly understood. If it is true that 'God sustains and rules all things as with his hand', that means that we must see God behind all that happens, not only behind the good but also behind the evil that happens to people. As long as these evil things remain within reasonable proportions, or as long as we can attach some sense to them, that's fine, but there are also things which mock any concept, things which should never have happened and which haven't just been seen but sometimes even perpetrated by human beings.

That causes terrible problems – I can't call them anything else – for believers. Usually that only happens when they are personally confronted with a disaster: a loved one perishes in a stupid, senseless accident or a child from an incurable illness. 'How can God allow it?' someone then cries out in desperation. I think that this is a good question, but it needs to be thought about. For example when the evil affected your neighbours, or when you read in the paper that soldiers in Brazil burned down an Indian village with everyone in it because the land was needed for a large-scale project. The Indians were also people, with the same feelings, the same needs, the same sorrow. 'How can God allow it?' – once someone has cried that out, he or she can hear it echoed back a thousandfold.

The question illustrates the tricky problem posed to Christianity all down the ages by the rule of God over all things. The recognition of God's power over everything is included in this, otherwise you wouldn't ask such a question. So too is the lack of understanding, the complete incomprehension of how events fit in with the conception that we have of God. Why doesn't God do anything, if God has all the power to do it?

The bewilderment which lurks behind the question is the bewilderment of disappointment, of miscalculation. They have told us of a different God from the one we encounter in reality. What kind of a God is it who can allow genocide, who can let a boy be burnt to death in a haystack or a girl be drowned in a ditch? Does that have to be? Assuming that God can do anything. But is that the case?

There is an alternative: if God can't do anything, I need no longer call on God, since that makes no sense. If God can, but doesn't, for some reason unknown to me, then I don't want to call on God any more, because such a God is a scoundrel, a God of stone.

So the whole question of a God who rules everything ends up in a great question-mark over God. If you maintain God's rule over all things, you burden God with a terrible world, on a small (small?) scale round the corner, but just as much with the thousands of deaths from famine in black Africa, with the genocide in Cambodia or with Auschwitz. To 'rescue' God you should say: it simply can't be true that God rules the world. But what then? The alternative is that God can do nothing – and is that really any better?

4. Theodicy: attempts at a rescue

To burden God with such a fearful world – Marcion, a teacher in the early church saw things very clearly: if you want to avoid that, you have to begin with creation. Creation can't come from God, because it entails the 'sustaining and ruling of all things'. These two notions are inextricably intertwined. So Marcion cut the knot and argued that the Christian God was not the God who had created the world. In this way the Christian God was 'rescued': the fearful world

86

didn't come about through God but through a god with lower qualifications, a kind of bungler, who will be overcome by the real God, the redeemer God of Christianity. As church history shows, this was a seductive idea; it gets round a great many problems of faith. But a price must be paid for it. Ordinary life with its being born, living and dying, is no longer the place where we encounter God. To do that we have to be in the church. But in that case, as I've shown, faith loses its significance. So what you gain with this 'rescue attempt' of God you lose again on the other side. God no longer has anything to do with our misery except by redeeming us from it.

It can be less crude, for example, to put some distance between evil and God. This distance is already there in the term 'allow'. Anyone who asks how God can 'allow' this clearly wants to avoid making God the 'author of evil'. Such a person hovers between two ideas; God has to do with it in the sense that God could have stopped it, but not in the sense that God is the author of it. We can thus leave aside the question where evil then comes from, as long as God is opposed to it.

Of course this is unsatisfactory. In that case what is left of God's rule over 'all things'? Augustine knew better: you can't give that up. He says that evil happens against God's will but not outside it. Does that help us to sort things out? No more than a good formulation of the problem helps. You can live rather better with it: that's all.

What Augustine says led later theologians to distinguish between the 'will of decision' and the 'will of command'. When we talk about God's will, are we talking about God's bidding ('will of command') or his providential order ('will of decree')? God's will in the first sense is known to us, but not his will in the second sense. In his government of all things we come up against his 'hidden will'. The problem remains: the evil in the world remains God's burden if we maintain that God rules over 'all things'.

The only adequate 'rescue' of God in fact consists in making God stand outside. God has no hand in the ups and downs of our world. So God has nothing in hand, as one might say. The question how God can allow all this is irrelevant; we're looking in the wrong direction, indeed it isn't a direction at all. God can do nothing about it.

This is certainly a way out, but that's all. A God who can do nothing about anything is no longer God. There's no point in calling on God; it makes no difference. Faith and hope go up in smoke.

That's the solution which Harold Kushner offered in a book that was a bestseller a few years ago (which shows how the problem concerns us): *When Bad Things Happen to Good People*. The book is splendid when it comes to describing the suffering that can afflict people, but God is left as no more than a toothless tiger, a God without power, a God who can do no more than we can. What are we to make of such a God?

There's also a christological solution. Didn't God in Jesus Christ allow himself to be forced out of the world, and in so doing didn't God show that defencelessness, rather than 'power over all'? Why do we then bother about a God who doesn't understand our need? We don't understand God in need – that's the point. I shall return to it later (it has to do with a misunderstanding of Bonhoeffer), but here already I would reject this christological 'rescue' of God. God isn't defenceless, isn't on the way to power, isn't defenceless superior power – those are words which indicate our perplexity over God's governance, and we can't really mean them. If the God of Christian faith were really defenceless, and had to hand over rule over all things to human beings and powers, Christian faith itself would be finished. The christological solution doesn't take us further than Kushner's: if it's right, we must go on without God. Do we want to do that?

5. God behind the scenes: a puppet show?

I won't say for the moment what the choice will finally be. First we have to clear the way so that it can be made without misunderstandings.

In the previous sections, more than once I used the expression 'God behind it'. That's the language of the puppet show or the marionette theatre. We see the puppets move, but they don't move themselves; someone is pulling the strings behind the scene. So it *looks* as if the puppets themselves are moving, but they aren't. They're being moved. Is that a good comparison for 'God rules over all things'?

No. 'God rules' isn't the same as 'what we undertake is only apparently the free action of human beings; in reality we're only carrying out what God has determined in advance'. That has become a view of things in Christianity which is as popular as it's disputed, but it's unnecessary, unacceptable and seldom if ever carried through consistently. Christianity doesn't think in deterministic terms, and where it does so, it gets involved in internal contradictions. The popularity of predetermination rests on an obsession. To guide is to foresee, but that's not enough for God; in that case all kinds of things can also happen that God doesn't will. So God doesn't just *see* everything in advance; God already *determines* everything in advance. That means having everything in hand, and this is the way in which God governs his creation. Really? If we take this view seriously, then the power of God is rescued and human freedom is lost.

But that doesn't work; the history of human beings and the world isn't the implementation of a programme conceived of (by God) in eternity. 'It's all settled' doesn't match the picture of God in Christian tradition. Christianity believes in a Creator for whom people mustn't be stones, sticks or blocks, but free men and women who are equipped and literally forced to cope with their Creator, and predetermination is incompatible with that.

So I'm not beginning by saying that human beings are created free and therefore there is no predetermination; I'm beginning with God, who according to Christian tradition wants people who will respond in a way which is as it were worthy of a God. Therefore human beings are free: in other words, people who can act otherwise if they so choose.

So God's ruling power doesn't do away with freedom: quite the contrary, if there were *no* God – at least as Christianity describes God – everything would be fixed, reality would be a closed circuit and we would be caught up in the laws of what we call cause and effect. For Christianity, God's providential government implies that the world isn't closed, but open. Our existence runs its course in interaction with the Creator, who challenges us, lures us out of our tents, and leaves us guessing and working away, and thus not only gives us our freedom but also manipulates it. Where there's freedom – in the sense that I indicated – there's God, and where there's God, there's freedom. So these two, human freedom and God's government, God's providential order, can't go together without one of them losing its effect; God's rule is even the guarantee of our freedom.

To shed some light on this, I shall take an image from Milan Kundera's book *Immortality* and alter it for my purposes. It's the image of someone playing a computer game. God has composed a programme in which we are involved as opponents. After each of God's moves we have a turn, and after our moves God reacts. In other words, God encounters us in a hidden way in everything that happens, as power and as will, and we react to everything that happens as free men and women.

Let me emphasize that once again: as free men and women. This will occupy us again in the question where evil comes from. Here I simply want to emphasize the point so that we don't simply imagine that we're victims of everything that happens. Do we ourselves have a hand in things? That's not the whole story: of course we aren't *just* active subjects, but also a product of what others have done. That will us occupy again in due course.

However, God is far from being just the victim of our reaction, as though he could do no more than react. Action and reaction aren't the same thing, if we keep to the terms of the programmer and his programme: the two aren't alike. God is infinitely broader, more inventive, more creative in his action and reaction than we are. But that doesn't exclude the fact that we too are involved as serious players in the game. It does exclude the possibility that God could be against us or that God couldn't achieve his goal.

Let me emphasize that this is a metaphor. I'm using it simply to indicate that human freedom and divine power needn't clash. As Herman Berkouwer has argued, God and human beings work at different levels. God isn't one factor among others. The conclusion is that the notion of God's providential ordering isn't concerned to make him our rival. That such ideas could arise is connected with the concepts that are used, but goes directly against what people want to express by them.

So we've got rid of one difficulty: God's providential order doesn't put our freedom under pressure. But in that case, what about God and evil?

6. Were there no sins there would be no wounds

The great stumbling block is caused by evil in the world. By 'evil' I mean anything that we experience as a disaster, both the wickedness of human beings and the recalcitrance of nature. Where does evil come from? Down the ages human beings have racked their brains over this question. As I've already indicated, the Christian tradition has coped with it by attributing evil to human beings and their mistakes.

It could do this – despite appearances – because ultimately it didn't think deterministically about human beings and their freedom.

Human beings are sinners, incorrigible offenders, and, as a Christian proverb has it, 'were there no sins there would be no wounds'.

It won't escape anyone that this idea of things is in fact an attempt to free God from responsibility for evil in the world; not, however, by turning to God's rule over 'all things', but by putting evil wholly and always to the human account. God created human beings and the world good, without a spot or stain, but human beings have stubbornly resisted God and thus made the best the worst. We reap the bitter fruits of our own failures. According to this line of thinking, moreover, the question 'How can God allow it?' is always wholly misplaced. On the contrary, we can count ourselves lucky still to be here. God's support and governance of 'all things' isn't a neutral attitude but a sign of his patience with a fallen creation. The world continues to exist because God is a gracious God.

Here I'm reproducing a classical argument, in the appropriate terminology. Let me begin by giving it the approval it deserves. It's true that in Christianity we – we human beings – accept blame for the fact that the world has gone wrong, and don't foist it on God. Not in the sense that every human being is personally responsible for every evil that happens under the sun. Certainly we're all in a train going in the wrong direction, but it does make a difference whether those in it commit murder or help one another. This doesn't alter the fact that the Christian tradition has been unwilling to give up the idea of a collective responsibility. We afffect one another and we affect the whole creation (in the sense of 'createdness').

From this perspective the discussion focussed on Auschwitz (did God lose his eyesight in Auschwitz?) is wholly misplaced. We are so shocked at ourselves, at our absence when we should have been present, that we hastily blame God for Auschwitz by first of all making it a problem relating to providence instead of a problem about our own responsibility.

But our voluntary confession of guilt can't serve as an attempt to rescue God. First of all we can no longer share in the presupposition on which the argument is based. As was evident earlier, there never was a golden age in which human beings and the world were in a 'state of righteousness', a state which was changed by a historical incident, the Fall, bringing death and corruption in its wake. Death and dying are part of human existence. But that's not the only thing.

Millions of people aren't primarily the agents but the victims of greed, aggression and the deceit of their fellow human beings. Their wounds may then be connected with sins, but the sins that they suffer under are those of others. In a sense that's true of all people. We live our lives in a network of interactions, in which we are one another's victims and executioners. Anyone who blights another person's life does so because of a life which has already been blighted by others, and so on. The network is a power, a web, which we can't get out of.

But there's also a third argument, the most important one. There's a great deal of disaster and misery in our world which has nothing to do with human action because it can't be reduced to it, not even to that web of evil deeds which holds us in its grip and makes us powerless. Floods, earthquakes, hurricanes, lava flows, viruses, microbes – I could mention a series of catastrophes which have nothing to do with human action.

So the proverb about 'sins and wounds' doesn't work, if it sets out to be an explanation of what can happen to human beings and the world. Therefore it also fails as an attempt to rescue God, quite apart from the question whether such attempts are necessary. The evil in the world is too enigmatic, too alien to be covered by the concept of sin.

7. The dark course of Providence

So there's no alternative: things that we call evil belong in creation. That rules out the idea that we have to 'rescue' God. God doesn't need to be rescued. Rather, we must start from the idea that there can be no evil which comes from God's side. It seems to me a symptom of the exaggerated attention which people require for themselves from their Creator. More is involved in creation than just human beings. Furthermore, this is the demand of a very luxurious attitude, the product of Western men and women accustomed to thinking that their world can be coped with, who, in contrast to former cultures, don't know what to make of what cannot be changed, let alone being able to bear it. This last comes about because they have done away with the 'hereafter'. Everything must be sorted out here, otherwise we have nothing. Indeed, those who think in this way just can't accept what doesn't suit them any longer. So everything is connected with everything else; faith in God's providential ordering perishes (God may do no evil) if we've given up heaven (God may not make it good in eternity). And vice versa.

I think that here we've tailored God to our own measure, made God the servant of modern men and women. God can never be that, at least not the God of the Christian tradition of faith. This God certainly inspires respect through his love, but the Christian church doesn't succeed in finding this love in God's rule over 'all things'; no one does. Life is too ambiguous for that: creation is too ambiguous, and history too obscure. As a 'dark Providence' (so a hymn has it) God goes his unknown way and his purposes escape our grasp. There is blossoming in existence, youth, wisdom, joy; but also sorrow, contradiction, demented old people who cannot die and children who have to.

Incomprehensible? Indeed, life seems to be a series of signs that we try to interpret. But we don't get very far with that. In one of the couplets of the Dutch national anthem the author expresses distress at God's gloomy course. 'Count Adolf fell in battle in Friesland'; but – it goes on – 'when it was the will of the Lord', tyranny was driven from the Low Countries.

That's a touching attempt to make something of the situation, to discover a pattern, but it works only rarely, and even then we have to be very careful. When the Netherlands was liberated in 1945, a service of thanksgiving was held in the New Church in Amsterdam. The preacher was Cornelis Miskotte, and the title of his sermon 'God's enemies perish'. Few people will have had the feeling that Miskotte had gone too far in his interpretation, yet Miskotte himself was among those most aware of the mistakes that we can make when we begin to interpret history. We can't do otherwise; the whole world becomes grey; good and evil vanish if we no longer attempt to do this. But it remains a risky business.

Where does evil come from? The classic answer of the Christian tradition falls short. Not just from sin; there's more to evil than that. There's an enigma in the dealings between God and his creation. I think once again of Van Ruler's statement that God is more involved in his creation than we would like. There's also evil which is not to be put to our account, but to the Creator's.

We needn't find an evil good because it comes from God. In any case, it needn't be from God. Moreover, that would be dishonest to ourselves and an insult to the people whom it affects. Evil is part of life and we have to put up with it. That's the only thing that can be said. Any explanation, any fine talk, any attempt to make sense of disasters and catastrophes goes wrong, betrays the people who suffer, makes them subordinate to higher ends or wider perspectives. Perhaps they are, but it isn't given to us to know this. So we must reject all these attempts to attribute meaning, no matter what name they are given. A disaster is good for no one.

Two questions remain. Can God deal with us and the evil that we cause, or in this way do we frustrate his rule over 'all things'? And – just as important – can we live with God's providential order, with a God who governs all things(!) as with his hand?

8. *The crooked stick and the straight blow*

There is a Latin saying above the Federal Building of the Swiss Confederation: *Hominum confusione et dei providentia Helvetia gubernatur* – Switzerland is governed by human confusion and by God's providence. The meaning is clear: one thing (God's governance) comes about through the other (confusion).

There could also have been a reference to the story of Joseph, who as a young man was sold into Egypt by his brothers as a slave, achieved a high position there, and was able to provide food for his father and brothers when famine came: 'What you intended as evil, God has turned to good,' Joseph says to his disconcerted brothers.

Or perhaps the story of Jesus is an even more attractive example. Jesus is crucified, something which should never have happened, the cruel death of an innocent man. But see what comes out of it: 'What you intended as evil, God has turned to good,' says one of the apostles (thinking of the story of Joseph).

Does that give evil a meaning? No, the programmer can react in such a way as (still) to make something good out of something evil. Certainly what Jews and Romans do to Jesus is 'against' God's will, but it isn't beyond his will. God can strike a straight blow with a crooked stick, as the proverb goes.

Is that the case? Certainly. But if we're to be able to say this, we need an insight into history that is rarely given us. In other words, 'the crooked stick and the straight blow' isn't a solution to the questions posed to us by God's providential ordering; it's a hope, an expectation that we may cherish. God may go his unknown course; history may conceal him from us; his face may grow dark; but there is a hopeful model before our eyes: God can turn to good what we had thought evil. That makes the unfathomable character of God's rule over all things a hopeful act of faith for the Christian tradition.

We don't always see it. Certainly not at the micro-level of our small life. 'God tempers the wind to the shorn lamb' is an attractive picture of God's providential ordering, but things don't always work out like that. There are people whose lives go on undisturbed, so free of disasters or upsets that they almost get anxious about the fact. Of course that's nonsense; this anxiety is a kind of superstition which goes back to what Greek mythology called 'the envy of the gods'. The God of Christianity doesn't know envy. But there are also those who have to cope with almost all the blows that life can deliver. How do such people keep their faith? God may know what to do about us, but do we know what to do about God?

9. The right and left hands

Of course God's providential order isn't to be endured if evil, too, and not just good comes from God's hand. Unless this God is to be trusted in a way which can cope with the evil in the world. That in fact is the only way out: the God of providential ordering is the God who will provide for us in it – that's what the Christian tradition offers as a conclusion, and that's what this section is about.

Luther wrestled endlessly with the question which concerns us. He could make progress by distinguishing between God's left hand which strikes and God's right hand which welcomes. I know of no better way of expressing this, so I shall follow what Luther says.

Doesn't God seem fearful if God is behind everything, even hunger and death? Indeed, if we had to read God's face bit by bit off reality, we would end up with a terrifying countenance. The Psalms sing of God's friendly face, but if we look around us God has lost that friendly face. It's unrecognizable, at least from the reality around us. There Luther was right.

But Luther says something else. 'He doesn't mean it.' God doesn't really mean it. God does evil to us, but doesn't will it. At times God plays cat-and-mouse games with us, but not in order to catch us. God's face is terrifying, but it's a mask. God puts on a mask, he says literally. A 'face', as we children in Friesland used to call masks. God puts on a 'face', but it isn't God's real face. The whole of creation with its suffering and its glory is God in masquerade. Luther says that if you want to see God as he is, you have to look closer. You see God's true face light up in Jesus Christ. So a person needs two things to be able to live: the Psalms, for there we find the bitter and the sweet of life, praise and lament over God's ordering. And the gospel, for there we are shown God's true will.

Therefore believing is a feat, not remaining on this left hand but fleeing to the right. In the church things still go well with us, we hear that 'the LORD is merciful and gracious, and great is his loving-kindnesss', and we readily believe it. But still to believe that outside the church, in everyday life, with its bitter blows, with its disturbed relationships, with the joy which becomes bitter to say that this is a mask, that God's true face is a friendly face – that's the feat of faith.

That's what Luther says. I'm quoting him, but in other terminology I could also have quoted Calvin or the Heidelberg Catechism. They all say the same thing: the God of providential order is a perplexing riddle for whose purposes we sometimes grope in deep darkness; God plays cat-and-mouse games with us. But God is to be trusted; we have seen God's true face in the words and works of Jesus.

10. What is this faith for? Opposition and submission

God's providential order, God's rule over 'all things', also implies that all things come from God's hand personally to us – to our little lives. If you see something in the hand, then you see something in belief in God's providential order.

This order doesn't involve special treatment for believers. Anyone in search of that had better give up. Nor can we use it as an easy basis for assessing what happens to us – or others. An accident isn't a punishment from God, nor is a flourishing business a blessing. Punishment is already a highly questionable interpretation, but even the usual talk about blessing must have a question mark set against it. You don't need belief in God's providence for that either.

Even the interpretation of what happens around us and to us – however indispensable it may be – isn't the real reason for believing in God's providence. We needn't put together God's will from the course of events, since according to the Christian tradition it has already been revealed to us in Jesus' words and deeds. What we don't know is how everything fits together, how one thing matches another, what the concrete meaning of things is.

So what is belief in God's providence good for? For living our everyday life in converse with God, for being able to give thanks and pray for things, and for fostering a fundamental trust in God's purposes.

We've lost that trust. The problem of God and evil will have contributed to that; we've seen more evil than previous generations. But I don't believe that that's the whole story, or even the main thing. We no longer see the need for trust as former generations saw it.

True, they were farmers who depended on wind and sun for their survival. Their existence was insecure; they desperately needed God's paternal hand to get through hunger, suffering and sickness. We aren't in such a difficult state.

But this argument seems to me to be a tragic mistake, which is concealed by the flourishing exterior of our existence. I'm not dismissing this flourishing exterior: in full accord with the classical confession of God's providential order, I think that we have to give thanks for it. But any minister or priest can tell us that behind this facade there's a sea of unmentionable suffering, far more – and far worse – then we could ever have thought of. Is there no longer any need for comfort? That's what people say who look no further than their own front door; others know better.

I'm not too sombre. I can well understand being criticized for this – at the end of the chapter on providence – but I want to counter the criticism, and another time to be rather lighter. However, this must come first of all, the evil with which we must learn to live, and that's rather different from closing our eyes to it.

I would maintain that belief in God's providential order is what keeps us going, in good times and in bad. The farmers of Zeeland used to say at times of catastrophe, 'Minister, no stranger did that to us', a modest way of speaking of God and meant as a consolation: the 'face' is not the real face; behind it is hidden the friendly face of God. The comment needn't always be so modest. But the pendulum will keep swinging between resistance and submission.

So we must leave it at that: God, the almighty Creator of heaven and earth, sustains and rules all things as with his hand. That's the only reason why 'all things' are to be borne. God meets us at the heart of our existence, in daily things – great or small. Not as a stranger, despite his 'face'. Far less as one who is powerless, who can do no more. If God is pure tears, how can God dry tears?

God does so, but not always here nor everywhere. Things only work out at the end. God doesn't deal as gently with human beings and the world as we would like, but in the end shows himself to be who he is, welcomes us and keeps us safe for eternity.

Interlude

VIII

The Connection

'Without doubt everything turns on Jesus Christ, because in his sacrifice he solved the riddle of guilt. But one cannot draw from that the mistaken conclusion that everything is also about Jesus Christ' (*A.A.van Ruler*)

1. Creation as a condition of redemption

According to the tradition of faith, creation is followed by redemption. It's at least the most logical order, to begin from the outside. Insiders sometimes take the reverse order and begin from redemption. There's also some logic in that: in the church we come into contact with redemption first, since the church is there to proclaim the gospel of the God-who-saves (the name Jesus means 'God who saves' or 'God who liberates'). Moreover, we learn there that God-who-saves is the Creator, and then it's easier to trust in God's rule over 'all things'. It doesn't much matter what we choose, as long as we accept from the tradition that the Creator is the same as the Redeemer and vice versa. One thing is impossible: out of a need to honour God as Redeemer, we can't also call creation a form of redemption or liberation. At first sight that's very attractive, and has the attractiveness of the radical about it: we know of only one thing, God the liberator! We needn't divide our attention between two words about God, a word of creation and a word of redemption, but listen only to the Word that is called Jesus Christ.

However, the consequences of this view are very confusing. If creation itself already has to be called an act of redemption or liberation, or even an act of reconciliation – from *what* is creation the redemption? From Nothingness? In that case we get into very complicated speculations which moreover unavoidably bring us to the question where that something or nothing from which creation is redemption came from. In my view this question poses problems which are insoluble and which in any case go beyond the Christian tradition.

It makes sense to speak of redemption or liberation only if there is a something or a someone who has to be redeemed or liberated. The creation which gives us this impression must therefore come before redemption. Moreover it must come from the same God whom we meet in the church in the gospel of Jesus. Otherwise it comes from a strange god or itself is a strange, eternal opponent of the God of Christianity. Thus the Christian church can never dispense with belief in God the Creator; that's the fundamental presupposition of redemption. Belief in God the Redeemer can never take its place.

That's not the view of e.g. Karl Barth, who goes a long way in the direction I'm describing here. But he finds the Redeemer God so fundamental to Christian tradition that he makes the Creator a shadow of the Redeemer. Really the Creator is already the Redeemer, although there isn't yet anything to redeem!

There's nothing against putting it like this, except that we are then compelled to accept the idea that God knows everything from all eternity. God was already (in God's eternal thoughts) the Redeemer or Reconciler when there was no world to redeeem. Even more strongly, in order to become Redeemer and Reconciler – the heart of God's being – God created the world and let sin in. For various reasons that seems to me to be an unfortunate construction. In this way we know, or rather Karl Barth knows, too much of what God resolved in eternity. Moreover the difference between God and God's human beings comes to look like a put-up job. Can we still take ourselves seriously if we are so clearly programmed from eternity, sin included?

But above all: in that case the creation must become a kind of disguised revelation of Christ, and that means that it loses its independence. It's only an attachment; it has to be interpreted in terms of the church and is really there for the church.

This seems to me to be a reversal of the Christian tradition. It's nice for the church, which as a result becomes much more important, but the creation (ordinary life) loses its central place and God essential characteristics as Creator. We may learn in church that God is also Reconciler and Redeemer, indeed even learn it as a primary fact, but this is and remains in apposition to God the Creator, an apposition in which human beings and the world have their ongoing existence, to which they owe their temporal and eternal salvation, but still an apposition.

2. Redemption – from what? On salvation

If God liberates, the LORD saves (and whatever other classical characteristics of God we may use), the question which arises is: from what?

It smacks of naivety not to put this question or not to try to answer it from the Christian tradition. My criticism of some liberation theologians at home and abroad comes at this point.

The question from what, according to the Christian tradition of faith, God redeems human beings and their world brings us to the crux of Christianity. For as in all religions, so in Christianity, God's salvation (the salvation of the Christian religion) is defined by what human beings regard as great disaster. For Christian faith, that is the sin by which human beings have become debtors before God. I won't be returning to these terms, but simply mention them here once again as key words for disaster as understood by Christianity. Salvation from God, the authentic, definitive, eternal salvation from God that the Christian tradition has taken with it on its journey down the centuries, is redemption from sin and guilt, and thus the abolition of alienation between God and humankind.

Other forms of disaster are certainly not denied by Christianity: above all sickness, suffering, death. But exploitation, injustice and oppression also stand high on the list; according to the Christian tradition they even come from the Evil One. Since the 1970s some Christians have become so fixated on them that they want to see God's real salvation in the abolition of poverty, in political liberation and social equality. It even gets to the point of God becoming another word for a just society.

In my view that is to take things too far. Moreover, I can't avoid the impression that this way is to make a virtue out of necessity. It isn't easy now to maintain that the primal evil of human beings consists in something that they can't see directly and that its removal isn't something that directly (at least tangibly) stops the evil. There's a great temptation to dilute Christian salvation so that it becomes social salvation, since in that way at least the Christian church still gets a look-in. But this is no longer the look-in it had to begin with. Social salvation is also salvation, even salvation from God. But it's salvation that we could create for ourselves if we wanted to. Christians are also called to that by the Christian proclamation of faith. First, though, the salvation for which the Christian tradition has been called to life is salvation that we can't create for one another because it's beyond our capacities: the abolition of our alienation from the Creator, the source of our alienation from one another as human beings. What is first (in a logical order) thus comes first: first the primal alienation is removed, otherwise we remain as we are and social salvation can no longer be achieved.

A second characteristic of salvation in the Christian tradition of faith is that it transcends what I call contextual salvation. It is that, too: salvation for blacks, for oppressed women, for exploited mineworkers. But again, that's salvation with something missing. Not just because we give it to one another or withold it from one another, but also because it's salvation for a particular group or a particular social stratum of the population. Definitive eternal salvation is one and the same for blacks, women, men, whites, poor and rich – you share in it or you don't. But it transcends the groups: it's universal salvation.

Again I don't want to be too pedantic. Death and suffering are universal, like dirty hands. Therefore in the Christian tradition they stand right next to the real disaster of guilt and sin, and for the same reason redemption can also be understood as rescue from death or comfort over all suffering. But according to tradition, suffering, including suffering over death, begins at the beginning of all disaster, and that is and remains the broken relationship with God.

3. Christianity as a religion of grace

In studies of religion Christianity has sometimes been put among the religions of redemption or grace. Quite apart from whether this kind of division is generally appropriate and whether Christianity should be put among the religions of grace in particular, as one religion among others, Christianity clearly encourages this classification. You've only to step inside a church and grace encounters you like incense (if it's a Roman Catholic church) or stale air (among Protestants).

Two questions arise: why does 'grace' play so large a part (what kind of a word is it?), and does the classification 'religion of grace' fit with the central place of creation which I emphasized in the previous section?

To begin with the answer to the second question: it fits in very well. So well, indeed, that it has been possible to stress both creation and redemption fully in the Christian tradition of faith without there needing to be any competition, far less a kind of partition between the two.

As I've shown, Christianity, as a religion of grace or redemption, presupposes the Creator and his world. Redemption has no sketch to which it could be related if there were no creation. But that is as it were a logical statement, and I must give it more content.

The Christian tradition doesn't stop at 'creation', but adds redemption to it. Not because it has such a jaundiced view of life, but because it approaches reality realistically. The good life isn't as good as we like to imagine; in our hands it has become the destroyed life. That's quite obvious. The Christian tradition can simply appeal to a fact of experience. All that it does here is to deepen this experience.

First by making it 'sin' and 'guilt'. That means a confrontation with the Creator who wants to see his work protected and not destroyed. That's bad enough as the deeper content to this destruction. But it isn't yet the whole story. The devastation is so great that any well-intentioned (?) attempt at making good gets nowhere. If any of the devastation is to be made good, the initiative must come from somewhere else, because it doesn't come from us human beings. That, too, is a truth of experience. We haven't learned to stop making war; cheating and fraud continue; violence and aggressive behaviour are the order of the day, both collectively and personally. Not in a worse way than before – though with more effective means – but not in a less worse way either.

That's the background to Christianity as a religion of grace. As a religion of grace it excludes achievement as a basis for existence, for the simple reason that achievement has never helped us out of the morass. Doing – even more doing than we've already done – doesn't make things any better, and we can't do nothing either. What's left? With grace or without grace to be in the hands of a higher power which rescues us from our helplessness.

I think that the contribution of Christianity to culture primarily lies in what I've discussed here, i.e. in precisely what has led to its bad name: it's said to have spoiled the vital joy of existence with sin and grace. There's some truth in that, at least in so far as the vital joy of countless people is the dream of a life which isn't hindered by responsibilities, laws and doubts. But that life doesn't exist, nor has it ever existed. Nor does the Christian view of human beings and culture spoil a love of life; rather, it saddles us with a healthy doubt about all blueprints for a healed world which are given us free. Christians join in anything that can make the world better, but they do this without any great illusions. One needn't cherish any hope of success to set out on an undertaking, said William of Orange, whether to win or to endure.

In other words, grace means that according to the Christian tradition redemption is not self-redemption but an act of God the Creator, who will not let the world go out of love. Moreover the very term ('grace') is used in the Christian tradition with a variety of meanings. We can get on with some better than others, and some have already completely faded out.

The church fathers could speak of grace as though it were a medicine – a *pharmakon*, as they called it. But they also associated the term above all with the use of the sacraments, in which grace is as it were was transmitted to believers. The Reformation broke with this terminology (in this way the church already had too much control over grace), and regarded grace as forgiving sinners. Redemption comes through being given grace.

The people who are happy with that are those who are involved. The others continue to have problems all their life – and this doesn't seem to me to be too strange. It doesn't tell us anything about whether this bit of the tradition is true or not; it only indicates that the tradition also has recalcitrant elements which sometimes need a good deal of thinking about.

4. Creation and redemption: the connection

The classical Christian tradition saw a chance of linking creation and redemption by putting the Fall between them. Once there was a time when everything was still good: human existence began in harmony and innocence. Then came sin, which has corrupted the whole of creation, and nothing is good any longer. But God comes with his redemption and will bring a time when the stains and blemishes will again be wiped away from creation: God's future. So the tradition links two opposed views by putting the Fall in the middle: the golden age as past and the golden age as future.

In the meantime we've seen that there is no historical basis for a Fall. There never was a time when everything was still good. What I'm doing in this chapter is once again to consider the consequences of abandoning the historical model – as I already tried to do in the case of the creation. Perhaps I myself don't see them very well, but I'm doing my best to take account of the fact that with the best will in the world the Christian tradition can no longer work with them. Let me sum up the outcome here.

1. Creation and Creator are the fundamental notions of Christian faith. I identify that with a commitment to daily life, a commitment to the 'below'. Here we have our concerns, our joys, sufferings and glories; in short, it is here that things happen which move us to the depths of our emotions. In all these things we come upon God as our partner. God goes with us, guides our existence without doing away with our responsibility; on the contrary, God clothes us with precisely that and calls on us to be responsible for our conduct.

I shall sum that up for the moment as 'being there'. 'Being there' isn't just the basis for the encounter with and the discovery of God, doesn't just precede something that can follow later, but is the main thing both for us and for God the Creator. Why else redemption? Because creation is the reality where it began for the Creator. It is redemption which emphasizes that the creation is the main thing, the beginning and end of all God's ways.

2. God's redeeming work is imagined by Christian tradition as an act of rescuing creation. As grace or being given grace, it is even imagined as an emergency solution devised by the Creator. In its tradition about Jesus Christ, his cross and resurrection, the Christian church has given a detailed account of this. I shall do the same thing shortly, especially in the chapter on reconciliation.

Redemption is a single action: that's the first thing. In other words, Jesus Christ is a unique phenomenon, and his conduct is a unique action from God's side. Not only because Jesus is a historical person and as such is unrepeatable, but also because salvation in terms of reconciliation is a unique action – and that fits in very well. That makes clear the central place which Jesus Christ occupies in the Christian tradition. Without redemption the creation was lost. So we get to the point we reached earlier: in the Christian tradition of faith, creation and redemption are indissolubly connected because they presuppose each another. But the important point is creation, although it also turns on Jesus Christ and redemption. Or rather, *because* creation is the issue, it turns on Jesus Christ.

3. We learn to know Jesus Christ in the church. Here the unique act of redemption, reconciliation, is narrated further. It is continued by the church's proclamation – that has to happen with unique actions.

How does that work? To mention preaching – and I shall come back to this – is to mention the Holy Spirit (i.e. God who works on our spirit). So preaching is also called the Word (with a capital W). The Word is the Spirit which touches our spirit and changes it. For this reason, moreover, redemption is always envisaged by the Christian tradition as more than just 'being saved'. Through the Word that is the Spirit, there is a reconstruction of existence, of personal life. Of course this has its effect on the extra-personal institutions and structures of a society. But structures can't change; only people can change. In this sense belief is a highly personal matter, and will always remain so.

To sum up: according to the Christian tradition, where do we encounter God? As Creator in the ups and downs of our existence, in our 'being there'. And as Spirit, in the proclamation of the gospel of redemption, in the Word (the basis of the Christian church) and its effects, the renewal/reconstruction of our personal life. God in us? Certainly; according to the Christian tradition it's never been less than that. So does the Creator dwell in the creation? Redemption means that God dwells in it in such a way that God's Spirit goes with our spirit. Communication is restored; we again live in awareness of God.

About Jesus Christ

IX

Christology

'O Kloos, why did your God sit
so deep in your thoughts
and why did he not walk normally down the street?' (*Lucebert*)

1. Believing in a Christian way

Christianity owes its name to Christ, since according to the Christian tradition of faith Jesus Christ determines the face of God. God is love, but in order to arrive at the God who is love people have to go the way of faith in Christ. They have to recognize their false insights, their guilt, and be reconciled through Christ with God. Thus the Christian tradition of faith understands itself as a message of salvation, which calls for faith and conversion and allows people to live and die at peace with God. So the Christian faith turns on Christ ('Mediator' is also an appropriate title for him), but is ultimately about God. With the help of this word-play (taken from Van Ruler, see the heading to Chapter VIII) I can emphasize a few things which are important for the Christian tradition of faith.

Although it's called Christian faith, it's not as if Christ forces God out of his place. That's an important point to make when we think of dialogue with the world religions, especially with Islam. No matter how great the emphasis with which Islam speaks about the prophet Muhammad, Muhammad isn't Allah, nor even an extension of him, but is wholly and always on the side of the created world. The honour for which he is zealous in his proclamation is God's honour; he seeks no honour for himself. According to Islam, the great objection to Christianity is that it makes Christ God's rival for Christians. Christ is a demigod, if not wholly God, and if that is so, what remains of the oneness and unity of God?

Now the way in which Christians generally speak about Christ isn't without its problems. But if we begin from each other's intentions and not from caricatures or deviations, we can say that Christianity, too, like the other religions, begins with God, and that seen from this perspective Christ *could* not occupy the place of God himself. So we have a basis for inter-religious dialogue. The next step could then be to sound out as cautiously and as carefully as possible *what* the other religion has to say about God. Only then can we discuss whether we want to talk just like this or otherwise, and why.

So with this starting point I'm presupposing a common element, an element that underlies all religions: God is the concern of all people (in this sense God is subject and object), but not in the same way. Christianity is a faith like other traditions of faith, but it's believing in a Christian way. According to Christianity, in the reflection of Christ we see God's true face.

2. *The controversy over the way*

'It's about God but it turns on Christ' has another aspect that must be stressed. The Christian faith is a tradition the special character of which came into being among other religions as the result of a *controversy* over the way to God and his salvation, the controversy with Judaism. It's customary nowadays to speak of a Jewish-Christian tradition, and of course there's everything to be said for that. In any case, there's a concern to indicate the affinity between Judaism and Christianity, or, to put it even more strongly, the roots of Christianity in Judaism. Without Judaism there wouldn't have been a Christian tradition. That's true, though I don't much like this way of talking. First of all it sounds a bit like a take-over: Christians act as though they're also Jews and in so doing are taking over the identity of Judaism. That's not good for the Jews, but it isn't good for Christianity either. There's a difference between the two, and that very difference – over Christ and thus over the way – defines each religion over against the other. My second objection is that the expression 'Jewish-Christian' trivializes this controversy, and again, here too no service is done either to Jews, or to Christians, or to the dialogue between them. What's really being said is that there's no need for such a dialogue: in the main we're one tradition.

Now my view is that this dialogue isn't so necessary, but for very different reasons. I think that the Christian community, having plagued the Jews for centuries, should for the moment leave them in peace: no take-over and no religious dialogue either. Because of their guilt-feelings towards the Jews, Christians are very keen on dialogue, but if I were a Jew I would find that a problem. Doing things together – for the moment that seems to me the best and only way of taking the Jews seriously.

Is there such a need to emphasize controversies? Not if they have little to do with identity. But that's precisely the issue where the difference between Jews and Christians is concerned. The entire role that Christ plays in the Christian tradition of faith – though it may have been exaggerated over the centuries or even have gone over the top – can be reduced to that of another way to God than the way of Judaism. Is the Torah (Moses and the prophets) the way or is Christ the way? From the start the Christian tradition of faith has maintained the latter, with all the questions that it raises: does the new way abolish the old or take it up into a higher order? But there for the moment I shall leave questions aside and simply move to a conclusion. Christianity owes its name to Christ: it turns on Christ, who opens up access to God. The controversy is a controversy over the way.

However, not only Christians but also Jews have always taken this controversy seriously. It culminates in the question whether one has to be a Jew to belong to the people of God or whether non-Jews (Gentiles) can also enjoy that privilege. For Christianity, the latter was and is the case: 'Gentiles' like ourselves can also belong. The way to Israel's God is universal: it stands open to all men and women thanks to the way which is called Christ.

The formulation which I've just used shows how close Jews and Christians are to each other and also how bitterly they can offend one another in matters of religion. But that's not the worst thing; that sort of thing always happens: the closer people are to each other, the harder it is for them to live together. The worst thing is the history of misunderstanding, hatred and even violence against the Jews which lies behind us. At that point there's little for Christianity to do but to accept its guilt and go further.

3. Jesus Christ, the interpretation of a life

How can anyone be so important that a world community has come into being named after him? Here I'm taking up a second question: the community is named after Christ, but where does the name Christ come from and what does it stand for? To answer both questions we must take a step backwards.

Unlike Christ, Jesus is his proper name, the name his mother gave him. 'Jesus' denotes a historical person who went round the land of the Jews around the beginning of our era and who died a premature death on a cross. So in principle Jesus can be arrived at through historical research, like Alexander the Great or William of Orange. A few years a student magazine had an article in the style of a historical report which went something like this: 'Jerusalem, such and such a day, such and such a month. Today a certain Jesus of Nazareth, of no fixed abode, was executed on a charge of rebellion against the state.' The piece was meant to shock, and did so, but quite wrongly. From a historical perspective the event couldn't be presented better. Moreover we should have heard no more of J of N, indeed we wouldn't even have known of his existence, like that of so many who were crucified, if the whole story had been told as a historical report. That this didn't happen is at least food for thought.

Jesus of Nazareth isn't just the name of a historical person but also that of a person from a Jewish background. However remarkable it may seem, the founder of Christianity wasn't a Christian but a Jew in origin and religion. Is that important? I think so, for a variety of reasons. A historical person is always someone who is embedded in a concrete, limited world. Jesus wasn't black, wasn't white, wasn't a woman. As the one thing (his Jewishness) marked his historical existence, so did the other. The question whether he couldn't just as well have been a woman, black or white, or whatever, is nonsensical, because it tries to transcend the characteristics of the historical. You can't make just anything out of a historical person. We shall come back to that later, when we consider views about Jesus.

But there's something else. That Jesus was a Jew also means that he expressed himself in Jewish religious terminology. So in order to understand his words and actions, Christians always need to know something about Judaism. The more work was done in that area, the more striking the agreement seemed to be between Jesus' preaching (as recorded in the Gospels) and the preaching of the Jewish religious leaders (especially the Pharisees). That they really became involved in a controversy right from the beginning is the story told by the first followers of Jesus. They had a different view of him from that of their Jewish surroundings.

That brings me to a second name, Christ. This doesn't come from his mother but from his followers, as an interpretation of his life, with all the questions which that raises. If they got its meaning right, must we give the same interpretation? Are other views of Jesus possible? And why this name of Christ in particular? At all events, this name was essential for his first followers.

What sort of a name is it? The word is originally the Greek translation of the Hebrew (Aramaic) 'Messiah'. Preachers and priests nowadays readily translate it Messiah and then speak of Jesus Messiah (or Messiah Jesus). That sounds refreshing, particularly to those who know the Jewish tradition. In the tradition in which Jesus was brought up – in whatever version of it we imagine him – the Messiah is the one marked out by God who brings in the end-time, the person of whom people will say at his appearance: 'This is the one who was to come.' But the remarkable thing is that the earliest Christian traditions didn't translate this name back. The New Testament indicates that Aramaic and Hebrew were known in the Christian churches (*abba, maranatha, amen*), but Christ didn't alternate with Messiah. This doesn't seem to me to be a coincidence. The non-Jewish peoples to whom the message had to be taken hadn't been brought up in a messianic tradition and would have had to undergo a complete training in Jewish religious expectations for the future if 'Messiah' were to have the associations for them that it does for Jews – down to the present day. That was reason enough for the first followers to be careful with this religious term.

But I think that there's more to it than that. 'Messiah' has associations with this fitting into the future, the messianic kingdom as the final end of God's ways. This future certainly hasn't disappeared from the New Testament; it's also attached to Jesus and his work. But the greatest concern isn't so much for Jesus as the end-point as for Jesus as the way, because this very way that he is (in his person) runs so contrary to current ideas. Hence 'Christ' in the New Testament and not 'Messiah'. The terminology reflects the specific feature of Christianity.

4. *Christ in apposition to Jesus*

Now the word 'Christ' certainly also caused knotty problems for non-Jewish hearers. Literally translated, Christ (of course like Messiah) means 'anointed'. Here the Jewish world thought of the Messiah who brought salvation, 'anointed' by God (as kings in ancient times were anointed with holy oil) to bring in his kingdom. But what did non-Jews think of? According to the New Testament scholar De Zwaan, many Greeks could only understand this word as a 'man with slicked-down hair', just as for us 'anointing' has associations with lotion and oil. Strangely enough, it didn't prevent 'Christ' from becoming a name which has been used down to the present day.

To begin with the going was difficult; the name had as it were to find a place for itself. Given the significance of the word, there needn't have been a problem. As we've seen, 'Christ' meant the bringer of salvation at the end time appointed by God. For the first (mostly Jewish) followers Jesus *was* that, and it was natural to call him 'Christ'.

But in the Greek-speaking world this couldn't be taken for granted (for a long time people preferred to call Jesus 'the Lord') and it took some time for 'Christ' to become established. That only happened when it had become a kind of proper name, a second name: Jesus Christ or also Christ Jesus. The original significance was then forgotten.

For many people, both inside and outside the Christian church, that's still the case: Christ is just a surname. But originally that certainly wasn't the intention, and anyone who still reads the Heidelberg Catechism will find that the name has a confessional character. Jesus is more than J of N. He is (the) Christ! Is Christ, then, a particular idea of particular people about Jesus? Indeed, just as to refuse to give him the name denotes a particular view. I can now say that Jesus is always spoken of in terms of a particular ideal. That's already the case in the New Testament. He is called 'Son of man', 'prophet' or 'Son of David', and that's still the case today: the minister speaks of him as Saviour, as Lord, as Redeemer, as Liberator, as 'the Lord Jesus', as 'Messiah' and so on. Each term has its own content (you can recognize from it which view the minister prefers) and is meant to be a closer definition of Jesus as a historical person. These are just the various colourings of Jesus' person and work within the spectrum of a broad, recognizable tradition of interpretation of, say, the Protestant Netherlands. There are other, less accessible, traditions.

What I call 'colouring', 'interpretation', 'exposition' of Jesus' life here is expressed by a technical term: christology or teaching about Christ which people hold as a view of faith. We can speak of the christology of the apostle Paul, of the early church, of Augustine or Karl Barth – and so on *ad infinitum*. The ministers whom I've just mentioned also clearly show different christological preferences in the different ways in which they speak about Jesus.

But we mustn't exaggerate this difference. Sometimes there are just nuances, sometimes preferences which aren't meant exclusively;

sometimes also real differences which can give (and often have given) rise to controversies and even to schisms and heresy-hunting. Moreover there are libraries full of theological literature in which all these christological schemes are studied, discussed or criticized. No wonder that often the question has been and still is raised: wouldn't we do better to keep to the simple man from Nazareth, Jesus, and take the interpretation which the disciples gave of his life for what it is, 'clothing' which we can easily dispense with or, even more, which obscures the view of the real Jesus? What Jesus said and did, his fate and his actions – isn't that more important than what his followers made of him? And above all isn't that far more accessible to simple, secularized people like us?

5. Jesuology in place of christology?

That sounds an attractive proposition: scrap the 'clothing' and return to the ordinary Jesus of the Gospels; he's already miraculous enough. To begin with, I shall make two comments on this proposal.

First, I shall refer to a presupposition which forms the basis of this idea. It begins from a contrast between 'purely historical' and 'clothing provided by the narrator'. But this contrast is untenable. A story about someone is by definition something which is told, and telling already involves giving a meaning. The so-called historical approach of the Gospels is thus by no means as purely historical as is often imagined. Simple investigations confirm that. The Gospels, too (in particular), give an interpretation of the life of Jesus.

Secondly, the preference for the man Jesus of Nazareth (in terms of a return to him) is also a colouring, though one which tries to strip off other colourings; however, that only happens by providing a new one. It's like the person who wants to transcend the division among the churches by founding a non-denominational church and in so doing increases the number of denominations by one.

I can also say that if for the moment we call the tendency to make the historical person of the Gospels central a form of Jesuology, then only one conclusion is possible: even a Jesuology is a christology. I shall explain this in a moment: it's a curtailed christology, which doesn't fulfil the expectations attached to it.

It seems to me undeniable that the need for a Jesuology stems from a very legitimate motive. The Jesus Christ of the church's tradition is so buried under tradition and church that it's impossible to have any relationship with him. He's become a stranger to us. Who can make anything of 'Son of God', 'God's only Son', 'Christ the King'? But one can make something of the Jesus who saves the poor, heals the sick, teaches the authorities a lesson. So why not put this Jesus at the centre?

The motif – perhaps it would better to say the need – behind the 'move' towards what are supposed to be the more historical Gospels is, in other words, that of the attraction, the relevance of Jesus for people living today. With Christ, the church doesn't make any impression on contemporaries, and sometimes is itself at a loss what to do, but it can make something of the historical person of Jesus and can also put him forward: people can recognize him. I'm aware that I'm now playing off Jesus and Christ against each other, and of course that's impossible. I made that clear earlier. But in doing that I'm following a tendency which I want to bring out and make conscious.

What are we to think of this need? In the first place, it isn't new. The history of Christianity is a real patchwork quilt of 'colourings' depending on need or usefulness, all of which are attached to what (it is thought) is the more historical person of the Jesus of the Gospels. The eighteenth century saw Jesus as the rational teacher of God, the nineteenth century suspected that he was a wisdom teacher of humankind, the beginning of a world morality of brotherly love, and the twentieth century has already seen a whole series of variants, beginning with Jesus as the first truly free man and ending with Jesus as a politician and social liberator.

It would be interesting – but I don't have the time or the competence – to investigate how Jesus was 'coloured' outside European Christianity. At the least it seems that for blacks he has negroid features, and in Chinese paintings you can see him with 'slit eyes'. This is precisely what we do, since for us he is a white man. But is this colouring limited to the colour of his skin? Doesn't it go deeper? Any culture, like any time, evidently sees something different in him, something of itself and its own aspirations. That sometimes makes Christians nervous. Can all this be? Where does it stop?

Of course it's all possible; we see it happening before our eyes, and what can we have against it from the Christian tradition of faith? Nothing. On the contrary, the answer to how it 'can be' is that the stories about Jesus evidently have so many sides that each age can find in him what they are fascinated by, and this then results in a new view of his person and work. Does that rest purely on the imagination of the beholders? That seems to me to be almost impossible. To give just one example: Jesus can be recognized as a social and political liberator because his story can also take on this colouring. But isn't he also the true king David, who leads his people out of oppression? And aren't his people also the poor and exploited? It seems to me that Christianity misunderstands itself if it doesn't realize that this kind of 'recognition' also constitutes the greatness of Jesus. However, the question is whether it's enough to take from the person and work of Jesus to represent the Christian tradition of faith. I think not, and I shall produce arguments in support of my view.

6. Useful or necessary?

1. The rapid succession of views about Jesus – whether we call these christologies or Jesuologies – is connected with rapid historical changes. Or should we put it differently, and were expert historians right to call the rapid changes no more than ripples, superficial ripples – which therefore come quickly and also go again quickly – while history itself is a broad stream in which changes really worthy of the name take place very slowly? I have sympathies with this view. I've already said that people aren't very different from what they used to be. No better and no worse, nor more murderous; they just have more refined weapons. Nor is their need for consumption greater, either; there are simply more people who have a chance to satisfy it, and so on. Ripples. The successive reinterpretations of Jesus' life and work can be fitted seamlessly into this picture: they're also ripples, sermons by way of present adaptations of the tradition of faith to particular situations, the next ripple bringing a new sermon.

2. Recognition is pleasant, but by definition implies that we already knew what is recognized and therefore didn't need to learn it from Jesus. We were, as it were, already doing it: with a policy in favour of the oppressed, with opposition to throne and altar – and look, there we also meet Jesus!

That prompts an interesting question: in that case why is Jesus so necessary? Are we busy reading *into* him what we ourselves find important? Are we seeking approval of our ideas and actions from above? That's not imaginary. But even if we exclude this possibility, the question remains why Jesus is still important for something that we ourselves have already discovered. Why bring Jesus into it? If it's a matter of 'importance', Che Guevara was also important, and Gandhi, and Martin Luther King, and Mother Teresa. Why be specifically orientated on Jesus?

There's no longer an answer to this question, at least if we don't want to go back to the christology of the tradition. Except that Jesus is useful. But 'useful' isn't the same as 'necessary'. Others can also be useful, or rather, others certainly are. At this point of 'usefulness' or 'necessity', moreover, the ways part.

What I've called recognition doesn't take us further than the usefulness of Jesus for purposes and values which we ourselves already know. In saying this I'm not saying anything against these purposes and ideals: perhaps they're good, perhaps they aren't, but that's the next stage. The point is that we find ourselves unexpectedly outside the Christian tradition of faith, for this doesn't think Jesus especially useful (for whatever purpose) but necessary. And in a particular sense. What sense?

The unambiguous answer of the Christian tradition of faith brings us to an essential presupposition: the alienation between the Creator and his people. Without this presupposition the Christian tradition is robbed of its essence. Jesus removes the alienation between God and his creatures: he isn't useful for that, but necessary.

3. How, with your good intentions (back to Jesus of Nazareth), can you go off the road when it comes to the Christian tradition of faith? Because only one historical relationship is possible and this never goes further than that of an inspiring model, an 'attractive figure', in short a moral model.

My question is: isn't Jesus, then, according to Christian tradition, an example to be followed? Certainly, but following by means of an imitation of Jesus as a person from the beginning of our era rests on a misunderstanding and leads nowhere. Moreover the striking thing is that the New Testament authors (who were still very close to Jesus' historical appearance) saw discipleship in a much more restrictive sense than is often imagined. They limit it to following his tenacity and readiness for sacrifice in his suffering. 'Who when he was reviled, did not revile in return; when he suffered, he did not threaten', as we read in the apostle's admonition.

To get back to the argument. I called Jesusology a curtailed christology. Of course it's a form of christology, since it attaches significance to Jesus of Nazareth. But Jesus takes on significance because we put him in a framework of reference (that we come upon or even make), and for a historical person that framework can never be more than the framework of inspiration, admiration and stimulus for action that is focussed on humanity and the like.

The proclamation of love of neighbour and justice then remains a basic value for Christianity. As a by-product of faith that's no small thing. On the contrary, Jesus preached these values and the Christian church followed him in them. But the Christian tradition of faith saw infinitely more in Jesus than the proclaimer and model of values. That's why I called Jesuology a curtailed christology, a christology in which there is only what we already knew: morality. It can tell us what Jesus is good for, but no longer why he has to be.

I can also put it like this: morality is a necessary characteristic, and in this sense an indispensable ingredient, of Christianity; we even need to make it the criterion of faith. But morality isn't the key. To that is opposed the christology of the Christian faith. This is about the way to God who is love, and says that it is rather less simple to get there than we thought in our innocence.

Classical christology doesn't deny that Jesus was a historical person, quite the contrary. But the relationship with him is not the relationship that we have to a historical person. That calls for a thorough explanation.

7. The prince in disguise

The story is well known and appears in many versions: a scruffily dressed, unattractive young man, who on his entry into the village at best gets a sympathetic smile, proves in a situation of crisis – perhaps by a heroic action which no one had expected from him – to be a prince in disguise. According to the Christian tradition of faith, was Jesus such a prince in disguise, who didn't at all look like it (so that people could make a mistake about him), but was in fact the Son of God?

A notable trend in early Christianity maintained this. God's only Son, indeed God himself, comes on earth in the guise of a humble person who is done away with with a curse and a sigh – apparently. An ancient Gnostic writing says that the evil powers failed to recognize him. Just as a fish gets caught on the hook which is hidden in the bait, so the evil powers – sin and death – swallowed Jesus up. Only when it's too late do they discover that they've misjudged his mortal exterior and are forced to submit to the Son.

Two important themes in this dramatic version of things – though it wasn't accepted in this form by the Christian church – will go on to occupy us. First the dramatic element. It puts the alienation between God and man outside human power and responsibility: it comes upon people from outside. At most their blindness can be removed, but fundamentally they're victims. Moreover they're rescued by a demonstration of power. The question which this view of things prompts is: does it fit? Are people basically victims of evil, or are we being rather too innocent here? I shall return to this theme in a later section.

Here I should just add that the world of Gnostic ideas (even then) had far too many mythological features to be able to get a footing in the Christian tradition. A drama indeed takes place between God and human beings to the degree that people are caught up in the power of evil – Christian tradition has never denied that – but God doesn't gain the victory by a trick. The Christian tradition has thought that beneath God's dignity. At the same time that's a criticism of the 'trick'. But what about the second theme, the prince in disguise? Officially the Christian community of faith didn't accept this notion either. That God himself was present in Jesus in one way or another was beyond question (and still is) for the tradition. But not disguised as a human being, since then Jesus would be nothing but a garment which God put on when he appeared on earth, and that doesn't do justice either to God or to Jesus. The whole complicated christology of the early church, which is known as the doctrine of two natures – one person (Jesus) in whom two natures (divine and human) are united – is intended to exclude this idea of a prince in disguise. The only question is whether it succeeds.

I think that in all honesty we must say that it doesn't, or barely does so. Not only because the popular piety of the Christian church – down to the present day – walks a tightrope and isn't at all rooted in the doctrine of two natures, but also because this teaching, for all its good intentions, takes us too far into the terrain of theological practice. Believers aren't by definition theologians and needn't be theologians to be believers (just as, conversely, theologians aren't by definition believers). Theology is there to give an account of the tradition of faith in terms of a particular time and culture. If we make it more, then the teaching is too quickly used for its own sake instead of serving as a chart for finding God. The classical christology of the two natures has become *par excellence* a model of such concentrated theology that it ends up in 'teaching for teaching's sake'. Those steeped in it have already forgotten that they were in search of God; even worse, orthodoxy in the doctrine of Christ becomes a decisive criterion whether or not someone is part of Christianity.

Thus the doctrine of two natures provides too much theology, and that's not all. It's also a theology in which people eventually get stuck, as I shall show in the next section.

8. *The doctrine of two natures*

What precisely is the doctrine of two natures, and what was meant by it? Seen in terms of the purpose it was meant to serve, it's less complicated than might be imagined. If it wasn't outlined as a repudiation, it was meant as one, as a kind of counter-model to that of the prince in disguise. The great objection to this idea – which was felt very clearly – was that the humanity of Jesus became a pseudo-question; it was only a shell, and it was really God who went around in it. But how could one avoid this all-too-fantastic view of things and at the same time maintain what it was thought necessary to maintain: that in the person of Jesus God became man?

Anyone who thinks in terms of the prince in disguise has no problems at this point: Jesus is really God, and that's what it's all about. Mary is then the mother of God, so in the early church devotion to her gradually developed. But in that case what becomes of the humanity that is due to Jesus? If you take that seriously, Mary isn't the mother of God but of the man Jesus, and the question becomes how a human being can at the same time be God. For this last is what all parties wanted to maintain at any price, and not just because popular piety required it: if Jesus isn't God, he may not be worshipped. But also because the essence of the Christian tradition of faith stands and falls by it; in Jesus Christ we encounter God himself. How?

I shall spare the reader the complicated intellectual convolutions of the doctrine of the two natures which have to show that two natures can be combined in one person without running into each other (the divine mustn't swallow up the human), but also without giving rise to two separate persons. It gets stuck in its own presuppositions. I shall make that clear first. After we've talked less than is usually supposed necessary.

An insoluble problem for the doctrine of two natures was that two 'I's have to be assumed, a divine and a human 'I'. That ends up in two persons in Jesus. If that's not the intention (and of course it isn't), we can say that the 'I' of Jesus is taken over by the 'I' of God, but in that case Jesus is no longer his own person as a human being, but a 'headless' person. We've then certainly arrived at one person, but there's no longer any question of two independent natures: the divine has again taken on the human as a garb (as in the case of the prince in disguise). The problem is insoluble: we sacrifice either the unity of the person (two natures become two persons) or the duality of the natures (one of the natures must give way to produce the one person). It's become a theological puzzle, and a puzzle which can't be solved. That's the price that has to be paid for avoiding the prince in disguise.

For this reason alone we can't use the doctrine of the two natures. I've yet to talk about the terminology which it employs. We use these terms (nature/person) in quite a different sense from the church fathers, but already at that time the different content that they were given led to a complete misunderstanding between theological trends. Moreover, with the best will in the world we can't require people to steep themselves so much in theology that they can describe in everyday English what was meant by these terms. The problems are insoluble.

Is that a bad thing? Not at all. We're straining over a problem that we ourselves have created. The doctrine of two natures is an attempt at a reply, an attempt by venerable church fathers, but with the aid of their own ideas and in terms of their own time. If such an attempt fails, then we can happily leave it aside. We aren't condemned to choose between one person (but no longer two natures) or two natures (but no longer one person).

9. Incarnation as bridging

Where does this fixation on two natures combined in one person come from, and what did people want to achieve with it? I've already said what people didn't want to lose from the idea of the prince in disguise: that in the person of Jesus, God became man. The classical Christian tradition coined the term incarnation, God's becoming human, for it. Both the notion of the prince in disguise and that of the two natures go back to that basic datum of the tradition; they're both notions of incarnation. But they work in different directions. Gnosticism envisaged incarnation as a sort of disguising: in human guise, God fights against evil and wins. Redemption takes the form of a drama. The classical church tradition had in view another image of redemption and thus used other terminology. So has the alienation to be overcome by Jesus? Now the doctrine of two natures seeks the solution in the person of Jesus himself: if God and man come together in him, then he really has accomplished everything. No more is necessary; with the union of the two natures the job of bridging – if

I can put it that way – is finished. God and man together again in the one person Jesus Christ: what more can one want than this miracle of grace?

In the next section I shall show that in addition to the bridging of the alienation by the union of the two natures, the Christian tradition of faith knows a second form of bridging: reconciliation as the work of Jesus Christ. Whether and to what extent the two bridgings meet remains to be seen. Here we shall see what we must think of the incarnation as a bridging of the gulf between God and man. Are we compelled to accept it if we don't want to get rid of faith? I don't think so. The gulf between God and human beings isn't bridged in such an abstract way (the divine nature is united with the human nature). Moreover it depends too much on the doctrine of the two natures: if this presents an insoluble problem (self-made), then the incarnation in terms of the union of the divine and the human nature isn't a 'must' for Christianity.

That doesn't mean that in reality, i.e. in Jesus' person and work, there was no occasion to raise the problem. The first followers of Jesus weren't such visionaries that they saw God where only ghosts were to be seen. But they didn't see an incarnation.

We can still best see the incarnation as an intellectual model made by Christianity, a failed thought-model for a mystery. Models in this sense aren't meant as a reflection of reality but as ways of making it possible to discuss reality in a satisfactory way. Here the model has taken things a long way. Almost all ideas of the person of Christ begin more or less openly from the notion that Jesus came to earth (so he was first already somewhere, in heaven), that he came for something (to perform a service), that God had sent him, and so on. Each in itself is an idea which can provide much clarification, but if they're pressed into the incarnation model, then everything goes wrong. Was there then already a man called Jesus before Jesus was born? And does Jesus go somewhere when his work on earth is done? Where is he, then?

Of course yet other questions emerge. When God became man, what became of God? Did God cease to be God (for a while)? The early church solved that problem, as we shall see, by saying that the second person of the divine Trinity became man. In this way, in the incarnation God need not cease to be God.

What isn't understood can of course still be a mystery. Can't we give the incarnation a place in this way? Of course, in a sense it has already got this place, namely in the liturgy of the church. There the mystery fits; there we also speak another language, not the language of understanding but that of worship, praise, rapture. There's nothing against allowing the incarnation its place there. Our Christmas (a latecomer among the Christian festivals) is itself devoted to it.

But there it must stay, since as a thought model the doctrine of two natures is well meant – there is indeed a mystery which must be expressed in words – but not successful.

10. What then? Talking about Jesus as about God

Jesus' first followers discovered something of God in him, and when the early church reflected on it they translated that 'something of God' into 'the divine nature'. Why should we follow them there? It's true that 'something of God', taken by itself, is unsatisfactory. There is something of God in everyone. It's already somewhat better if we say – for the moment – that according to Christian faith God was present in a unique way in Jesus, as compared to other people. But that, too, is quite vague and requires to be given more content. Just as is also, of course, the case with 'Son of God'. Human beings, too, seem to bear this name in the Christian tradition, and yet in Christian faith by preference we reserve this title for Jesus. He is not God himself, but so much God that we call him God's Son and, to stress the difference with others, God's *only-begotten* Son. Of course that's a metaphor, transferred language. God has no Son, or sons, in the way in which human beings do. 'Only-begotten' stands for a unique relationship, for a place which can only be occupied by an only-begotten Son.

Where does this get us? In one of the earliest literary products of Christianity (the Second Letter of Clement), the unknown writer says that Christians speak of Jesus 'as of God'. That's an attractive formula. It doesn't say that Jesus is God, God's own self. That can't be; Jesus may identify himself with God (in the Gospel according to John), but that doesn't cost anything: anyone can do that. It has the 'power of proof' only if God also identifies himself with Jesus. And according to Christianity, that's what God did in the resurrection of Jesus from the dead. That's why this plays such a great role in the opening of eyes to the mystery of his person. Of course Jesus' disciples also noted his love, his authority, his righteousness, but would they go on to speak of him 'as of God' on the basis of their experiences of him? I don't believe anything of the kind. So was there 'no splendour or glory' to be seen in him, as the prophet puts it? And surely he ended on the cross? But no, Christianity speaks of Jesus 'as of God', because God identified himself with Jesus. By identification I mean that he is occupied by God; 'occupied', full to the brim with God; hidden, of course (you can miss him), but made manifest in the resurrection.

Anyone who finds that too little may reflect that the early church was evidently so fascinated by the notion of the union of God and man as the union of two natures that as far as it was concerned that was the be-all and end-all of the message of salvation. But that now seems *to me* to be too little. The gap between God and man cannot be filled in so abstract a way as incarnational theology imagines: nature assumes nature. At Christmas Christianity doesn't celebrate the doctrine of the two natures, nor even the dogma of the incarnation. All that is terminology, expressive material which the Christian church has used to speak of its faith, but in itself as broad as it's long. The Christian message of salvation didn't really emerge with so little. It filled out the unique manner in which God was present in Jesus – surely we were looking for a good description of this – in a concrete and practical way: 'God was in Christ reconciling the world to himself, not counting their trespasses against them.' That (and everything else that it implies) is why Jesus is the light in the darkness. As far as I'm concerned, 'The light of this world appeared to save' and 'The day dawns in the east' are a better expression of what began at Christmas, at any rate better than incarnation and better than 'two natures united', and even better than 'celebrating the birthday of the Lord Jesus', as the kindergarten teacher tried to tell my children. They didn't see anything in this. The one who 'unites heaven and earth' has his own way, another way than the union of two natures, of bridging the gap between himself and his people.

All this certainly has its point. We needn't be embarrassed at that vague feeling that there is a peace 'which passes all understanding' at Christmas. On the contrary, Christmas is a confirmation of it. 'From here to God, no one sobs about our fate, no one' – however splendid this line by the Dutch poet Leo Vroman may be, what he says isn't true. In our best moments we endorse the Christian tradition which says that someone does. God was concerned at our fate and did something about it, regardless of the cost. Bach begins the *Christmas Oratorio* with drums in the night. That comes closer to it than Vroman's line.

X

Reconciliation

'. . . when the burden of our sins and of the wrath of God brought out the bloody sweat on him in the court; where he was bound that he might unbind us; after he had suffered countless shame that we should nevermore be put to shame; though innocent was condemned to death, that we should be acquitted before God's judgment; indeed, had his blessed body nailed to the cross that he should put his signature to our sin . . .' (*Formulary for the Service of the Holy Eucharist, 1618/19*)

1. Reconciliation: the sour summons of Christianity

'Why reconciliation? I didn't know that there was a war on!' Such an exclamation seems natural to me. In its honesty, at the same time it reveals the state of things: the pivot on which the Christian proclamation of faith turns no longer wholly matches up with our emotions – fails to do so at all. Reconciliation presupposes two parties, presupposes that there is something between these two, at least a form of dispute. But do we have a dispute with God? We aren't aware of any evil; moreover the forgiveness of sins doesn't make us jump up in the air (or if it does, only seldom), and peace with God is no great news. I'm exaggerating to some degree, but I'm not saying anything unrecognizable. The only thing left is: though we have nothing against God, can God have anything against us?

According to the Christian tradition that is indeed the case. So we must first be told what is at issue between God and human beings before we believe it. And even then we find it difficult to remain emotionally involved.

In this section I shall make an attempt to explain where this relative lack of concern comes from. In my view there are two factors which play a role, both of which have to do with the most essential features of what in Christian tradition is called reconciliation.

First let me take up the point that God has something against us. If that's the case (and it's the starting point for the Christian tradition), it's obvious that we're the ones who have to restore this relationship. This idea is deeply rooted in us, as is witnessed by the great place that sacrifice has in numerous religious traditions. Sacrifices are there for making good again. The unique thing about the Christian sketch of God – Christianity is rightly proud of it – is that God is the one who makes good again. So it's put the other way round. The reason which Christianity has given for this reversal isn't so crazy: we are helpless to do it ourselves.

However, this surprising reversal creates a complicated situation. It's certainly not the easiest solution. To mention just a couple of questions. How does God then make things good? And no less urgently, what about us? Are we also involved, or does this reconciliation take place over our heads? Such questions call for an answer which must be built into the notion of reconciliation. There it – and thus the way – becomes complicated, more complicated than we would like.

There's a second factor: reconciliation not only presupposes that something has gone wrong with the relationship between God and humankind but also *what* has gone wrong. In this chapter I shall call it alienation: God and God's people are alienated from each other. This alienation is on the human side; human beings withdraw from God. Why? Because they don't dare a real confrontation. And what's behind that? We have a bad conscience, and that makes us anxious before God as judge. There are therefore really three presuppositions on which the conception of reconciliation rests: 1. there is a gulf between God the Creator and God's people; 2. it's caused by human beings who – to put it briefly – sin against God and God's creation; 3. God doesn't hold the sinner innocent. These aren't pretty, attractive things for people, but essential presuppositions for what the Christian tradition means by reconciliation. Reconciliation is the sour summons of Christianity that we must bite on before we get to the sweet.

2. Tragedy or guilt?

It's quite risky to say that human beings withdraw from God. God may well be far from the prayer of the average Westerner, but if you interpret that in terms of 'people avoid God, get out of God's way', you're making human behaviour the criterion of your own theory, and then you're always right. Just as Marxists are always right: if you don't agree with their social criticism, then in their view it's because you live in a corrupt society; you just *cannot* see what they see. Similarly, the Christian tradition says that the reason why God makes no impact on people is because they've had something to do with him and don't *want* to be reminded of it.

I've an abhorrence of this kind of argument, but have to confess that it's an essential view of the Christian tradition about human existence. 'Adam, where are you?' But Adam was nowhere; he (and Eve) had hidden behind the bushes because he was afraid (quite rightly) to meet the Creator.

I concede that this is difficult to swallow. The only thing is to call experience to our aid. There's something like a two-sided relationship between us and God: sometimes we call on God, sometimes we forget God, sometimes God is something and sometimes nothing. That goes through all cultures. There is no culture which doesn't give content to the sense of God in terms of a broken relationship which must be healed.

The Christian tradition interprets that fact – a fact of experience – in its own way. The break isn't a misfortune, nor is the gulf a tragic fate of which human beings are the victims. In the Christian tradition of faith that kind of interpretation is called a 'displacement' of what is really going on. Human beings aren't victims: aren't mere victims, I mean, but guilty parties who daren't look at and see their own situation, and therefore evade God. It's very ambiguous, to use that word again, for at the same time they're doing their best to approach God in all kinds of complicated ways. But they don't succeed in this because they don't take the gap seriously, or rather, they don't arrive at, or find it very difficult to arrive at, the insight that the gulf is their fault and not the Creator's.

Christianity claims at least to know the depth of the gulf (fully realizing it is another matter). It derives that insight from the bridging of the gulf in reconciliation. If God has to step over the gulf in what is called 'reconciliation', how insurmountable it must be from our point of view! Note that the removal of the alienation takes place outside us, as an action which comes from the other side. That's again difficult: in the first instance we aren't even involved. The reconciliation (the filling in of the gap) is told us as a story, as something which took place earlier in which we were standing on the sidelines, more object than subject. That's difficult to assert, it seems to me.

What were we told then? The life of Jesus Christ, which ends with his death on the cross. In the Christian tradition *that* is the reconciliation; that's where it takes place. There's a sequel, the story isn't told without a reason; it's transformed into the message of salvation by further telling, into what the apostle Paul calls 'the word of reconciliation'. The reconciliation is, in other words, a kind of two-stage rocket: first we aren't involved, and reconciliation takes place in Jesus' life and death. But after that, when the story of Jesus and his cross are retold as a mesaage of salvation, we are involved. I shall be discussing this in detail at the end of this chapter.

But this message continues to have as its content that the reconciliation comes about without our being involved in it. Christianity has become the religion of the way because, according to it, the way goes through Jesus Christ and his cross.

3. The cross: from story to symbol

The Gospel narratives are one-sided: they don't give a balanced historical picture of the life of Jesus but hasten towards the cross. For all four evangelists, in so far as they set themselves up as narrators, that is where it clearly began. But they aren't, of course, just narrators; they've presented their story as a message of salvation, and each does so in his own way. They go once again over the interpretation of the life and death of Jesus, of his cross and resurrection, as we find this in the apostle Paul (he wrote his letters before the evangelists wrote their story), but now by means of an ordered historical account. So it isn't the case that in the Gospels we find the simple stories and in Paul, for example, complicated dogmatics. The Gospels are just as 'dogmatic' as the letters of the New Testament and we encounter the same vocabulary ('sacrifice', 'lamb of God', 'ransom for humankind', etc.) in them. But they aren't there for nothing! The Christian tradition has no better or more vivid way than these stories about Jesus and his cross which are so dear to us of showing how reconciliation is primarily a matter outside us and for our sake.

What does the cross stand for in these stories? For the sacrifice that Jesus makes in his person. He was led like a lamb to the slaughter; like a sheep which is dumb before its shearers, he didn't open his mouth. That's a quotation from the prophet Isaiah, which goes on:

Surely he has borne our griefs and carried our sorrows;
yet we esteemed him stricken, smitten by God, and afflicted.
But he was wounded for our transgressions,
he was bruised for our iniquities;
upon him was the chastisement that made us whole,
and with his stripes we are healed.
    All we like sheep have gone astray;
we have turned every one to his own way;
and the Lord has laid on him the iniquity of us all (Isaiah 53.4-6).

Why this detailed quotation? Because these statements fit the story of the suffering and dying Jesus so amazingly well. The earliest Christian tradition was already struck by this (see Acts 9). I leave aside here the exegetical questions about the correctness of this application and the conclusions which have been drawn from it over the course of the centuries. If we want to know what the Christian tradition thought of the cross, the suffering and the dying of Jesus, then we must cite the statements of Isaiah that I quoted above. The chastisement which brings us peace was on him; with his stripes we are healed. Jesus speaks of the judgment.

This concentration of the Christian message of salvation on the suffering and death of Jesus explains the central place which the cross has been given in the Christian tradition. It has become the visible sign of redemption. Jesus saves sinners from judgment by going to the cross for them. Jesus is the lamb of God that takes away the sins of the world. Jesus has borne the unrighteousness of all men and women, and he is broken on the cross under it. That doesn't involve any dogmatics; it's in the narrative as it was told by the evangelists, has been read out for centuries in the churches and celebrated in the eucharist: 'This is my body which is broken for you: this is my blood which is shed for many for the forgiveness of sins.'

Once the visible sign of redemption, the cross has become a symbol that stands for Christian faith, a mark of identification, as the crescent has become for Islam. Nothing is then left of the cross as a means of executing criminals (emotionally speaking, a kind of gallows, but even more cruel). It becomes another word for suffering (bearing your cross), an ingredient of rituals (setting up a cross). In short, like all symbols, it begins to lead a life of its own, comes to stand on church doors and graves, on coats of arms and on noblemen's clothing. As an amulet it has to offer protection against the powers of darkness; as a crucifix it adorns the walls of churches, homes and monasteries, and as a silver pin I wore it, when I was a preacher, on the lapel of my jacket. That's a far cry from Simon of Cyrene who carried the cross for Jesus, but it's still to be seen as a pointer to Christianity. Until even this reference is stripped away. In a trinket shop a girl asked for a chain with a cross on. When shown a few, she said, to my surprise: 'No, I mean one with a little man on.' End of the crucifix. The Christian church mustn't have too many illusions about the symbolic value of the cross.

4. God was in Christ reconciling the world

Reconciliation isn't the speciality of Christianity. Judaism, too, begins from the need for reconciliation. What distinguishes Christianity from Judaism at this point is the link between reconciliation and the person of Jesus Christ and his cross.

'God was in Christ reconciling the world to himself', runs the classic formulation of what happened in the suffering, crucifixion and death of Jesus Christ. I would work that out like this.

God himself was in Christ. There, then, we finally have the unique significance of Jesus for us, in comparison with other people. God wasn't in Martin Luther King or in Mother Teresa or in any other saint, ecclesiastical or secular – at least not in this way. These may all be there and have their function in human existence: saints are the indispensable models by means of which we organize our lives. But they aren't like Christ, for in Christ God was reconciling the world to himself. God *was* active, I said. In the past. We shall see later the way in which this past time takes on significance for us who live in the present. But first I shall follow the trail we're on.

'Was' (past tense) refers back to the cross of Jesus of Nazareth which is interpreted by all Christianity as a sacrifice. Does Jesus make the sacrifice of his life? Certainly, but we mustn't imagine that Jesus, dying on the cross, thought: 'Now I'm bringing about reconciliation between God and human beings and soon I shall rise again from the dead.' If he did, the drama on the cross would become a game, if not a charade. What Jesus thought on the cross was something quite different: 'My God, my God, why have you forsaken me?' His way began as that of a prophet who knows that he is appointed by God to bring in the kingdom of God; perhaps Jesus identified himself with the Suffering Servant of God whom we encountered in Isaiah 53. But he ended his life as a religious leader who was left in the lurch both by God and by his own followers. And yet his followers said: he is the one we thought he was, the bringer of salvation from God, but in another way. The kingdom of God enters the world with him, but not in the way we had expected. He did what first had to be done to reconcile God and man, to undo the alienation.

The Christian tradition thus puts the cross of Jesus in quite a different framework. Of course it's also the outcome of what human beings did to the scandalous prophet from Nazareth. From that standpoint the crucifixion of Jesus is a crime against humanity, one of the many in which our history is so rich. But that's just one side of the picture, the one that we see; according to the followers of Jesus, the other side is that God used human plans to fulfil his plan to bring redemption.

Of course it didn't happen just like that: attributing to someone's death on a cross the significance of filling in the gulf between God and man. The interpretation could only come after they had experienced what they called 'God has raised him' (I shall return to that under the heading of resurrection), and then they saw his life story with quite different eyes. Just read the Gospels: they're written after this experience. That's the only reason why the story of the cross wasn't the story of a failure but could become the story of reconciliation.

So far I've read 'in Christ' as 'through Christ' and seen God as the active person. But is Christ only passive, then, the sacrifice which is offered? That needn't be the case; we can also understand 'in Christ' to mean that Christ himself is the active person, and then it becomes that in Jesus Christ who offered himself as a sacrifice God was active reconciling the world to himself. The two phrases aren't exclusive; they overlap. That happens because they've both contributed an indispensable element of what the early church understood by reconciliation. 1. God himself is the giver of reconciliation, but 2. just as indispensably, the way by which it comes about is that of the sacrifice that Christ brings.

To whom is the sacrifice then made, and who requires it? Does God have to be made to change his mind by this sacrifice? But how can that be if God is the one who sees that the sacrifice is made? I shall postpone these questions for discussion to another section and first return to the notion of reconciliation.

5. Reconciliation as a metaphor

So far I've assumed that reconciliation and sacrifice are notions which cause no problems. But of course they do. We can see what they mean by here, too, remembering that they're metaphors, pictorial language which seeks to transfer something of a known situation to an unknown situation. But if reconciliation is one enormous metaphor, where does that get us?

We begin – again – with alienation as an undeniable reality and – dissolved into factors – consisting in sin, guilt and helplessness. For the moment I shall sum this up by saying that human beings are sinners. What must happen to sinners? The outcome of the previous sections was that they fall under the judgment of God. But must that be? Why doesn't God forgive sinners, so that they can get back on their feet again? But that can't be; sin is something in the past, and whatever else can happen to the past, one thing can't: you can't make the past not have happened. The past can't be undone. Even God can't do that. There's nothing for it: if it can't be undone, it must be reconciled. In other words, not got out of the way, but rather 'covered'.

In the religious rites of which the first followers of Jesus made use, the covering happened by a sacrificial ritual. A sinner can't get rid of the past other than through reconciliation as covering, reconciliation by means of a sacrifice. It's from here that the Christian tradition takes up the metaphor by means of which it interprets Jesus' crucifixion: also a sacrifice that 'covers', but now made 'once for all'. Guilt is covered for good.

That isn't yet the whole story; it brings us to another question. Sacrifices are offered with blood, and the Christian tradition speaks of the blood of Jesus Christ; even a complete blood mysticism has emerged from it. Did God then want the blood of Jesus? That has sometimes been supposed. It led Adolf von Harnack, a well-known historian at the beginning of this century, to lament that God had the doubtful privilege of being the only one who might not forgive without having first seen blood.

What is a caricature here, and what is meaningful Christian tradition? That depends on how far we take the metaphor. As an illustration, let me take up an example that I used in the first chapter. In one of the Gospels (Matthew), we read that Jesus (the Son of man, it is said) did not come to be served but to serve and to give his life 'as a ransom' for many. To whom did he give this ransom? To the devil? To God? That isn't stated, and down the centuries readers have racked their brains over the right answer. But it isn't there. The metaphor isn't concerned with this question. What it indicates is that a ransom usually consists of money; however, Jesus didn't put a sum of money at the disposal of others but himself, *as a person*. I don't want to go further, though I have to recognize that people are equally justified in doing that (and indeed have done so). I find the insolubility of the problems in which we 'go further' a good argument that here we're asking too much of the metaphor.

In the case of 'sacrifice' we have to apply the same modesty. To cover by means of a sacrifice, certainly, but sacrifice is a term which is used in a transferred sense, like blood; you can easily go further and end up with ideas which are both impossible and tasteless, while the object of concern threatens to get lost. Blood indicates how seriously the sacrifice is a sacrifice, a real sacrifice. And reconciliation doesn't mean that God wants to see blood: rather, the sin is so serious that it must be covered with or through an authentic sacrifice. And who covers it? God covers the sins of the world in and through Christ. In this way I'm reducing the metaphor of reconciliation to: sacrifice = cover = is a manner of forgiving. Reconciliation says that God forgives, but that God does this by covering. That seems to me to be the essence of the Christian tradition of faith about reconciliation.

But my interpretation hasn't exhausted the metaphor. Like all religious metaphors, it has further connotations. Why should anyone have to stand by what I read into it? The conversation about what it does and doesn't set out to say remains open.

6. Reconciliation and substitution

The metaphor of reconciliation has another aspect which is worked out in the tradition of the church, the aspect of substitution. I can't distinguish between representation and substitution, though I find the first expression more attractive. Anyone who has difficulty with the aspect that it indicates has just as much difficulty with both terms. And there is a difficulty! Where does representation come into the picture, and what does it mean to apply the concept to reconciliation in the way that the Christian tradition does?

For that we must return to sacrifice. For us it's become a spiritual term, the description of an attitude, but originally it denoted a ritual in which a sacrificial animal was used. In some sacrificial rites (but not in all), the animal replaced someone who had become a sinner, without knowing it and (we assume) contrary to their intention. The reason why the term substitution has become so dear to Christian tradition is that it provides an opening for a sacrifice which is used willingly and knowingly, the sacrifice of Jesus out of love for the sinner.

That brings us to another thought-model: yet another, but again a model which puts reconciliation and sacrifice at a particular point. This point is the exchange between the sacrifical lamb and the transgressor. It's an indispensable element in the tradition of reconciliation, even an essential element, since without 'exchange', sacrifice is meaningless. It simply means that we can also express reconciliation in terms of 'exchange': Jesus changes places with the sinner. Jesus is then the active person. Or it can also be that God is the active one: God makes Jesus and the sinner change places; God hands him over for all of us.

All this is metaphor, transferred language. It's given with the pictorial language of sacrifice, and if we can't do without this pictorial language, then we can't do without the language of substitution. But we must see what this notion does and doesn't mean. Must there be a sacrifice, a covering? Certainly, says the Christian tradition. And is that a form of exchange? Again the Christian tradition firmly says yes. Moreover representation and reconciliation belong together.

The significance that the Christian tradition attaches to the death of Jesus is thus connected with this. With his death on the cross Jesus is more than just a victim of his calling, a victim of political or religious powers. He is that, too, but that's not the whole story. He doesn't just die as a 'victim'; his death was also a 'sacrifice', an offering. Therefore I think that it isn't an exhaustive description of his crucifixion to say that it was meant to give a shock to the transgressors ('are we capable of that kind of deed?'). The cross also has that 'shock effect', as I've shown, but if that's all there is to it, then forgiveness has dropped out of it.

So the idea of reconciliation has to include sacrifice and representation. If it doesn't, it loses its point. But the one by whom this covering must be is the one who offers himself for it, changes places, is himself sacrifice: God, reconciling the world to himself in Christ. This is certainly quite a complicated way, but I shall be coming back to that at the end of this chapter.

Here I simply note that we mustn't conclude from this metaphor that Jesus already knew Christian doctrine and thought of the sinners whom he would save with his sacrifice as he hung on the cross. The language of the tradition isn't that Jesus so loved sinners that he went to the cross for them, but that God so loved the world that he gave his only-begotten Son.

'In our place' is an expression which fits into the mouth of the sinner and means 'they planned the wrong thing', 'he has to stand there for me'. In this way substitution doesn't amount to putting someone under supervision, but to confessing sin, and confessing sin is something which presupposes adulthood and an awareness of relationship: you can only feel guilty towards someone whom you know.

7. Be reconciled with God

The cross of Jesus is past time: we can only have the historical relationship to it that we have to all the events of the past. I can find the battle of Waterloo exciting or even decisive for the fate of Europe, but it cannot become a part of my existence; I myself can no longer be involved in it. However, the Christian tradition of faith says that reconciliation can become part of our existence. How? By reconciliation being as it were included in the word of reconciliation, in the proclamation of reconciliation. So it gets detached from the past and from the place where it happened in order to go into the world of history. Today God, according to the Christian tradition, is active reconciling the world to himself in the Word of reconciliation. If we neglect this element of the tradition, the cross remains stranded in Palestine. Riding on the Word, it detaches itself from that and comes within any time, including ours.

What we have to hear – the word of reconciliation – is expressed by the Christian tradition in an enormous breadth of variations, but at the same time it amounts to one and the same message. 'They preached Jesus and the forgiveness of sins' is said of the earliest Christian message. But it can also be said that they preached that the judgment had been made, the exchange had taken place, the sacrifice had been offered and sin atoned for. We have to know that, but knowing isn't enough. Surely this is also a reconciliation in which I myself am involved, with the abolition of the alienation between God and (also) me? That's the reason why reconciliation (then) is transformed into a message of salvation (now). The past reaches us in terms of information-with-a-summons, 'Be reconciled with God'. Here are some indications of what the answer to that might look like.

1. Of course reconciliation is only a message of salvation for those who need reconciliation. It isn't the healthy but the sick who need a doctor. It's as simple as that. Moreover we don't worry about those who don't need it or think that they have it. The Christian tradition has done this, but in doing so has overplayed its hand. According to the church father Origen the threats that the biblical authors put in the mouth of God, Jesus and the apostles, are pedagogical measures. God is only playing; God isn't really cross, God's not like that. So they were already aware of this threatening language at an early stage. But I would want to follow Origen. Origen gambled on a reconciliation of all things, but we can't say anything about that because we know nothing about it. Let's maintain that the Christian tradition has no need to make people anxious. What does a faith driven by anxiety have to offer?

2. I translate 'letting ourselves be reconciled' as: accepting a verdict on our life that has already been made (a pre-judgment) and at the same time puts us on a free footing. That's not easy for people who aren't aware of any evil. So must we do our best to feel how bad we are? Yes, but we may as well reflect on whether we are as good as we thought. Here the Christian proclamation helps us. It's diagnosis and therapy at the same time. Anyone whose eyes are opened by the word of reconciliation wants to be reconciled and return to God.

3. 'Accept' is another word for 'believe'. That completes the circle; we're back to the way. How is the alienation removed and peace made with God? 'Through faith', Christianity can say in a kind of shorthand, and in so doing indicate the way to God by marking it off from other ways.

4. In classical terminology, to indicate faith as the way is called 'justification by faith'. This is a complicated chapter of Christian tradition; however, it means no more than that the way isn't paved with good intentions (which haven't been carried out) but consists in taking reconciliation seriously. Freed from judgment, rescued from a bad conscience and living in peace with God – that is 'being justified by faith'. Not because the judgment ('God doesn't make it') subsequently proves to be a fairy tale or rested on a misunderstanding, but because it has already taken place in the lamb of God who takes away the sins of the world.

5. In the past much has been made of the contrast between 'faith'

and 'works'. It isn't outmoded, but in the form in which we know it it's been very badly defined, first through the controversy with the Jews and later through that between Rome and the Reformation. I think that in any case this latter controversy is no longer an issue, at least not in the classical way. What remains positive and incontrovertible is 'the freedom of a Christian man', as Luther called it. Faith brings freedom, makes a person the slave of no one – not the state, far less the church authorities – but the servant of all. So a person could become a Christian for the freedom for which Christ sets us free.

6. 'By faith' is nothing unusual; it's the same as 'through Jesus Christ', and again that's interchangeable with 'not by our works', with 'freely' and 'by grace'. The terminology may be well-worn, but it's completely clear: we return to God without having made things good ourselves.

Moreover, it isn't meant in a limiting way. 'For all who believe' doesn't mean just for people who believe, but simply means that the gates are open. There are no condiitons.

7. Is that cheap? In his book *The Fall*, Albert Camus left no doubt that that's what he thought. I don't believe in this white-washing, says the main character, by which he means the forgiveness of sins. I concede that everything can be made cheap, but taken by and large the notion of reconciliation in faith means the opposite: there is no 'cheap grace'; forgiveness has a price, both for God and for human beings.

8. The new person

Being reconciled with God means beginning another life. That needn't be; it's simply the case and can't be otherwise. A person changes as a result; he or she has gone over to another state of life. A good comparison is the way in which someone who gets married goes over to another state of life. He or she is the same person, but now different from before. Christians believe in their new status; they're recognizable by that belief; they've a name for it and call themselves 'child of God' or 'new creation' – at least they would like to call themselves that.

A change in status changes a person. 'Since he got married he's a different man.' I know that the comparison goes wrong, but it gives us something to think about. Change of status brings with it inner change. So we end up with this 'new person' as the outcome of reconciliation: God makes us new persons. Let me give some idea of this by using two expressions of the apostle Paul which are both mystical and curious.

'Anyone who is in Christ is a new creation.' That's about the new person, but what is being 'in Christ'?

I take it as a poetic expression for a home in which you live. We need such a home, made up of reassuring thoughts which bring security, a stable home. The philosopher Karl Jaspers did much to show that everyone uses such 'homes' for living. In his view the question is only whether the 'homes' survive time. Christians, too, need a home; they live 'in Christ'. He is their home, and because by 'Christ' we really mean God, we can say that God is our home. This not only endures through time but also makes new people of those who live in it.

But what does 'new' mean in this context? The apostle Paul can also put that in a very mystical way. With his letters he works on his readers, he massages them 'until Christ takes form in you'. That sounds very intriguing, but what does it mean? Let me point out what it certainly cannot mean. Here Paul doesn't mean that the historical Jesus has to take shape in us, since the historical Jesus is far away from us. He lived in another world and another time, and *if* we know anything of his historical existence, it's little more than the handful of stories that the Gospels tell us. So the new person isn't Jesus of Nazareth.

Of course the apostle doesn't say that either; he says very express-ively that Christ must take shape in us. Christ is the new person. What we must think of here is the reconstruction of our life by Jesus Christ. In a later chapter I shall explain how Christian terminology has reserved the expression 'the Spirit' for Jesus after his resurrection. The risen Jesus *is* the Spirit. So I can even (and better) talk of the reconstruction of our existence by the Spirit. And to the degree that by the Spirit we mean God, but in that case God at the spiritual level (Spirit works with spirit), I can also say that God reconstructs our life and uses Christ as a model that must be expressed in it.

We haven't got much further. New = Christ and Christ is new. We're going round in a circle. Unless we want to keep to pure mysticism (and there's nothing against that), we must begin to provide some content, precisely because the apostle Paul gives content to 'new' by means of all kinds of rules of life. Rules of life? That sounds rather disappointing. This new person comes to stand one step lower on the ladder of our ideals. Now clearly we're concerned with something like the Christian life, and that's time-conditioned, not as new as all that. We ourselves have got out of the habit of the rules of life which the apostle Paul offers, and Paul wouldn't have thought much of our rules. I'm noting that here. In the chapters on God's commandment I shall be returning to this historical definition of rules of life. Christian life is constantly given new content and *must* constantly be given new content. That's not an anxious under-taking, far less a departure from Christian custom, but rather – conversely – a call to Christians. Christians don't allow a slave's yoke to be put on them again; they're Christians, and therefore in every age they investigate anew what is Christian and what isn't. If we do accept a yoke, we chain not only ourselves but also others to what our grandparents found Christian, and that becomes slavery in place of Christian freedom.

What does this amount to, then? The new person is 'Christ in us', but we have no other form for such a relative entity than the Christian life. In the chapter about the Christian expectation of the future we shall see why things can't be otherwise.

Thus only a bit of the 'new person' can be seen; the Heidelberg Catechism speaks – modestly – of a small 'principle' of the new life. That all sounds somewhat worrying, but I think that it adds up. To be Christian is also to fight enthusiastically for a better society, to fight against injustice and poverty, but we engage in that very naively if we don't also enter into a struggle against the wrong, the lies, the deceit and the rubbish that we discover in ourselves. 'Work on yourself' (which used to be called 'conversion') is not only possible, but necessary. But that is to fight. To become a new person is to die and rise at the same time.

9. The 'way' is a detour

There's no denying it: the idea of reconciliation is quite complicated, and certainly not the first thing that we would want to take from the Christian tradition if the choice was ours. Must we really believe in it?

Let me begin by saying that of course there's no must. If you can't make anything of it, you can't. No more needs to be said. But what do we mean by 'I can't make anything of it'? That usually means that something doesn't arouse any emotion in us. But it needn't do so. That's not what the tradition is for. Emotions are aroused when the tradition is actualized in sermon, prayer or ritual. However, we have no power over that, any more than over a performance which is gripping.

What is clear is that the Christian tradition stands and falls with reconciliation. That's why I've gone in such detail into the question whether we can make anything of it, anything personal. At least it makes us think: about God, about our neighbours and about ourselves. Except that we don't shoulder the guilt ourselves, but always foist it on someone else. Without reconciliation wouldn't we all become moralists?

The complication is aptly put into words by someone from the Third World: 'Only by the detour of sending the Son and then leaving this Son in the lurch on the cross – how can such a God be my support and stay?'

Apart from the fact that this remark is a splendid example of metaphors which begin to lead a life of their own and say something totally different from what they were ever meant to say, it's a good indication of the complication of the Christian way: the way is at least a detour. What's the point of that?

The most satisfactory answer is that the way looks so complicated because people are so complicated. We don't find it easy to believe that we are bunglers who are destroying the creation (and ourselves with it) and finally have to talk of forgiveness. To convince us of that, according to the Christian tradition God set a whole machinery in motion which leaves God God and human beings their greatness as human beings: they can become guilty before God.

God can do everything – certainly. God can renovate people as you renovate a building. But people aren't houses: they have their dignity as people and God leaves them this dignity. Therefore according to Christianity the way is complicated. We are saved *as human beings*, and therefore we are reconciled. And a reconciling God retains his dignity as God. Just wait, says reconciliation to the eager, 'fools rush in where angels fear to tread'. Transgressors can't just appear before God, if I may go over to a metaphor from etiquette. First they must wash and put on clean clothes. Anyone who believes in reconciliation through Jesus Christ has become a modest person before God.

Finally, as I've said, reconciliation is proclaimed, and proclamation takes place, in church. That's the only reason why the church is important, but it's enough. In the church, in the preaching of reconciliation by Jesus Christ, God confirms what and who God is.

'Merciful, gracious and full of loving-kindness' – that's true of the Creator; God has always been so, and continues to be so. What I mean is that God didn't just become that through or in Jesus Christ. Through the person and work of Jesus Christ it becomes clear that forgiveness isn't cheap, or obvious; not for God, far less for us human beings. If the Christian proclamation of the forgiveness of sins isn't to perish through superficiality, then it must be preached in the framework of reconciliation.

XI

The Resurrection

'Death, thou shalt die!' (*John Donne*)

1. The crucial role

There is no doubt in the Christian tradition about the crucial role of Jesus' resurrection. If Christ isn't risen, the Christian proclamation doesn't have a leg to stand on. That's because (as I shall go on to say) the resurrection isn't just one article in the assortment of Christian notions of faith – although it is sometimes presented as if it were – but is incorporated into a greater whole (even into more than one) from which it derives its significance and of which at the same time it is the cornerstone. What frameworks are those?

Let's begin with the framework of christology: who was Jesus, according to his first followers? They could only give an answer to this question after his death. It's always like that: you only realize someone's significance at the end of their life when you can see it as a whole. After Jesus' death the first disciples felt that his painful end on the cross wasn't really his end, but rather fitted into God's purpose to reconcile the world with himself. Something contributed to that which happened to the person of Jesus in a decisive way: his first followers said that God raised him. His cross wasn't his end; his story, with himself as both object and subject, goes on, and is what Edward Schillebeeckx has called the story of a living one. Here God has established what human beings denied, namely that he was the bringer of salvation sent by God. God didn't abandon his Son. You can even say that God made him Son by not leaving him in death.

I would recall that Son isn't really Son in the Christian tradition (God has no Son), but a metaphor which indicates the close link between two persons. Within such a metaphor it doesn't matter whether this close bond was already there or whether it only came about through his rescue from death.

In anticipation of the sections to come I shall already note that in perplexity people have wanted to put it the other way round: Jesus' first followers weren't convinced by Jesus' resurrection, but their conviction created the story that Jesus had risen. Of course that could have happened. But it then becomes quite incomprehensible how a myth (for that is what the story would amount to) could last so long, and even more incomprehensible that (in contrast to such myths) it should have had such an effect, down to the present day.

A second framework in which the resurrection belongs is that of the salvation brought by the bringer of salvation. He is the lord of death; death doesn't have the last word, and that opens up perspectives. All the more when we realize that in the earliest Christian tradition death is seen as a punishment from God. Sin came into the world (to follow the historical model), and with sin death. Death sits there as a kind of payment. From this perspective, to gain the mastery of death is a colossal event. The Jewish tradition regards it as the dawning of the new world. When the dead rise, that happens. The Gospels, too, have the resurrection stories as their conclusion.

Regardless of whether the preoccupation of Mediterranean culture with death and burial (down to the present day) did or didn't make its contribution (but any culture seeks a solution to death and the grave), Christian tradition has expressed the saving significance of Jesus' resurrection in terms of the 'conquest of death' and celebrates that at Easter. Above all in the Eastern churches (the heirs of Mediterranean culture), Christians began to celebrate Easter very elaborately. The definitive farewell to the old world, the argument goes, consists ultimately in being definitively redeemed from death.

How we must see Jesus' resurrection as a conquest of death remains somewhat vague. The precise question is easy to suppress in the midst of the festivities that mark Easter: why must we still die, if death has been overcome? One classical formulation of the answer is that for believers death is a transition to life. Christians have learned, as Pannenberg puts it, 'to hope beyond death'. I shall leave it at that for the moment and return to the matter at length.

Both the frameworks that I indicated give meaning. At the same time the resurrection functions in both of them as a cornerstone. If Jesus isn't risen, then there's nothing, and the Christian tradition is built on a fairy-tale. Similarly, if the Christian tradition isn't a form of conquering death, frustration is and remains the last word. Then at death it's all over; the person is blown out. In the eyes of Christianity that's too little; there's a sequel with the value of eternity.

2. Our problems of possible/impossible

A student made friends with a young Reformed Christian, and since she knew nothing about Christianity she went to the chaplain to ask what it was all about. The pastor made a start, and finally came to the story of Jesus; when he had described Jesus' end she asked, 'And did they ever see any more of him?' For the pastor that was an open door; he immediately became enthusiastic and talked about the resurrection. I've never forgotten the response (for I was the pastor): 'If that's true, I'll become a Christian!'

But is it true? To put it mildly, we have great difficulty in accepting it. Of course for more than one reason, but perhaps these reasons are to be summed up in the idea that here are miracle stories which we rightly dismiss; we no longer have anything to do with that sort of thing. Worse than that, they prejudice us against the narrators. In our view, no angels come from heaven to open tombs; a person can't emerge from the grave after three days, since by then – certainly in hot countries – the body will be in an advanced state of decomposition. And no one comes back to visit after death – unless the spiritualists are right. So these are objections to the actual features of the event that the Christian tradition describes as the 'resurrection of Jesus'. The frameworks giving meaning to these facts within the Christian tradition share in this fate. Is it real to think of a new world and to see this ushered in by the resurrection of the dead? What is that? Can physical people become physically alive again? Surely they're composed of the matter of people before them? We end up in quite nonsensical problems! And as far as the christological context is concerned: you must already believe in Jesus as the bringer of salvation appointed by God if you're to be able to believe in his resurrection.

It would be a distortion of the situation if we were simply to reduce these difficulties and problems to unwillingness. These aren't the questions of outsiders – and that speaks volumes; we meet them just as well within Christian communities. It's an aspect of the culture in which we live: we regard the resurrection as actual event with scepticism, and think that something of this sort can't really happen. It no longer fits into our concept of reality.

So is our concept of reality the criterion for what can and can't be?

Certainly not, but we can't put it aside for the sake of an idea which is dear to us either. That would smack of dishonesty, and moreover, what good does it do?

I can demonstrate the division by a famous miracle story from the Old Testament, the story of the floating axe. A group of young men from a school of prophets was cutting wood, and one of them dropped his axe in the water. Disconcerted, he turned to the prophet Elisha for help – the axe was borrowed. As happens with famous prophets, on being shown the place in the water where it had fallen, Elisha made the axe float, so that the young man could get it back again. A story to the greater glory of the prophet Elijah, since axes do not float.

'You've become a victim of our modern culture, because you deny this miracle,' said a student who had heard my exposition. Is that true? It's very easy to believe that God can make axes float; the question is whether God does so. If that were the case, and tomorrow axes could escape the force of gravity, no train would be able to run again. So we don't reckon that it happens; pieces of iron don't float by themselves and therefore we get into a train or a car with a peaceful mind. So what's the use of a discussion about wonders here? None, as long as wonders are defined in terms of miracle.

3. Christian rescue attempts

Solutions have also been put forward in Christian circles to the problems I've described. They often cause a stir because rightly or wrongly people see them as an attack on the factuality of the event.

That brings me straight to a first proposal. 'Is factuality so important?', some Christians ask. 'Surely we can maintain the significance of the story of the resurrection and leave the facts aside? All this emphasis on factuality can even be damaging because it makes the outlook meaningless.'

This is a solution which has good credentials. People go on relating what they think important. But here the 'go on relating' always done in terms of the view of the event which the narrators present, a view which is connected with their view of human beings and the world as a whole. So this also includes further relating of what happened (if it's important for them) in terms of what they believe to be possible and impossible. For the narrators of this time, resurrection was not only important but also possible: hence the resurrection narrative. Today we live in a culture which, because of a quite different view of human beings and the world, has the utmost problems with Jesus' resurrection specifically at the level of the possible/impossible and much less at the level of important/unimportant. But what is narrated is well worth the trouble of narrating it. So why not detach factuality from significance?

In fact that's sometimes a very meaningful proposal. I shall return to it in connection with what in the Christian tradition is called the ascension. But unfortunately in the case of Jesus' resurrection that isn't the case, for the importance of this event lies precisely in what was possible for the narrators but not for us. So 'Didn't really happen but still is true' isn't a solution. In that case, of course, we remain faithful to our everyday view of what can and cannot happen, but we've got rid of what the tradition says about Jesus' resurrection. However, the term 'true' also takes on a separate meaning. It means something like 'revealing'. That's a special concept of the truth, and the question it leaves open is why Jesus' resurrection should be revealing if it didn't end up in an event. Is there then no longer any need for an account of the resurrection? If there is, then more is involved!

Even retreating to the resurrection as a unique event doesn't solve anything. The meaning of the term is clear: it must indicate that the resurrection of Jesus Christ is an irruption of God's world into our world. It doesn't fit into our frameworks of space and time and therefore can't be tested by means of criteria derived from space and time. In short, it can't be discussed as we discuss other events: it's historically incomprehensible, and even unhistorical or suprahistorical in the light of our frameworks. What are we to say to this? It isn't wrong at all; it's true to the degree that we know no event which can be compared with it. But this puts the resurrection far outside any comparison. What's unique is unique, and moreover can't be fitted into concepts and views of life. It's really the same as 'undiscussable', and that can't be the intention.

Furthermore, the term 'unique' can be used to defend any improbable event: anything is possible, the floodgates are open, and we're back to the point when a miracle no longer has any significance. So I think that it's better to keep off rescue attempts: we believe it or we don't. The only question is: *what* then do we believe?

4. Follow the trail backwards

The resurrection of Jesus from the dead (really his 'raising' from the dead) was without any doubt related by his first followers – and we must refer to them for things concerning Jesus – as something that happened to Jesus. 'Jesus' cause goes on' we can say, but only because Jesus himself 'goes on'. The view that Jesus lives on after his death in the faith of the Christian church (he rose = people began to believe in him) also falls short of what the first followers want to impress on us. If Jesus didn't rise, we can indeed believe, they say, but in that case it is a senseless belief. Even the statement 'He is risen in the Word that is proclaimed to us and brings us to faith' falls short. It's much clearer and more to the point, but doesn't exhaust the original witness. Why don't these first followers say that straight away, without going round by the resurrection as something which actually happened to Jesus? Or was this last some fatal mistake on their part?

If we don't opt for that – though if we did, we would make things much easier for ourselves – what can help us to understand these first followers better? What in their view happened, and why was it so important? You could say, 'I accept the fact of the resurrection in good faith', and leave its content open. But that robs this faith of its significance. A 'that' without a 'what' says nothing. If it's true of any theme that it lives by transferred terminology, it's true of the resurrection. Resurrection is a metaphor, a word that is transferred from a known to an unknown situation. However, the great problem is that the unknown is so unknown that we ask 'metaphor of what?' If it's about something that we don't know, yet want to understand, then more than ever we face the possibility that we're letting the pictures themselves construct the event. In my view, this is the reason for the great variations in the Gospel stories about Jesus' resurrection. In some stories Jesus even eats bread and fish to show that he's real. Here the metaphor clashes with reality even in the story.

But, something happened to Jesus of which they were sure: the story of Jesus doesn't end like all other stories with the death of the main character, but goes further. I'm not saying that it goes on normally, since in that case the resurrection of Jesus becomes an ingredient of a human biography, and that can be said of the cross; but the resurrection goes beyond that.

The most illuminating metaphor is that of the grain of corn and the ear. It's used, for example, by the apostle Paul, and makes quite clear why the resurrection narrative isn't a drop in the ocean that you can't do anything with but is relevant to all people who believe deep in their hearts that there is hope beyond death and the grave. 'Grain of corn and ear of corn' applies not only to Jesus but also to all who die. Moreover I shall speak of Jesus' resurrection and of resurrection as a saving gift without making any distinction between them.

The metaphor of the grain of corn and the ear of corn excludes the view that the resurrection is about the resuscitation of a body. What is sown must in some sense first die before it rises, but what then comes up looks quite different from the grain of corn that we put in the ground. And yet there's continuity. The corn is the seed and the seed is the corn. First I want to emphasize this continuity. Resurrection means that what is raised is the same as what lives. Otherwise surely it's not the resurrection of *Jesus*. To put it vividly, the one who says 'I' is the same. Moreover we mustn't understand resurrection, however much it's also a creative action of God, as the raising of a 'new' person in the sense of someone who hadn't existed before. There's something that passes over, otherwise it's no longer us. So the doctrine of the immortal soul isn't completely wrong. In any case, while all those protests made by present-day Christians are understandable (the resurrection mustn't become a matter of course), at the same time they're exaggerated. If there were nothing of us which returned on the other side, *we* wouldn't be risen.

But just as important as continuity is the otherness. What is raised is a reality which is no longer like what is sown, the person who is buried. The Risen One is other, other in every respect; no longer of the same form as the picture that we acquired of a person.

5. Bodily resurrection?

So in the case of the resurrection we certainly mustn't think of a human body as we know it, coming out of the grave in which it had been laid. What puts many Christians on the wrong track here (one might say) is the Gospel story about the resurrection of Lazarus. Of course the story has the clear aim of making it clear to hearers and readers that in the person of Jesus we encounter the one who has power over death. So Jesus has only to call, 'Lazarus, come forth', for Lazarus to emerge (as we read in John 11). But we can't read out of this what the Christian tradition means by resurrection. For Lazarus then died again; he himself died twice if we are to take the story historically (so I don't think that we should, because God wouldn't make anyone die twice).

Resurrection isn't the resuscitation of a corpse. That has consequences for the way in which we talk about it. The current (and often vigorous) discussion, for example, about the empty tomb mentioned in the Gospel accounts, misses the point. Here I would stress that this idea, modelled on Lazarus, came into the Easter account and was meant to fill a gap in the chain of events: he (Jesus) is no longer where they had put him. But Jesus isn't Lazarus. He isn't brought to life again, but rises from the dead. That's something different, something incomparably different.

Therefore the Jesus of the resurrection (and the resurrection itself) escapes our perception, very much in keeping with the model of the grain and the ear of corn. So we needn't rack our brains about the manner of the 'appearances' of Jesus. Whether they were real appearances or visions is something that we can't discover. He is other; he is taken 'out of time'; and the stories which the Gospels tell about him are already a metaphorical attempt, like the rest of the Easter stories. But we can at least talk about them.

That's necessary, since what the resurrection means for Jesus himself it will also mean for us. Not exactly, I must add: for Jesus, the resurrection means that God confirms him; he is the one for whom humanity had waited. Christianity has seen the resurrection as so to speak proof from God's side. That's an aspect of Jesus' resurrection that we don't take part in; it's his own personal, biographical story. But his return to the God from whom he came, a return to beauty, wholeness and purity, is indeed something of and for us. Resurrection means that for us, too, death isn't the last word; we escape death and return to God who has created us. This is what God wills; God is not a God of the dead but of the living. God wants our company.

For this God passes over everything, frees us from being no more and takes us back 'as new'. That's something quite special for transgressors who had to fear the worst! So resurrection from the dead amounts to what elsewhere in the Christian tradition, at other points, is called being recreated. It emphasizes the break between now and then. The new person hasn't been hidden in us all this time; the new person is a recreation from God's side. We are taken 'out of time' on dying; the house of our tent, as the apostle Paul can say vividly, is broken and in its place we have an eternal house, not made with hands, a dwelling with God, indeed a return to God himself.

6. Resurrection of the flesh

At this point I must make a critical comment. 'Resurrection of the flesh', the literal translation of the original Greek of the penultimate line of the Apostles' Creed, is thus a contradiction in terms. It's a credit to the Christian church that it wanted to weave this notion into its tradition. Corporeality ('the flesh') wasn't rated as low as people imagine. That the church fathers wanted to make it part of the resurrection is a sign of respect. But the idea doesn't fit: flesh and blood – at least in the meaning in which we use these words, and we don't know any other – don't inherit the kingdom of God. To survive death and move into God's society as new means saying farewell to flesh and blood. As is clear, we don't coincide with our flesh and blood. People who as far as flesh and blood is concerned are left out in the cold here will be glad there.

Moreover, this isn't at all a relativization of human and thus bodily existence, but an emphasis on its historical character. It's the only thing that we have, and it's transitory. That makes all that we do as people of flesh and blood important. It counts as it were for eternity.

But surely a person without a body is no longer a person? Indeed, bodies make us persons. The Christian tradition has known that and maintained it for ages. Though the body might be spiritual or heavenly, it must be a body. What Paul is trying to say with this strange kind of expression is that we remain authentic persons. But not flesh and blood; these will never inherit the kingdom of God.

What I'm stressing here is important for belief in the bodily resurrection, the criterion for orthodox Christian faith. If 'flesh and blood' will not inherit the kingdom of God, it goes against the grain of the Christian tradition to regard the resurrection of the dead as a destiny which will befall our earthly body in its time. It will perish as Jesus perished – that's what Christianity believes.

Here I return to the statement with which the previous section ended: what the resurrection means for Jesus, it also means for us. The tradition calls Jesus the 'first-fruits', or also 'the firstborn of the dead'. He has the primacy; he is already there, so to speak, and we are to follow. Not in the sense that all people before Jesus' resurrection from the dead came to nothing and afterwards, so to speak, they survive death. Jesus was the first in the sense of a 'sample', a model that shows what happens if people die reconciled and in peace and friendship with God. We might therefore put it better if we said that the feeling that everything isn't over with death is confirmed by the resurrection of Jesus.

In our best moments we may feel that. That's also how I would interpret John Donne's solemn language which I quoted at the beginning of this chapter, 'Death, thou shalt die.' Death has no more hold on us; it can no longer be the great enemy, or better, as a great enemy it's destroyed, since it's no longer the great divide between God and the sinner.

7. Some doubted

In the meantime the fact remains that Jesus' resurrection makes heavy demands on our faith, both the text and the context, its factuality and the framework which gives it significance. So some doubted, as is already stated in all honesty in Matthew's Gospel.

It seems to me worth stressing this. A current misunderstanding about belief ('Take it or leave it') is that belief amounts to swallowing notions and conceptions without batting an eyelid. But that's a caricature. 'The freight should be proportioned to the groove', says Emily Dickinson somewhere, and I agree with her: the burden of believing is lighter or heavier depending on the length of the distance we have to carry it.

I can't imagine anyone not being racked by doubt, at least at times. Certainly over death and resurrection. There's nothing we can do about this. We must try to bear it and look to happier times (which thank God also exist). But I must allow myself just one comment at this point.

The New Testament relates a dispute between Jesus and his contemporaries about the resurrection from the dead. The classical Jewish tradition, represented by the Sadducees, wanted to have nothing to do with this – in contrast to the 'progressives', i.e. the Pharisees. 'You fools,' Jesus says to them, 'you do not know the scriptures or the power of God.' Resurrection is connected with God; God isn't a God of the dead but of the living. The passage should in any case provide food for thought for today's Sadducean Christians (the phrase comes from the theologian Piet Schoonenberg).

A second comment: as in other questions which the Christian tradition saddles us with, the easiest way of solving the problems that we come up against here is to manipulate ideas. No blood is drawn, and little is gained. But Jesus' resurrection isn't something like: 'Faith says Yes to Jesus of Nazareth and therefore he lives on'.

Faith certainly does that, but it does so because according to this same faith God has first said Yes to Jesus.

Nor is it enough to reduce our own resurrection to saying 'Present'. That's attractive: living on in the community (or rather, being kept alive by the community), but however heart-warming it may be, it isn't what the Christian faith meant by the resurrection. To refer to what I said elsewhere: where are the millions who have no name or whose names are forgotten and for whom no one calls 'Present'?

Another comment. What happens if you can't believe that Jesus was raised by God and we shall follow him? Does God then get cross, and are you lost? Both answers are equally nonsensical. The love of God isn't earned by dutifully maintaining a few compulsory ideas, nor is it forfeited by being perplexed about them. What can be said is: you're missing something; you could have believed that a person survives death and comes to God. If you don't believe that, then you have only yourself.

Moreover, not to share in a belief or only partially to do so doesn't by definition mean 'I don't believe'. Belief and the accepting of notions of faith go together; that's the way things happen. But that doesn't mean that giving up a particular conception implies that you no longer believe what this notion seeks to convey. Notion and matter never fit together smoothly; there is and must be a margin between them.

XII

The Ascension and Sitting at the Right Hand of God

'On a chariot of light,
the Lord is taken from earth,
he goes to his heavenly throne' (*Children's verse from primary school*)

For ages Ascension Day has been one of the Christian festivals, but at most no more is left of it than a holiday in some places. This shows that the Christian world doesn't really know what to make of the ascension of Jesus Christ.

That's not surprising; the ascension is a subordinate theme. The 'didn't really happen' has no consequences, for although the event is told in just one Gospel narrative, it's clearly comparable to a Jewish midrash. This isn't a story which is told because it really happened – it didn't – but because it fits in well with the person about whom it is told. It *could* have happened, so it demonstrates who the person involved is. Elisha is a great prophet, and what can you expect of great prophets? That they know what to do in emergencies. So Elisha rescues the axe which a poor 'prophet's son' had dropped into the water. The Old Testament and Jewish literature teem with stories with a midrashic character.

But the story of the ascension isn't a real midrash. Like the virgin birth of Jesus it's more like a logical legend. Its aim is to fill in what was felt to be a gap in the logical order of the story, and we could call that a form of theology.

What hiatus does the ascension story deal with? We can read that from the Apostles' Creed, which has the ascension of Jesus Christ ending up with his 'sitting at the right hand of God'. First of all let's try to discover the significance of what to us is a rather strange idea.

'Sitting at the right hand of God' is metaphorical language which we have to understand against the background of the culture of the time. God doesn't have a right hand and Jesus doesn't sit anywhere in the universe. 'Sitting at the right hand' stands for occupying a position of power. The bringer of salvation, the humiliated Jesus, through whose crucifixion reconciliation is achieved, is raised to the heights by God. He is given all power in heaven and earth.

That's an expression (taken from the Gospels) which needs a few comments. First of all, we mustn't imagine this picture as involving a sharing of power or, more strongly, as indicating that God has transferred his power to Jesus and retreated into the background. Jesus at God's right hand means something like Jesus having executive power. Furthermore – again we see that metaphors have their limitations – we mustn't think of a real throne, far less of two persons sitting on it. There aren't two someones; the Christian tradition never thought that and never will. But what can it mean for Jesus to have 'all power'?

The answer has to do with the nature of this power and thus with the way in which it's exercised. It's not the power of the 'pantocrator', the ruler over all, of which we must think, the power with which a ruler tramples his enemies under his feet. At least, for the moment we needn't think of it like that. Must we call it the power of love? But what is that? I would opt for something else (which doesn't conflict with this) and think that we should say, rather, that it's the power of the Word. The Word leaves people free, and the church with the Word can never be a tyrant; at all times it remains a servant of the Word. But the Word does have power over people. The Christian tradition believes that Jesus as the Word that is proclaimed has all power on heaven and earth. He makes free but also leaves free.

Back to the notion of the ascension. In order to sit at God's right hand, Jesus must first get there. This is the filling in of a hiatus by telling a story.

One question I can't avoid: why call the ascension a logical legend, but not the resurrection? Because there's a great difference between the stories. I've tried to make it clear that on the basis of the tradition itself it's impossible to see the resurrection as an event with a miraculous character. But the ascension – as an event – can only be miraculous. And there's something else. The resurrection is essentially something that happened to Jesus, something that took him 'out of time'. The story of the ascension presupposes that the most essential thing has already happened, and no more needs to be added. Except that – as the Word which liberates – he has all power in heaven and on earth.

XIII

The Last Judgment

'Signs are taken for wonders. "We would see a sign!"
The word within a word, unable to speak a word,
Swaddled with darkness. In the juvescence of the year
Came Christ the tiger' (*T.S. Eliot*)

1. *Dies Irae*

These days we hear little of God's judgment. Has it been abolished,
or did Christianity make a mistake and there's no such thing as a
judgment? You sometimes hear that said. Today's church preaches
God – at least for the most part – as redeemer, liberator, giver of all
good things, in short the God of salvation (and we think that churches
which don't do that aren't authentic). But in that case what's become
of judgment, the idea of Jesus' return to judge the living and the
dead?

The Middle Ages were well aware of judgment. The *Dies Irae* (Day
of Wrath) that we know from the world of music (for example, the
Requiems of Mozart or Verdi) comes from this time: it's an impressive
prayer for mercy on the day of God's wrath.

> *Quid sum miser tunc dicturus*
> *Quem patronum rogaturus?*

What can I say when the trumpets sound and the graves are opened?
What plea can I make for myself?

Not only the Middle Ages but also the New Testament can evoke
in bright colours the picture of God as judge who pours out his wrath
upon the peoples of the earth. And isn't Jesus there the intercessor
for whom the poet of the *Dies Irae* asked, Jesus 'who saves us from

the wrath to come'? What's become of all this? Is the Last Judgment, or whatever name it goes by, a fable?

No. The notion is indeed 'fabulous', but that's because it's a picture shaped by the genre of apocalyptic. The ascension of Jesus, his sitting at the right hand of God, and now the conclusion of this passage, 'from whence he will come to judge the living and the dead', belong with this imagery. On the clouds of heaven, of course, for surely he ascended in his 'chariot of light'?

It's remarkable that here (the passage comes from the Apostles' Creed) Jesus holds the last judgment and not God. But I shall come back to that. First of all the question, what is apocalyptic?

Anyone who wants to get a good idea of that should read the book of Revelation. Apocalyptic is in fact concerned with fantastic pictures of the future events which will introduce the downfall of the old world and the dawn of the new. Fantasy? Without doubt, unparalleled fantasy. But not without a deeper meaning. What fills the heart is projected on the screen of history: the dispute between God and Satan and the conquest of God 'on the day of the vengeance of our God'. That is the day on which he will make the judgment, and will separate the sheep from the goats; will finally bring bliss to the oppressed souls who, lying under the altar, do not cease to cry out 'how long', and hurl into the abyss the oppressors who have steeped themselves in their blood.

Is all that authentic? In other words, can we expect that kind of event? There used to be large groups of Christians who regarded all these fantastic pictures as historical predictions. And of course there are still some today who keep a finger on the text of Revelation and look at the world events of today to see how far we've got. Is the end in sight? Nearly the end? I won't make any negative comments on this except to say that while it can't be bad, no good will come of it. No one knows how history will turn out, nor is there a forecast in the apocalyptic passages of the Old and New Testaments. That's a misunderstanding of such literature. Apocalyptic is pictorial language about what takes place in history (according to the writers concerned). No more and no less. What apocalyptic envisages is quite plausible: if a new world is to come, then the old world must pass away.

So the Christian tradition has also dropped a good deal of this imagery. Except for what we are now concerned with: the return of Jesus to pass judgment on the living and the dead, the Last Judgment. Rightly so. But didn't I say 'what fills the heart'? The judgment is deep within us. People don't do other than condemn others, and also – if no one is around – themselves. Life consists of accusing and excusing. The last and definitive judgment is projected on the screen of the eternal God. *Quid sum miser tunc dicturus?*

2. The judgment as reckoning

The picture may be apocalyptic by nature, but what it presents, the judgment in terms of a definitive reckoning, isn't nonsense. Even the notion that it takes place at the end of time is an extremely important characteristic. It means that according to the Christian tradition the history of the world isn't itself the world's judgment. The fate that everyone meets isn't the Last Judgment. Fortunately, because that would lead to a sea of injustice. The judgment can take place within the world but, as everyone knows, it doesn't always happen. Sometimes the good get their reward, and the evil outcome of the life of a bloodthirsty oppressor satisfies our sense of justice; sometimes the opposite happens and the evildoer gets off and the victim is irreparably crushed.

The Christian tradition says that the real reckoning doesn't take place in and through history but will take place at the Last Judgment. Then everything will be definitively put right. The poor Lazarus will fare well and the rich neighbour who didn't see him sitting there will fare badly. Sheer compensation? Yes indeed, but why should we be troubled about that? Must Lazarus draw the short straw to the end of his days, and the executioner have an eternal advantage over his victims? Jesus thought differently: see his story about the rich man and poor Lazarus.

Certainly, I can point out that the Last Judgment is at the same time meant as a form of retribution: all get their deserts. This sense is also deeply rooted in our hearts. Why else do people say on their death-beds that they've lived a good life, and done their best to be good? They fear the judgment and are covering themselves.

Retribution is a term from penal law, I'm using it deliberately. Our sense of justice can't do without it, and it's also deep within us. So the discussion about retribution in penal law is never over either. There's much in favour of forgiveness instead of retribution, certainly if the idea of retribution is inspired by feelings of vengeance. But we can't live without the idea of retribution, whether here or in the hereafter. It's a simple demand for justice that the oppressor shall not reap the fruits of oppression for ever and that the oppressed shall know nothing but oppression for ever. And that's the situation if there's no Last Judgment.

The Last Judgment is 'last' because it's the judgment of the Last, of God. That means 'utterly serious'. God in no way regards the guilty as innocent, to put it in the terminology of the Old Testament. That's a disturbing fact for all those who destroy creation, but it isn't at all irrational. People damage each other and their world, which they haven't made themselves; they maltreat another's property. Will the Creator stand for that? No, the term judgment indicates that they will be brought to book for it. Greater and lesser injustice isn't just something about which *we* get cross – at least in our best moments and above all when we encounter it in others; it arouses the wrath of the Creator. In the tradition it can even be said quite forthrightly that the sinners (viz. those who damage creation) shall perish from the earth. That seems logical.

I'm not overlooking the positive side of the Last Judgment; we remain human there; we're held accountable for our conduct. Take away the judgment and we're children with no accountability. Easy, but not what we are or want to be.

However much we may dislike it, then, there is no avoiding the fact that the judgment of God is essential for the Christian tradition. So essential, indeed, that little or nothing would be left if there were no divine judgment. The Creator would be a non-value, a being who can make no difference to what his creatures do. But what according to the tradition is the fundamental significance of Jesus is also wholly orientated on the judgment of God. Reconciliation, the forgiveness of sins – it's left hanging if we could just as well leave out what the tradition says about judgment.

3. The Judge is the criterion

What is the criterion by which, according to the Christian tradition, we shall be judged at the Last Judgment? A word needs to be said about that if we aren't to end up with the classic representation of hell and damnation. Where these last went wrong wasn't the notion of a judgment, but the content of the criterion at it. It was such as to make talk of divine judgment a convenient way by which the church could keep sinners under control. It led to a grisly caricature of the Last Judgment.

I think of the preoccupation of Roman Catholic clergy with sexuality. 'You'll go to hell if you play with your genitals' and more of that sort of obsession with the bodies of the faithful. With the judgment of God in its hand the Christian church could exercise its authority even in the bedroom. A sanction on the morality of the church – a historically determined morality – or on what was regarded as socially fashionable; that was all that was left of judgment. Although the Roman Catholic church has long since moved away from this deadly sin, countless people think that this is still how things are in the church and therefore perpetuate the caricature – perhaps out of laziness.

But to begin with, God's judgment isn't a matter for the church but a matter for God. Or, remarkably, for Jesus Christ. The judgment stands in the context of christology: 'from whence he (= Jesus) shall come to judge the living and the dead'. So if we follow the tradition, the Last Judgment is postponed, or rather entrusted to Jesus Christ. Very surprisingly, the lamb of God becomes a tiger and shows his teeth: 'Christ the tiger'. How does that come about?

During his travels through the land of the Jews, Jesus spoke at length about the Last Judgment and called on his followers to feed the poor, care for the sick and visit those in prison. For when he comes again to judge the world (that's again the language of apocalyptic), he will say: 'What you did to the least of these, you did to me.' He identifies with the poor, the sick and the oppressed. Thus the judge already stands before us in the poor and the little ones; we look straight in the face of the one who will judge us. And the criterion is no problem either. Judge and criterion coincide. So we needn't wait until the last day to know where we are. Jesus doesn't need to 'come again'; we know it already.

It's clear that to pass over the little ones and the poor is no small matter; on the contrary, it's something of such importance that we bring the Last Judgment upon ourselves with it.

To make it quite clear, then: what is the criterion? Not the 'dolls' sins', as Luther called them, but humanity. Nowhere can the Christian tradition say more clearly than here that humanity is the criterion, the only authentic criterion, elevated by God to the level of an eschatological power. To ignore the poor and the little ones makes the lamb a tiger; we call down the judgment upon ourselves. That's firmly established in the Christian faith; the all-or-nothing of humanity decides our eternal weal and woe.

4. Lost for ever?

These last words bring me to a difficult point. At least according to the story, the judge who divides the sheep from the goats has the sheep going into eternal joy and the goats going into the outermost darkness. No less a person than Jesus speaks of this, and that makes us think. Is there really such a thing as the wrath of God?

We aren't the first to ask about that. The judgment and wrath of God are connected from the beginning, in the Old and New Testaments. But according to the church fathers this wrath cannot be. A God who gets angry can never be the true God, since by definition God is immune from passions. You have to be ashamed of a God who gets angry. Such a God remains below the norm that we set ourselves. Indeed, here we get to a favourite point of the early church, the struggle against the desires, the passions which unsettle a person and can even put a whole life out of joint. God as unmoved mover was therefore better than a God who reacts emotionally. Do we agree here with the early church?

There's nothing wrong with the wrath of God. It's an ancient but attractive word and fits very well into the usual metaphors of God in human terms. God isn't at all God's creature.

There are greater problems in the question whether God's wrath corresponds to God's love. Perhaps we have to see it as the reverse side of love: only those who love can hate. That's a quite obvious idea, so it's been retained down to the present day. Much less plausible, but really more exciting, is the view of the church father Origen that I touched on earlier. God doesn't really mean his anger, Origen says; it's a pedagogical trick, just as fathers put on a cross face when their children do naughty things but mean them no ill when they punish them. Eternal damnation, too, is a deterrent, and isn't meant seriously. People need to be treated like this.

Will all then be saved? Yes, says Origen, all. Even the devil (it can't be otherwise, because he has a spark of spirit, and spirit is something of God and therefore can never be lost). So hell isn't compatible with God. What is compatible with God is a place of purification where sinners undergo temporal punishments commensurate to their misdeeds. Origen is the inventor of purgatory. I find this a sympathetic view, a kind of middle way. Purgatory meets the earnestness of the judgment; that's not denied. But at the same time it brings out the perspective that this isn't a banishment for ever; a place of purification takes the place of hell.

Of course Origen didn't know anything about this, any more than we do. But he did reflect on it (it cost him his status as a church father), and arrived at a view which certainly isn't nonsense. That's why I've quoted him. We see him wrestling with the wrath of God and with judgment, so in the light of the tradition we needn't be ashamed if we're at a loss. We aren't the first.

Finally, and to the point: is there a Last Judgment, or is it a metaphor? That's an impossible alternative. What I wanted to say above is that it's a metaphor, but that doesn't mean that the judgment isn't reality. Only we've no more than the metaphor. We don't see the end of time, and don't even know whether there is an end. We only know our own end. So with the farmers of Zeeland I think that after our death we shall appear before the tribunal of the Judge. For us that is the moment of the Last Judgment.

Will we come out of it all right? The judgment hasn't become a piece of Christian tradition for people to fear. It stands in the context of a God who takes us seriously, but that can be combined with forgiveness and reconciliation. So can we sleep peacefully: is there no such thing as 'eternal punishment' or 'eternal death'? I find eternal death an appropriate term. God wants our company, but it won't depend on him whether we return to him. However, it may well be that anyone who doesn't want the company of God will remain in death. That is to be 'lost'.

XIV

The Trinity: Father, Son and Holy Spirit

'That we speak of three persons is not in order to say something, but in order not to be completely silent' (*Augustine*)

1. Mystery or speculation?

According to many people, the Christian tradition of faith stands out for its talk of God as the triune God. That's certainly an unusual way of imagining God, which can result in a wealth of possible misunderstandings and incomprehension. It makes me bold enough to ask whether the Holy Trinity – the solemn formula – must now be seen as a mystery or not rather as a theological speculation which was later turned into a mystery.

At all events the Trinity (to talk in these terms for the sake of brevity) began as a theological answer to an intellectual problem. Once we've said that God became man in Christ (the classical doctrine of the incarnation), the question arises whether God is no longer in heaven. Or, to put it more strongly: if God really became man, what was left of God? No one wanted two Gods (God and Jesus), but people also wanted to address Jesus as God. So are there two? All kinds of solutions were offered. To mention just a few: couldn't you say that Jesus was a kind of mask which God put on when he came to human beings? Indeed, but in that case, in Jesus we would no longer really have to do with God but have a masquerade, albeit a sacred one. The idea that Jesus was God's power on earth suffered the same fate: attractive, but again there was too little of God (as a person) in Jesus. Most solutions in which a human being could still be recognized had the flaw of leaving too little of God in Jesus, yet it all began with the assertion that God was in Jesus. So does two make one and one two? The teachers of the early church argued over this for centuries, and in the course of this discussion they noted that the earliest Christian tradition also speaks about God's Spirit as a someone, a person. So the question became: how can 3 = 1 and 1 = 3?

During the first centuries the three persons were still somewhat confused, but as an answer to the question, in the course of time the doctrine of the Holy Trinity came to be crystallized: God is one (and not two or three), but the one divine substance consists of (or better in) the three persons of Father, Son and Holy Spirit. Since then this has become a fixed part of the Christian tradition. For some people (down to the present day) it has become the occasion for engaging in colossal speculations about God, humankind and the world, and for the Eastern church it's the real mystery of Christian faith, but for most Christians it's an uncomprehended, incomprehensible and unimaginable concept of faith. When I once tried to explain to students what the tradition meant by the divine Trinity and came to the three persons, a girl asked in amazement, 'Three? But surely there are four; isn't there also a Substance?' Such kinds of misunderstanding are unavoidable. What the early church meant by substance isn't clear, let alone what it meant by 'person'. In any case it was quite different from what we mean by person.

2. Asking too much

Not understood, incomprehensible and unimaginable – that doesn't seem to me an exaggeration. It's an occasion for fundamental misunderstandings about the Christian faith. Islam can't see this as other than the fact that Christianity worships three Gods in place of one God; the Jews assume the same thing, and Jehovah's Witnesses time and again retort with the logic that three cannot be one and one cannot be three, while Unitarians have left the mainstream of Christianity because they found it impossible to acccept this idea.

Nor am I talking about the malicious misunderstanding of someone like the Dutch novelist and poet Vestdijk, who in one of his poems presents the Trinity as an escape for God himself: he delegated his suffering to his Son, 'but you yourself never hung on the cross'. I call that a malicious misunderstanding, because the doctrine of the divine Trinity was specifically intended to show that God did take suffering upon himself, wholly, by being present in Jesus Christ and – as far as the human nature is concerned – by taking the cross upon himself.

Once again: not understood, incomprehensible and unimaginable. Is it meaningful to make such a notion a crux of the tradition? I think that that's asking too much. People have to have studied theology for years to be able to understand the ins and outs of the matter. Most Christians don't have these years to spare. Then is it to be accepted without being understood? The Eastern church took this direction, and turned it into liturgy: the most holy mystery of the Holy Trinity as the centre of the celebration of God's presence. We can be content with that: mysteries needn't be understood, they're worshipped.

But the Western world wanted to see a doctrine here, and doctrines serve to prompt understanding. The doctrine of the Trinity isn't capable of that, yet what it is stating is fundamental to the Christian tradition of faith. God was present in Jesus Christ. That is and remains the distinctive feature of Christian faith. But to put that in terms of a complete doctrine of the Trinity, and then elevate it to be the foundation of all reflection on God and his salvation is theology: holy speculation if you like, but speculation. This is not only legitimate, but also necessary; we honour God when we know what we're doing. However, Augustine was already honest enough about his own statements about one Being and three persons to say: I'm not speaking in order to say something, but in order not to be completely silent. That sounds very modest. Here Augustine recognizes that he is making no claims, yet wants to say something. Let's make that the characteristic of the doctrine of the Trinity. It's a way of talking which Christianity has if it doesn't want to be completely silent. But is it a doctrine which brings insight or offers an answer? The idea of one substance and three persons seems to fall short of that.

3. Jesus another word for God?

The Christian tradition may originally have spoken about Jesus as about God, but how can that be if we maintain that Jesus is a human being as we are? That's a question about the person of Jesus which amounts to: 'How can the man called Jesus at the same time be both God and man?' I went into this in the sections about 'The prince in disguise' (it wasn't meant in this sense) and the doctrine of the two natures (in one person).

But it's also a question about God: how can God at the same time be the man Jesus and yet remain God, or, as I put it elsewhere: how can the man who is called Jesus be God without God disappearing from the scene? We must either have an answer to this question, or we must stop talking about Jesus as though he were God and leave it that Jesus was a very important human being. However, as the famous theologian and Dutch prime minister Abraham Kuyper said, you can't pray to a human being. If we do, then we're doing the same thing as the early church, and for us too Jesus has become another word for God. How do we justify that? That's also what the doctrine of the divine Trinity is ultimately about. Here I've restored it to its real purpose and given two answers which we can find in the tradition.

1. The first consists in a kind of development. 'God is unthinkable for us without Jesus Christ' (that's true, some Christians say) is developed into 'God was never without Jesus Christ'. From eternity he was already 'laden' with Jesus Christ and therefore the birth of Jesus can be spoken of as the 'coming' of Jesus to earth. He was already there, but as God the Son, who had not yet appeared in the flesh.

2. Jesus wasn't in God 'from eternity', but the eternal God identifies himself with the rejected, crucified Jesus. He does that in time, in our history, at Jesus' resurrection from the dead. So we must take God's self-identification with Jesus literally; God's took Jesus up into himself. To put it crudely: Jesus wasn't the Son but became the Son. These are all metaphors – that's clear. But they express the most intimate bond that the classical language knows.

Both version 1 and version 2 indicate that not only is Jesus inconceivable without God, but God is inconceivable without Jesus. So both versions say that you can talk about Jesus as about God. If you want to do him justice, then *you must* talk about him like this. The difference is that the first (crude) version incorporates Jesus into God from eternity (as the Son), and the second also incorporates him, but through an action of God in time.

Why we need have less of a dispute in Christianity than has often been the case is because in both modes of speaking Jesus determines the profile of God. So Jesus can be regarded as a 'revealer' in the Christian tradition. 'No one has seen God at any time, the only begotten Son has shown God to us' is a statement which is more in line with 1, and 'whoever has seen me has seen the Father' (viz. seen the Father at work) fits 2 more closely.

In this discussion I've answered a question which I haven't yet put. Jesus as another word for God implies that God has two faces: God as he was and will be as Creator, and God as he has a face for us when we see Jesus. How are these two faces of God related to each other?

We can't have God exhausted in Jesus Christ. That's meant well, the good intention of love. But love exaggerates. If someone like Bonhoeffer says that the whole of reality is Christ, then that's an exaggeration.

It's just such an exaggeration to say that God the Creator begins all over again in the way and work of Jesus Christ, and that in that case we can forget the creation, because it's no longer relevant. Even church teachers say that out of love for the person of Jesus Christ, but again it's at least an exaggeration.

It's one step too far in this direction to say that human beings and God come into contact for the first time in Jesus Christ. According to the Christian tradition human beings and the world are already from God. God was already there and was already in the world; he comes in Jesus Christ in a different way and with a different, new intent, but – he came to his own.

Continuing along the same lines, it's quite untenable to present Jesus as a substitute for God. We live in a culture in which God is no longer necessary, and people can no longer make anything, or can make hardly anything, of God. But that doesn't matter; we have Jesus. Thus necessity becomes a virtue! But that only seems to be the case. In reality this damages Christian faith. In the Christian tradition Jesus is important because God is important. Take God away, and Jesus has lost his significance. Is he there to give people a sight of God again or to give God a face again? The instrumental significance of Jesus – Jesus the Mediator – is and remains a fundamental notion. Not Jesus but God who is all in all – that's how the story of God and human beings ends.

4. The Holy Spirit

The Christian church proclaims Jesus. That's new, perhaps news or even good news. At all events we have to listen to the church to get the story. But there's something remarkable here. Jesus is proclaimed, but he's no longer here; he is past time, at least if we follow Christian tradition, which doesn't present him as a prince in disguise but as a real person. How then can the Christian church think that proclaiming Jesus has any influence on people, that it renews their lives and puts them on a new way, and so on?

With this question we come to the tradition about the Holy Spirit. Is this an incomprehensible chapter of Christian faith? It needn't be. By 'the Holy Spirit' or 'the Spirit' for short, Christianity in the first instance means none other than Jesus Christ. But here it is Jesus Christ who has passed from the past time to the present and 'is there' in terms of the Word that is preached and effective in the personal life of a Christian. In short, the Spirit is Jesus Christ as we encounter him (or he encounters us) in the proclamation of the gospel.

In the first instance the Spirit is none other than Jesus Christ, as I've just said. But wasn't God in Jesus Christ? Indeed, and in this way for the early church God, Jesus and the Holy Spirit came together. You could say that by 'the Spirit' the Christian tradition means God, but God who is concerned with us 'spiritually', I might say from Spirit to spirit. In a spiritual way, I might also say, the way of the powerful Word.

Not every word is powerful, but this word is: the word that has Jesus Christ as its content. For that has the presupposition that I've just mentioned. It's the Word with a capital W, the Word that has become Spirit.

So it's no small claim that Christianity attaches to the proclamation of the gospel of Christ. This does something, has an effect, sometimes spectacular. Eyes are opened, a person is illuminated, hidden pages from his or her existence come to be uncovered, prople get out of the morass in which they were caught and jump for joy. Sometimes, or rather usually, this isn't particularly recognizable but gradual, as happens with influence in most cases. By 'proclamation', moreover, we shouldn't think purely and simply of the pulpit; proclamation is also telling, talking about it. But this invisibility doesn't take away the power.

So the Spirit and the church belong together: that's already clear. And that's how it's always seemed through the Christian tradition of faith. Not exclusively, as if the Spirit were only in the Christian church, but in the Christian church the Spirit *is* present as a word that is effective, intervenes and changes.

The claims of the church are in turn bound to its preaching. It's not that preaching is important because of the church, but *vice versa*, that because of its preaching the church is important: it's a creation of its own preaching, of the Word which it has to serve. To the degree that it serves, it's strong, and may be strong. It needn't be afraid; it's led by the Spirit.

Not automatically – I shall come to that in the chapter about the church. But the Spirit is a reality that the Christian church needs. We're no longer Paul or John. The source began to flow and the tradition came out of it; christology is itself, as I said, a creation of the church. It's obvious that this sort of observation disturbs many Christians, but in my view it needn't. The Spirit goes with the church from land to land. With the whole church, I would note in passing. The Reformed aren't the whole church, any more than the Roman Catholics are (despite the Pope and his *magisterium*). So the leading of the Spirit, as it's said, has its conditions. A church which trusts in it can make great mistakes, but isn't going beyond its brief.

XV

Election

'You can be a man of God and yet be dead. You can be called, and yet go the wrong way. I understand that that could also happen to me. You can be baptized, and a believer, and yet be rejected. Few, very few, was the number of the elect, as I heard now and then when I went to church with my father and listened to Reverend Venema. And I ran more risk of being one of the damned since I was Reformed' (*Maarten t'Hart*).

1. *Chosen or rejected?*

The classical nightmare of many Reformed adolescents is election or predestination. Interpreted – I must go on to say – as a predetermination which can't be changed in any way: I'm saved for eternity or I'm damned for eternity. Chosen or rejected, that's the question. If God has resolved on the former, then I needn't make an effort, and if the latter's the case, then I needn't either. When I was a preacher in Zeeland, a housewife assured me that she was lost for ever. 'Would you like another cup of coffee?' she added. Another member of the congregation sat there knitting; she said that she felt one of the elect, knew that her middle sister had a faith she fell back on (i.e. that was still there), and that the youngest sister was damned for ever. The youngest sister was also sitting there.

Where does this caricature of election come from? From a misunderstanding about the Christian tradition especially caused by Calvin. God loves his own from eternity and that can only mean that he hates the others from eternity. Calvin conceded when pressed some people are created for eternal judgment. No wonder that people see little in faith if from childhood onwards their ears are assailed with this kind of theory – more or less seriously.

However, this whole way of thinking is utter nonsense, and it isn't so difficult to show that from the Christian tradition itself.

I'm not claiming that it began as nonsense. What the Reformed fathers in particular emphasized was the 'from eternity'. It's a term which was long used to express the fact that God belongs to another order, the order of the lord and king who rules 'eternally' over his creatures. If something is resolved on by God 'from eternity', that means for example that it isn't a fleeting idea, as is often the case with human decisions, but comes from God himself. Therefore it's also certain that what God wills comes before anything else. So 'from eternity' is literally the same as 'from beforehand', but means something different, emphasizes that we have to do with God.

It's not incomprehensible that the Reformed branch of the Reformation, on the prompting of Calvin, should have gone astray over the expression, but what they made of it, election or rejection 'from eternity' (in the sense of 'from beforehand'), is no less a ghastly misunderstanding. Not the only one, though. 'Jacob I loved and Esau I hated' – a well-known biblical passage in this connection – confirms the suggestion made by the 'from eternity'. What kind of chance do you have if 'from eternity' God loves some and hates others? This is to heap misunderstanding upon misunderstanding. I shall go into these in the list which follows.

2. God has a preference

1. In all contexts where there is talk of election (loving one and hating the other), love and hate don't mean what we mean by hating and loving but express a preference. God has a preference? Indeed, according to the Christian tradition of faith. God puts some above others.

2. 'From eternity' doesn't mean that before my birth, indeed before all times (whatever that may be) all things are already decided by God and so it's also settled whether I'm saved or damned. Quite apart from the use of such terms (though they belong in the argument), and apart from this pedantic examination as to whether one is or isn't saved, this view makes God's rule over 'all things' a form of determinism which expresses a fatalistic sense of life. Both are a fixation of some Christian communities, but can't be reconciled with Christian faith. In the chapter on God's rule over 'all things' I've explained this as far as I can.

3. What then? 'From eternity' means that it (the preference that we have to deal with) comes from the heart of the Eternal One, from

God's eternal heart. So God's choice isn't a whim, a superficial welling up of love; on the contrary, God means it.

4. So what is election? God's preference. Therefore according to the Christian tradition God isn't neutral. Indeed! God isn't democratic either. Not every option weighs equally heavily with God, has as much right to exist, gets as much of a chance. The Christian God follows his own preference.

5. Anxiety about that would be justified only if we knew nothing of this preference. But it isn't hazy or misty, doesn't leave us uncertain, doesn't mean that we never know where we are with the God of Christianity. On the contrary, it's clear, transparent as glass. Election in the sense that 'God has a preference' thus does the opposite of what people claim; it doesn't make us uncertain but gives us certainty about God and God's purposes.

6. Then for whom, according to Christianity, does God have a preference? For the sinners and the beggars. The despised are chosen to shame those who exalt themselves or have all too much imagination about God. 'They'll fall flat on their faces' may not sound gentle, but it's a good Christian statement. So God's preference kills two birds with one stone: those who can't help themselves will be helped by the God of the Christians, and those can do everything themselves will be left with empty hands.

7. Aren't sinners and beggars different kinds of people? Certainly, but both are the focus of God's concern, at least according to the Christian account of God. The sinner finds forgiveness in God and the beggar – what does the beggar get? Does God make the beggar rich? Is that what the Christian church offers the poor: you'll all be rich? I don't think so. The parallel between sinner and beggar is taken from the parable of the rich man and poor Lazarus. What does Lazarus get? He's compensated for his poverty in the afterlife, however offensive that may sound to people who want to see everything levelled out here: otherwise they don't believe in it.

8. So does the Christian church consist of sinners and beggars? Certainly, but others may join in if they show that they're seeking God in a lively way, a way which goes hand in hand with humility towards the sinner and a helping hand towards the beggar. It isn't a matter of 'Look, we too are for the poor, just like God'. That becomes holiness by works, and sometimes even pseudo-holiness. An attempt is the same as a lowly prayer to be allowed to join in.

9. That the poor or sinners as such have a better knowledge of God, of what human life is, of what may and may not be, has no

foundation. God's preference isn't based on the qualities of the poor, any more than it's based on the qualities of the sinner. They cherish themselves and may know they are cherished in and through God's preference. That's all, and as far as God's concern goes, that's enough. Only afterwards can both the sinner and the beggar best say who God is, since they've experienced God in his glory.

10. So what is election? According to Berkouwer, it's the style by which, according to Christianity, God is to be recognized. We know where we can find God for preference.

The Church

XVI

The Church as a Summary of All Frustrations

'I would not have God as Father if I did not have the church as mother'
(*Augustine*)

'There is no more bitter people than the saints' (*Martin Luther*)

1. The trauma of the church

'I believe in one holy universal Christian church' is a line from the
Apostles' Creed with which Christians are thought to agree. But there
is a disappointment in each of the words used here. The church is the
great disappointment. The most pregnant formulation came from a
theologian at the beginning of this century: Jesus meant the kingdom
of God, and what came? The church.

Where does this disappointment stem from? Like all disappoint-
ments, from the discrepancy between the ideal that we have in our
head and the reality that bitterly opposes it. We are incorrigible
optimists, and we also (and above all) judge the Christian church
from that standpoint. A truly human society? Forget it. Living as an
example for others? Not much sign of it. A delight to belong to? I've
yet to meet anyone who says that. I shall simply pass over the
historical problems. When people needed it, the church lacked a
social face, so the workers left it. Artistic people couldn't make
anything of it with its snugness and its slavery to the letter, and also
left. And how is it faring today? The citizen who has come of age has
experienced social freedom, and has no other memory of the church
than manipulation and pressure, an institution which was apprehen-
sive about losing its influence. All the frustrations of whole, half,
quarter and assimilated Christians come together in the theme of the
church; the church has become a focus of opposition to the Christian

179

faith. 'Écrasez l'infâme' was Voltaire's cry. I know plenty of people who would echo him.

What can the Christian tradition of faith set against that? In principle, two ways are open. We can put the ideals rather lower, perhaps give them up altogether, or do more to correspond to them. And of course there can be a bit of both.

I shan't be taking either course, although my account allows anyone to opt for a particular side. My purpose is to make as clear as possible what the Christian church is good for and what it isn't, as a given entity, indeed as an institution amidst other organizations and institutions. That first of all involves unravelling a confused and confusing terminology. After that, there's only small scope for the Christian church, not much left. But we can't do without it. That's the strange paradox of the recalcitrant obstacle called church: we can't do with it and we can't do without it.

2. *The church 'as it really is'*

We can mean all kinds of things by 'church'. Some people immediately think of the building, of going to church on Sunday and all that was or is associated with that. For some it smacks of festivity and for others of the plague of iron rituals or the compulsion of what can and cannot be done on Sunday.

With expressions like 'the church teaches', 'the church says' and suchlike, we find another side. In that case, at least in the first instance, we aren't talking about the building but about the church as an institution (almost imagined as a person) that maintains views in which you must believe. That's true to the degree that in the 'church' as an institution we encounter the distinctive form of organization of the Christian religion, based on its own interpretation of itself. Christians aren't shut up in the institution; they also function as Christians outside the church, or rather they only function there. But then they don't feel themselves to be the church, or feel at most what Abraham Kuyper called 'the organic church' as opposed to 'the institutional church'. But there we don't have a trauma; there we have the church 'as it really is', the institution.

By institution I understand a form of organization which regulates interpersonal relationships according to fixed patterns that have grown up over history, have proved meaningful, and therefore established themselves, sometimes over centuries. Marriage is a good example: you don't need to choose your partner afresh every day;

that's already regulated by the institution. So the church regulates the relationship in faith between its members and God and between one another; that's the special feature of the institution called 'church'. How to pray, to believe, to practise love of neighbour and so on – all that is prescribed in fixed forms of teaching, liturgy and life.

Institutions help us and make things difficult for us. If we had to make new choices in every situation every day, we would go crazy. But fortunately we don't need to; most of what we undertake is prescribed in the institutions in which we're involved. I've already mentioned the man/woman relationship, but that also applies to work, family and even how we spend our leisure time. We keep fitting into a pattern of behaviour which is already present, including the rights and duties which go with it, and we benefit from that.

But institutions, including the Christian church as an institution, have another side. Through their fixed, patterned regulations they have something oppressive about them and become more oppressive, the more subtle, sensitive, emotional the relationships that they regulate are. So people get more at loggerheads with the institution of marriage than with that of work. To the degree that personal relations play a great role in faith, this rule also applies to the church as an institution. Its regulations are already too precise, and that's certainly the case when a church *magisterium* or synodical supervision exists to apply these rules rigorously.

That's what the church has shown too much of in the past: too many unnecesary regulations directed at the wrong points. Especially doctrine and (sexual) morality have fallen (and still fall) victim. They're constantly kept under control by supervisors who vigorously apply the teaching that regulated their own attitude.

To manipulate the organization of the community of faith by means of a hierarchically ordered institution has been a masterpiece of strategy, one which is still practised by the Roman Catholic church. The institution comes to stand above the person; people have to adapt, and if necessary are trimmed to match the institution. If not voluntarily, then by force; otherwise they're expelled (if they haven't already left of their own accord). I'm exaggerating by looking above all at the past, but a hierarchical institution still remains what it is. There is flexibility only when the practice is flexible.

So the question already arises: why not begin with the people in place of the institution? Surely institutions consist of people? That's incontrovertibly true, but a community of people falls apart like a pile of sand if it isn't kept together by a bond of an institutional kind. If it's to survive, the institution is indispensable – for any community. We should find something like an institution that gives freedom; at all events an institution without compulsion. The only question is whether such an institution exists.

3. The invisible church?

Since all these objections and frustrations relate to the institutional church, the 'church as it is', it isn't surprising that Christians down the centuries have tried to retreat to the invisible church.

That can happen in a subtle way, as it were imperceptibly, but also by creating an official invisible church – in terms of doctrine. I shall begin with the first way, which is connected with a kind of 'bewitching' of our terminology. The other way naturally follows from that.

In some tractates or catechetical leaflets we can read that the church is 'the body of Christ'. Or also that the church lives by the Word of God, that the church is the refuge for the poor, doesn't let itself be tied to the chariot of the state, and so on. Those are normative statements about the church, by which I mean that they don't say how the church *is* but how it *needs to be*, what it *must do*. It's simply not on to describe the church with the help of normative statements; at all events it will inevitably turn out badly, and indeed does. It's fooling your fellow men and women. For in that case you're talking about the church on paper, the church as described by the Christian ideal – or at least as you see that ideal. You can go on talking about it for hours, days, months and years without catching sight even for a moment of the 'church as it really is'. You're talking hot air, about a conceptual house of cards, and no more. Of course this talk doesn't get in the way, doesn't do any damage, unless you've been thinking that the whole time that you've been talking about the church as it 'really is'.

Of course normative views of the church are vitally necessary, I don't deny that: but only if we regard them as a stimulus or as a criterion by which to measure the existing church. The very best statement about the church ends up in chaos if we move at will from 'is' to 'must be' and vice versa.

To escape into what the church *must* be is to take refuge in an invisible ideal, and in this sense in the invisible church. That's not the same thing as what the Christian tradition meant by the so-called 'invisible' church (an established concept), but it comes close to it. 'Invisible church' indicates (and indicated) that we must regard the Christian church as a datum of faith. You can say that the church is God's dwelling-place but not see it; we're talking about something that can't be seen from the outside. Hence the term 'datum of faith'.

In that case, do these data of faith fit? As the term indicates, Christianity *believes* that this is the case; it believes that God dwells with human beings and that this dwelling-place is to be found in the church. That means at least that you can't control it and that's appropriate. But conversely, you can't read anything out of it, so it becomes all the more precarious to call yourself the dwelling-place of God. Such talk can have a ghastly outcome, as indeed it has done over the course of the centuries. 'Dwelling place of God' isn't a fact, though I called it a fact of faith. Nor is it true because it stands in the doctrine of faith; it's true only *when* it's true, and that depends on what people make of the church which really exists.

So what does this add up to? The word 'is' is also tricky in this second context. If you don't understand 'is' in the sense of 'may be', you get confused about the church and everything else. The church 'as it really exists' is automatically loaded with God.

That's the source of the self-understanding that the mediaeval church maintained and that is maintained down to the present day by the Roman Catholic *magisterium*. The word 'is' isn't understood as 'may be', and thus is applied without qualification to the Roman Catholic church as it really exists. In this way the Roman Catholic church does itself too great an honour: it makes itself the one true church, which as such is justified in demanding unconditional obedience to the church government.

The crude 'is' even returns in the sacraments: in the Roman Catholic view they are literally the housing of God. God *is* there in the tabernacle, whether you believe it or not.

That's what the Reformation had against them, the automatism. 'Where God is, there the church is.' If 'is' doesn't mean 'may be', that unavoidably becomes the case.

If the church is the dwelling place of God, it can't fail either. But that, too, is a disastrous development. The church is always right, and criticism, even fundamental criticism, in the way in which Savonarola, Johannes Hus, Luther and Calvin and many others expressed it, is impossible. We can see from the examples that I've mentioned here how such a concept of the church is also disastrous for believers: they are mercilessly put outside the church and can count themself lucky that it's no more than that.

4. Belonging to the church: what does that feel like?

Where do you belong if you belong to the church? I'm now asking about the experience. Not the experience of being a Christian in general. There would also be interesting questions to ask about that. Black experience is different from Western experience, Chinese experience different again from Latino, and so on. But that's another matter.

Still less do I have in mind the theological responsibility of the church, or the theology of the church. At least not in the first instance. That, too, is interesting and important enough to investigate, but it would take me away from the area with which I'm concerned, that of the tradition of faith.

What do people feel if they're members of the Christian churches? What I really mean is how it feels. The answers indicate a great variety of attitudes and emotions. I shall just make a selection and also mention that none of them describes attitudes exclusive to a particular church community.

1. We're a different kind of person, a third 'genus' alongside Jews and Gentiles. That's what one of the earliest Christian writings says. This is an expression of pride: there's something novel about the Christian church. Elsewhere it's said that we're quite different. To use Augustine's words, in a sense the church is the appearance of the kingdom of God on earth. The feeling is almost like a feeling of victory, as in any case it could be in a martyr's death.

2. There's another emphasis when the church is compared with Noah's ark. Anyone who is in the church is saved – as in the ark. To belong to the church is to belong among the saved in a 'crooked and perverse generation', among the 'little flock' that has escaped God's wrath and is waiting to enter eternal bliss.

3. Yet another emphasis: the true church consists of God's elect. That lays on them the task to live accordingly. For how do you know whether you're elect? By perceiving within yourself that you're taking it seriously. So what must you do to become certain of your election? Practise it in an appropriate way of life.

4. More martial is the experience that being the church amounts to being in the service of Christ the king. I use to have to listen to talk about being 'soldiers of the Lord Jesus', and Abraham Kuyper coined

the saying that there is 'no inch of ground' in the sphere of life of which Christ does not say 'Mine!'. Elsewhere, too (in the Spanish Roman Catholic church), talk of Christ the king is rife. And in the German Protestant churches people readily identify the church with the 'Lordship of Christ' – however spiritually that is meant.

5. We are strangers and sojourners in an alien land. Anyone who has that feeling in their church is living on the edge of culture, indeed over the edge. As pilgrims on a journey to eternity, church people no longer have a a message for the world. Many Protestant 'sects' give this pilgrim sense to belonging to the church. The world is a 'land to pass through'.

6. A less hidden and self-effacing variant is for people to see themselves as pioneers of the kingdom of God, the forerunners of Life with a capital L. The church is not itself the kingdom on earth, but it is beginning to turn the earth into the kingdom. So being the church is to be against the old and for the New (capital N). If the new is identified with another political order, a political variant develops, as for example in some liberation theologies.

7. Over against that there is a mystical sense, where people see the church as the 'body of Christ'. The church is then a world in itself, a world behind the world, in which one tastes and tests what isn't enjoyed elsewhere. The sacraments play a great role in this experience; in fact being a member of the churh is tantamount to being drawn into the sacramental reality.

8. Related to that, but less individual, is the experience of belonging to the 'people of God'. That can go in the direction of a new 'genus' (see under 1), but usually it represents a world of feeling in which the church is experienced as a community on the way. On the way where? To a new world. Is that coming, then? The church as the sacrament of the world stands surety for that; it experiences itself as a living sign and promise that the whole of the world already lies in God's saving hands. Therefore a precise boundary is drawn between church and non-church.

What does this list show us? It shows us two things. First, that the way in which people experience the church corresponds to what they understand by believing. A whole range of variants of faith can in fact be read off practice. Secondly, these variants are simply there: they need no legitimation; the tradition has openings enough through which they can come (which doesn't mean that they will all get as far). But the most important thing – and this is my third comment – is that there is a binding element. This whole list of relationships, however different they may be, is concerned with a feeling that has to make use of the word 'world' to express itself. No church without the world – that's the heading under which they all fit. So it's time for a few sections under the heading 'church and world'.

5. Church and world (i) A self-interpretation of the church

First of all, what 'church and world' cannot mean in any event. If we take 'world' in the usual meaning of the term, the world around us, culture, then the 'church' is of course also 'world' and the contrast collapses. Without culture there isn't even any church. Therefore a church always presents itself in the garb of the culture in which it's established: Black churches are coloured by Black culture, Western churches have a Western form of Christianity, and so on. That doesn't mean that the church can't come up with something that wasn't there first, but it can't tell its story other than in terms of the culture in which it moves.

But that's not of course the question that 'church and world' is about. Here world is something standing over against the church, not-church, an entity outside the church, and in this sense is a creation which the church needed, and needs, to make its own place in the culture clear to itself and others. So a particular self-interpretation essential to the Christian church underlies this terminology.

I can best explain this by taking up the original significance of the Greek word for church which the apostles used: being called out. In the same way – we have to think – as Abraham was called out of his land and people to go to the land that God would show him, to become a great people there. So the church is also a people, a new people in a world which is in the grip of evil. On the one hand it's the bringer of the message of salvation which calls people out of an old life that is nothing but a dying by stages, into a new life that is a gift of God. On the other hand, it's a product of this message, a *creation* of God's saving word, a new creation which will survive the old world. So the Christian church isn't there for nothing. It preaches God's salvation and explains itself as the first pledge of that salvation.

What I'm presenting here is an indispensable claim of the Christian church. The church doesn't coincide with world, or with society (although it is the church *in* a society), but is by definition different from it. Should the church lose this belief, it would mean that it declared itself to be unnecessary and thus superfluous. It stands and

186

falls with the reason for its existence; it is this way, and then abolishes itself.

So the Christian church cannot imagine itself as other than necesary for salvation – to use a classical term.

6. Church and world (ii) No salvation outside the church?

'Church and world' is a contrast which – to use a classical term – presupposes the necessity of the church for salvation. Here I shall try to clarify what is meant by this (and whether it's true). I must first distinguish it from an equally classical expression which comes from Cyprian: 'outside the church there is no salvation'.

Of course that's an extremely crude and pretentious exposition of the need for salvation. It was extremely effective in consolidating the church's power (the church leaders were never averse to it), but horribly lacking in solidarity. Noah creeps into the ark and lets the rest drown. Do we really want to join him?

If we express it like that, no, but I've put it in such a crude way to explain why the Christian church has never felt – nor can ever feel – completely happy with its interpretation of itself. Moreover, creeping safely into the ark is, historically speaking, a caricature. The opposite has happened. A failure to show solidarity? Down to the present day the Christian church has refuted this allegation (or its own uneasy conscience?) by two completely different counter-moves. The first is the apostolate (what used to be called evangelization). The great activity here – extending to mission – is inexplicable without the necessity of the church for salvation in the background. The message of God's eternal salvation must be delivered; that's what the church is for. People must be called to faith and conversion in order to add themselves to the Christian church as the community of believers. So in terms of apostolate 'church and world' means: we don't deny that the church is Noah's ark, but we don't creep into the ark without taking account of others; on the contrary, we proclaim the saving message of God and call on people to do the same.

The great activity of the apostolate has meanwhile passed, and even the term has fallen into disuse. It's something from the 1950s and 1960s.

The second counter-move is much more modern. The Christian church moves on the horizontal level of giving aid and humanity, the level where everyone is in need, not just 'spiritual people'. Here it can be shown that the church, although a bit of an odd one out, nevertheless isn't as strange as people think. In any case the world doesn't leave it cold. Here, too, 'church and world' is meant to express solidarity. But that search for a link would never have assumed such almost solemn form had there not been behind it the feeling that the church is something quite different from the world.

One step further and the show of solidarity disguises the contrast. So the church is there for human salvation? But surely it's also salvation to live together better, to be good neighbours, and so on. Certainly, there's nothing but good in that, and churches, too, can do much here. They're useful for that. But are they also necessary? We're back to the question we began with, the necessity of the church for salvation.

Two comments on that. To begin with, we can see the great importance of the concept of salvation that we hold. If better life together is the salvation that our world needs, then little or nothing is left of the necessity of the Christian church for salvation. The church will never be able to deny the salvation that is called 'life together' without losing itself, but it has more to it than that, a speciality which cannot be found anywhere else, and that is peace with God through Christ. If that's no longer an attraction, what then?

That doesn't end up in 'outside the church there is no salvation'. Of course, if by the church you mean a society of true believers which is invisible to us but visible to God, then salvation is where the church is. But we aren't God, and so we can't work with such an invisible church; we reckon with its existence because we don't want to look at the visible, 'really existing church'. As the church father Augustine said, as far as that is concerned, there are many sheep outside the church and many wolves within. So what goes wrong here is when 'church' (where the church is, there is salvation) is taken to mean an institution; it is then quite wrong to limit this institution to a particular institution, say, the Roman Catholic church. According to official Roman Catholic doctrine, the church is entrusted with 'the guidance and government' of grace. Therefore there is no salvation outside it. That doesn't mean that those who enter into it can also be certain of salvation; no, salvation is only to be *found* there. Thus both statements fit the Roman Catholic view: outside the church there is no salvation (it is to be found only within) and therefore the church is necessary for salvation. In fact that means that the clergy (who control grace) are necessary for salvation, and that in turn means a hierarchy. Above are the clergy and below the laity.

I would suggest that we do better to abandon the statement that outside the church there is no salvation. It's open to too many interpretations. So we're left with 'necessary for salvation'. But in what sense?

7. Church and world (iii) 'The mother of us all'?

The term church presupposes the term 'world' as its counterpart. Without 'world' there is no church, and without 'church' no world. But that isn't the whole story, even of the necessity of the Christian church for salvation, the source of this terminology. We can see two sides here.

Augustine coined the expression that the church is 'the mother of us all'. Now if the church is necessary for becoming a Christian, then there's truth in that. The church has brought us into the world – that's what it's about. But there's a dilemma here. As Augustine puts it, it seems as if we're only there when we're Christians. Before that we were non-existent, not yet born. Indeed, not only does that seem to be the case, but for Augustine – and all who reflect on this point of Augustine's – that is indeed the case. Hence the people who are included along these lines get a name only when they're baptized. Before that they have no name, because they don't exist. A person takes on real existence only in the church. Ordinary, worldly existence, natural birth from our parents, isn't of course denied; it's a necessary condition for our existence. But all that takes on significance only when we join the church. So the world is ultimately there for the church.

I don't approve of this way of giving content to the necessity of the church for salvation; it comes too close to 'outside the church there is no salvation'.

There's another way of giving content to the necessity of the church for salvation, in such a way that the world isn't there for the church but the church for the world. By itself the world itself is perishing, it's not doing well; God's creativity is thwarted by human bungling, and all this must be remedied by the Christian church, which calls on people to be reconciled with God and begin a new life. Human existence or, more broadly, creation doesn't have to become 'church' or 'churchly'; on the contrary, it must again become world in the true sense of the word, God's unfrustrated creation. But precisely for that reason everyone must go to the church to be liberated from the delusion of their own righteousness, to be converted, and as new human beings recreated by God to go on to make what they can of the world. Here I'm referring to a classical Reformed current in the Christian church. If we want the creation to retain its own importance, then we must choose this last option: the church is there for the world, not 'before', but for.

There is in fact a certain duality about this notion of things. But it's as logical as it's unavoidable. It's about the world and it turns on the church. Just as it's about God the Creator and turns on Christ. Jesus Christ is the Mediator between God and man, no less and no more, and in keeping with that the Christian church is a means and not the end of God's ways. It's an indispensable means necessary for salvation, but a means.

Of course we can try to reconcile this duality by incorporating Christ into creation so to speak from the beginning (for example in terms of a humanity which is not yet made). He is then an end-point towards which the whole of creation is developing. Alternatively, he can be regarded as the ferment which will make the creation rise as yeast makes dough rise. This then happens – that's the point – by bringing in the Christian church which knows and proclaims that mystery.

This is a favourite construction of Roman Catholic theologians in particular. It transcends the duality and still holds fast to the creation. But the price is that the whole of the world must ultimately become church; creation – if you plumb its mysteries – is really already church, and the church is both the means and the end of all God's ways. Attractive though this view is, for me it goes too far: the independence of culture from the church disappears and that takes its revenge.

So, is the church necessary for salvation? Yes, the Christian church has its indispensable place because of its proclamation of salvation in terms of the appropriation and transmission of faith. It has to see itself as the conduit of the Christian tradition of faith. Things can still go wrong, but at least a functional test is possible of what it says or does.

8. The institution must remain

If we may believe social historians, the Christians, gathered in their local churches, were originally a friendly people, not aggressive, living outside the mainstream and recognizable by their Sunday services in which Jesus was confessed as the Christ. At first this group wasn't under the religious umbrella of the state, but was rather what today we would call a cult group. The liturgy consisted of good works, inspired by the summons to 'be wholly other'. It was more a sort of escape from the world under the motto '*sauve qui peut!*', and certainly in the first century of its existence it was still stamped by the consequences of the idea of a rapid coming (or return) of Jesus as Judge of the world, complete with an interim ethic – preserved in the so-called Sermon on the Mount – in which it is given its last instructions for life in the atmosphere of 'this world will soon pass away'.

But things couldn't continue like that; the church became an institution, ministries and buildings developed, even an organizational structure with hierarchical features, and so on. But above all, the interim feeling disappeared, the church settled down and indeed had to settle down, with all the consequent compromises with the solemnity of the first hour. I am by no means claiming that the first hour was the true hour – that's a real question – but that every movement, including the Christian church, starts with an original (unordered) enthusiasm and subsequently gets caught up in the needs of its daily existence. A pity for the church? Some Christians can't avoid that feeling, but I see it more as nostalgia or a need for romanticism ('back to the time when everything was still clear') than as a sense of reality. The church would then become a kind of subculture, a community of people alien to the world with customs alien to the world, for whose children there's no option but to take to their heels.

Would we really want the Christian movement to have remained outside the great stream of history? Certainly not. The statement that Jesus intended the kingdom of God but the church came is, moreover, nonsense. But a price does have to be paid, and that is what we are concerned with in this chapter: the price that the church has paid and must pay in order to be in the world (its terminology) and of the world, but in a deeper sense also *not* of the world. The church as an institution which is self-sufficient, proud, compulsive, spiritual and material is too high a price to pay. The institution is saved, but the church seeps away. What is left, to use Nietzsche's words, is God's grave.

But everything has its price. If the Christian church is necessary for salvation, then the institutional church is also necessary, for without the structure of an institution the church runs away like sand between the fingers. So we're talking about the need for the 'church that really exists', if the process of appropriation and transmission is to continue. Not in any arbitrary fashion; I'm not giving any *carte blanche* here. Far less am I saying that all that churches ask for must be done by everyone at all times. You don't always need to do what was done earlier. Why shouldn't people also be able to be associate with the church in a more distant way? But 'necessary' means that you help it to continue, if only with the paying of annual dues.

9. The church as a provider of opportunities

The church cannot present itself more modestly than as a vehicle for the appropriation and transmission of the tradition of faith. It should keep its institutional form, necessary for its ongoing existence as a community; it should keep its ministries, but drop the pretensions and the power which are given with them. It provides an opportunity; that's all.

Anyone who provides an opportunity doesn't rule over faith but serves it in a way which leaves room both for participants and passers-by to make something of faith or 'to join in'. If appropriation and transmission are the reason for its existence, what must we then be able to find in the church (as an institution and building)?

1. Appropriation and transmission need a language, words and sentences, fixed terms and phrases and reconstructions of them. Language in this sense is a necessary condition of being able to think and talk about the Christian faith (hence this book). So the church maintains a doctrine which presents this faith to people in terms of catechesis and Sunday sermons. It's possible to repeat this, and to repeat is also to talk. To stop talking makes people dumb. Without a clear catechesis, of whatever kind, nothing is left of the church. Good works don't keep a church together. However important they may be, they aren't enough.

2. The preaching of grace is necessary for appropriation and transmission, though not in the form of the sermon which is so familiar to us, and so is the proclamation of the great commandment to love God with all our heart and our neighbours as ourselves. The proclamation of grace is none other than the preaching of reconciliation and the call to be reconciled with God. We must be told that, since otherwise we don't know that anything is wrong. And how can we become other men and women without reconciliation?

3. Appropriation and transmission presuppose contact between

the generations, not only between parents and children but also with generations who lie still further behind us. We stand on their shoulders, whether we like it or not (and shouldn't we say when we don't like it?). Nowhere does this become so clear as in a tradition of faith. It's brought to us in the church through the exposition of the Bible, through joining in by opposing our grandparents and so on.

4. Room is needed for appropriation and transmission, room for variations in spirituality. Among the classical Reformed that was called a 'situation': the word indicates that God's salvation isn't assimilated by everyone in the same way. There are dependent and independent Christians, thinkers and doers, mystics and those who live on the surface. They all may and must be at home. If there's no room for them, then the church gets empty.

5. Disposition needs a place. Where is mystical experience possible which stimulates appropriation and transmission? Where is prayer possible? First of all at home in our room. But in order to share with the generations which preceded us and the community which surrounds us, we must go to church. That puts demands on the building. Sadly, Reformed Christians have been too slow in seeing this and are saddled to the end of our days with glorified barns. That's bad for prayer; the classical prayers and litanies don't resound there.

6. I haven't yet mentioned hymns of praise, and celebration as 'the suspension of existence'. The churches of the Reformation have little sense of liturgy compared with the Anglicans and Roman Catholics, and a contempt for ritual. Sadly, this is an impoverishment. But at least hymns flourish. Anyone who sees (and hears!) Friesian farmers singing the Psalms knows that they know the seduction of songs of praise, of incantation. And where else can that happen if not in the church?

7. Finally, the community. Is the church the 'communion of saints', as the Apostles' Creed calls it? If we understand 'is' as 'needs to be', then there's no doubt about that. But the question is whether the church as it really exists shows so much community. I myself don't know whether I should be so concerned about this. First of all I like a certain degree of anonymity in the church (and certainly in the building). Not that family-like, chatty, we-all-know-one-another display. To hang on one another's words seems to me the opposite of community. I hope to find community when I'm in need: not earlier and preferably also not later.

10. Can anything still be made of the church?

The circumstances in which the Christian church finds itself, at least in Western Europe, have already been the occasion for a great many laments and sad predictions, from 'serious but not hopeless' to 'hopeless but not serious'. This justifies the question whether anything can still be made of the church.

It's clear that a 'lost generation' has grown up. The Christian church will have to resign itself to this in the sense that it has itself to blame for much (though not all) of this outcome. But there need be no reason for panic or lack of courage. Religious belief isn't as worn out as is often suggested. Men and women are active in it; they 'join in', as I suggested earlier. If the average churchgoer weren't so scornful here – can it only be as church and theology prescribe? – the church could do more. With patience, with faith in the necessity of the church and with the intention of not allowing itself to be 'made useful' (and thus excluded), a generation will again arise which accepts the Christian church into its pattern of life. For the moment I don't see being useful to the world as a way out of the impasse. Sadly enough, I would add, since the Christian church and being of service go together. But here the longing to be of service mustn't stem from a lack of clarity about oneself or one's interpretation of oneself. You can't on the one hand (intellectually) maintain a concept of the church which presents the church as necessary for salvation (hence 'church and world') and on the other (practically) only give the world what it already has. As long as the Christian church fails to do away with this imbalance because it doesn't first opt for the necessity for salvation and then (on that basis of this) for the ministry of welfare worker among other welfare workers, it can't expect to solve its own problems by multiplying the services it has on offer. That isn't what they're for.

The Christian church must put the bar somewhat lower, so that everyone can get over it and not just semi-theologians. 'Joining in' can be different; it needn't consist in mastering doctrine. It's written of Mary that she pondered everything that was said in her heart; she wasn't a chatterbox. We should attach more importance in the church to people who switch off at such chattering.

The church needn't become jolly, but grumbling mustn't be the only trademark of, for example, the Protestants, nor compulsion the characteristic of Rome. These seem to be conditions for the return of our lost sons and daughters. We need an institution of quality and free from pressure. The church will never become an example for the world, a shop-window of what God's eternal salvation does for people, but it can become a showroom in which one can see stands showing how people can be reconciled with God and therefore know how to forgive one another – there's perhaps something simple there. If that doesn't work in the church, what will happen elsewhere?

11. Christianity without the church?

In the 1960s there was interest in a Christianity without the church. Another flight into the invisible church! But is there such a thing? Let's take the desire seriously and look for the motives that could underlie it.

1. Those who want a Christianity without the church have clashed with the institutional church and its pressures, and when they hear the word 'church' can only think of the pastor or the minister or the pope or a synodical Diktat: in short, of the authorities which remind them of a concern for discipline, regulations and spiritual compulsion. These are all things which have been associated with the institutional church down the centuries and – to say it once again – have alienated large groups of people from the church. I've gone into this sufficiently enough not to need to say more on this point.

An institution without a trace of compulsion would be the answer, but honesty compels me to say that this is an illusion. There's always a form of regulation in any institution; otherwise there would be no institutions. It would help not to impose regulations as obligations. Church members would have to give up their anxiety about freedom and church authorities the anxiety that their church wouldn't survive the freedom of its members.

2. A second motif behind the call for a Christianity without the church is that 'church' means discrimination, by definition a lack of solidarity, setting oneself up as being different from the others, more pious, more holy. This seems to me one of the most important reasons why young people don't find it easy to become members of the church and quite easy to leave it. It's simply the issue of membership of a group which claims to be further on than others! Through grace, as the minister says. But whether through grace or not, they don't like hearing about it.

That distaste seems to come over me, certainly as I get older. I must say more about the hostility to an egotism of salvation which can lie behind this. For indeed, if you may be an egotist where God's salvation is concerned, you may be an egotist everywhere. Is an egotism of salvation authentically Christian? No. 'I would be willing to be accursed for the sake of my brethren,' we hear the apostle Paul say when he describes his sorrow at the distance between his Jewish contemporaries and Jesus of Nazareth. That's an expression of compassion, not of the egotism of salvation. Far less is it a suggestion that eternal salvation isn't worth seeking; on the contrary, it's worth it so much that the apostle would prefer to forfeit his share if that could benefit his brothers.

3. A third motif has also gained popularity in the recent decades. What you expect to find in the church, justice and love of neighbour, you often find outside. Can't there be something like a 'church outside the church'?

The answer to the question is first of all a matter of definition. If you say that wherever justice is practised, the church is there, then the church is present outside the Christian church in all parts of the world, in both Islam and capitalism. For not only does injustice prevail everwhere, but also justice. But that means that you're claiming people (and their views) for the Christian church who have neither accepted the Christian confession of faith nor want to do so. That's not honest to these people; you're including them in Christianity without their knowing it (if they knew it, then perhaps even against their will). Moreover it devalues the relationship of faith with Christ, which can only be practised as a conscious relationship. So the term 'anonymous Christianity' isn't a good term.

Moreover, the take-over takes place on the presupposition that doing justice should be a prerogative of Chrsitians. But that isn't the case; one can also find it in other areas. That must be recognized instead of being taken over. Why then take refuge in the 'church outside the church' on seeing so much that is true, good and beautiful'? Against this background there is still the spectre of 'outside the church no salvation', so everyone (and all things) which we value must come within the church. But that's unnecessary intellectual gymnastics. We don't judge other people's salvation, but see what is true, good and beautiful in our world as a gift of God the Creator and believe that God sees it the same way. So the world remains what it is and salvation remains God's salvation.

12. God's one church and our many churches

The features of the Christian church have been very badly dented by the splintering of the Christian community of faith. The church has fallen from its pedestal, multiplied into parts, each of which wants to be the whole. What's to be done, if you want to join the church? There are immediately ten, twelve candidates who want to be considered for this honour. This leads to abuses, the church on special offer. I would venture to say that the chaos in which the Christian church finds itself begins with its impossible multiplicity. The Christian concept of the church simply hasn't taken account of this multiplicity, and this puts the whole tradition of faith out of joint.

The different churches are very well aware of this, so they continue stubbornly to speak of 'the church' when they mean themselves. Sometimes this is automatic, a kind of naive terminology, but it can equally well be given a dogmatic foundation, as happens in Roman Catholic doctrine and in that of the Free Reformed churches (how remarkable that these resemble each other so closely!). It won't help; the multiplicity doesn't become any less, and the squared circle of what Berkhof calls 'God's one church and our many churches' remains.

Where does this multiplicity come from? To try to begin positively, the story isn't entirely a sorry one. In his time, Abraham Kuyper spoke of 'uniformity as a curse of modern life', and in so doing defended a distinction between the churches on the basis of cultural definition. In his view, the pluriformity of creation could be reflected in the churches. Kuyper was partly right. Today we see more clearly than before how churches show the colour of their context. Black, Mongolian, Batak, and why not also Latin American and Western? When Saul was converted and became Paul, the great apostle, he remained the hard-driven zealot that he had always been, but now as a Christian. So, too, churches remain communities of Christians who retain their European, Chinese or Latin American colouring. They can't do otherwise, but Kuyper thought that we mustn't want it otherwise. The creation leads to a colourfulness in the church which is a happy one.

What I'm saying doesn't of course amount to an identification of church and context. What it does mean is that if a church thinks it has anything to say in this context, it can only express itself by means of the cultural context. The wretchedness of the situation is, rather, the way in which the church has split apart into a number of confessions (Roman Catholic, Reformed/Protestant, Anglican and Eastern Orthodox, to name the largest) and within these confessions into a large number of competing groups – or just groups which negate one another. I don't deny the controversies that keep this division going; sometimes they're brush fires, and sometimes they're well worth thrashing out, but must they be developed to the point of dividing the church? Talking through the differences gets nowhere; anyone can see that. The identities and the established positions are far too strong. There's only one solution for this impossible multiplicity: to make the different church confederations orders within one over-arching association, just as down to the present day the Roman Catholic church has been able to integrate a great difference in spirituality into the one church by turning it into orders. In doing this we don't bring any disasters upon ourselves: the churches may retain their special features, the world goes on as usual, and what we gain is, if perhaps not direct recognition of one another (but we've time and eternity for that), at least recognition as churches, which is always much more than tolerating each other.

There's another point. The inter-confessional differences are in turn a brush-fire compared with the immense differences between the great religions. I see a splendid task for the World Council of Churches in this area. It should be able to leave the unity of the Christian churches for what it is – certainly if we begin to see them as orders within one whole – to prepare itself for inter-religious dialogue. First of all with Islam, one of the largest religious communities in many countries in terms of size. I would very much like to know whether I can also say 'Allahu Akbar' in place of 'God is great', and I would want to see the place of Jesus in the Christian tradition compared with that of Muhammad in Islam – to mention just global themes which it is very important for us to put on the agenda.

And when it comes to being of service: the world church is there to intervene for those for whom no one intervenes, for people for whom no political dignity is to be got, for the outcasts who have found themselves on the rubbish heap, the despised among humankind. Wouldn't this being of service be much more helpful if Islam and Christianity practised it together?

13. Plurality in the church

I see the emergence of plurality within the different Christian churches as a test case for the will to accept one another. For many church members, and also for those in authority in the churches, this is a new phenomenon, to which they aren't very accustomed.

Plurality is, moreover, initially evaluated and spoken of as a negative phenomenon, a form of the 'impoverishment' of the Christian church. Compared with the situation of thirty years ago this interpretation is accurate, but then we've introduced 'thirty years ago' or what other past time as a criterion for 'good', and that of course cannot be. Yesterday is never the norm for today or tomorrow.

We do better to begin with the recognition of the fact that the unity of doctrine and life has split into a multiplicity of views. That's plurality, with all the advantages and disadvantages that go with it and which we can't help even if we wanted to. But we can't want to any longer. Outside the church, freedom to speak, not to put what you want to say into other people's mouths, has become flesh and blood to us, to such a degree that we now also want to practise it in the church. And rightly so. The way itself could have been the opposite; in the church (at any rate in the churches of the Reformation) we learned the freedom that we apply in society. Political freedom began with freedom of religion.

The disadvantage of plurality doesn't lie so much in the multiplicity of views which have taken the place of unity as in the process of assimilating them. What some people find positive is for others apostasy and a sell-out. The learning process that goes with plurality imposes on us the task of keeping a legitimate place open for both reactions. Someone may call apostasy what I find to be progress, and not just the opposite. The problems begin when people are no longer ready to listen to one another's views. At best we still tolerate one another in the church, but toleration is the beginning of the end. Those who are merely tolerated draw their own conclusions and disappear.

Accepting one another, as Christ accepted us – that's where it must all begin. I would point out – it's a saying of the apostle Paul – that there is no call to accept one another's opinions. That would really be too crazy; some prophetically inclined people very much want that, but in doing so they spoil things for themselves and others. When you accept one another you needn't accept one another's *views*; you can quietly discuss these views – any views – with one another.

On this condition a variety of views about Christ, about baptism, about practical questions like health insurance, euthanasia, or whatever needn't become an occasion for leaving the church or dividing the church or even division in the community. There is room in the Christian community for any view about what is Christian that is held in an authentic way – as long as it isn't explicitly aimed at lovelessness or harming others; but that doesn't mean to say that such a view fits within the Christian tradition or falls outside it. Anyone who doesn't want so much room wants to dominate, and to dominate if possible with the authority of religion as a back-up.

I don't mean that plurality knows no bounds. I've already said that practical love is such a limit. Being active within the framework of the Christian scheme of God is such a limit, as is loyalty (quite different from obedience) to the group, the community.

To accept and assimilate plurality within one church community may not be simple; the church has to learn to live with it. If even pedestrians tire us, how shall we be able to cope with horses?

14. Mission

A chapter about the church which didn't touch on mission would be unacceptable. The two belong together, and we shouldn't have had a Christian church in Europe had there been no mission.

Nowadays, the way in which mission used to be carried on in the past incurs a good deal of criticism. The harsh judgment is that people didn't go to help but to oppress. I don't agree with this judgment, certainly not when it comes from the church side. I'm no masochist. A church which accuses itself will in the long term arouse resistance, not to say despair. There will have been many mistakes in mission, and especially the reliance on colonial power is to be regretted. Moreover it was possible to identify missionary and dominator in a way which in the long run would take its revenge on the churches and would lead to a bad conscience. But seen in the framework of time, mission seems to me to be a soft option compared with the hard hand of the colonial conqueror.

Why did these churches engage in mission? Because they began by taking it for granted that Christianity was true, as Islam does now. Pagans are without God in the world; they're idolators, and Christianity has knowledge of the true God. That imposes obligations: anyone who can drive away the darkness and doesn't do so becomes guilty before God and humanity. The literature shows that there was always also more feeling for the indigenous population. Certainly in the heyday of colonialism, the motive behind mission wasn't a sheer desire to dominate but rather concern with the eternal salvation and damnation of human beings.

But mission took place in terms of an unparalleled paternalism. The culture of the 'pagans' was regarded as remarkably backward; people had neither knowledge of it nor respect for it. Here were 'savages' who in God's name had to be redeemed from the thought-world in which they had become entangled. They fought against this because they didn't know what was good for them. Fortunately the missionaries were well aware of this.

Paternalism and compulsion were closely connected, certainly in lands where colonial powers had settled. Missionaries didn't recognize this. I don't mean that they made use of the strong arm of the colonial authorities, but that they didn't see how colonization and Christianization were interwoven. They brought the religious faith of the conquerors and thus imposed on faith a burden which to the present day concerns the self-interpretation of mission. The time of grateful Blacks is long past, but the churches still look back on it. It disturbs them, and so they go over to providing aid. There's nothing against that; on the contrary, this too is one of the prime tasks of the church. But can mission turn into it?

15. Do we need mission?

Over the last two centuries the Christian church – almost in an exaggerated way – has described itself as a missionary church. I won't be investigating the theories and motives behind this here. The church must be planted, because the word must be proclaimed 'to the ends of the earth'. From of old that has been part of the solemnity of the Christian tradition. Must that continue to be the case? Certainly, people may continue to relate what is important for them. That happens with philosophical profundities, with religion and with dirty stories. Freedom of expression ranks high on the list of Western values. Islam may talk freely in Western Europe about Allah and Muhammad; and while the time of the Baghwan may be over, we gave him plenty of scope and many people listened to him, even with reverence. So why shouldn't Christian mission – in the form of the believing individual or church – be able to talk about Christian faith?

So there's nothing against the mission of the churches by the criteria which are generally accepted. But why should the churches missionize? The Christian church must answer this question; it must know what it's aiming at and thus have good reasons for it. Moreover

– if it thinks that it has these reasons – it must apply criteria to mission which match.

1. Mission has its roots in a society. It will be true. One has only to read Maryse Condé's book *Segou* to follow the process of up-rooting with its far-reaching consequences. First comes Islam, then the West, and finally – in its wake – Christianity. By this time virtually nothing is left of the original fetishistic culture.

2. What is to be said against this? No mission? First of all, the uproooting seems to me to be unavoidable. Europe also became involved in this process and rose above it. Secondly, Christianity isn't the great malefactor, unless one identifies Western techno-culture with Christianity. But even if that should be true (and it is not), then there is still something unavoidable in the development. It's impossible in one world for cultures to exist which are miles apart where development is concerned: there may be (but should not be) rich and poor, but there cannot be people who are technologically highly developed and people who are technologically primitive. So the crucible will do its work.

3. The seriousness of the process isn't to be underestimated. Putting people out of joint and uprooting them will produce even more victims, will result in even more deaths, will rob even more poeple of house and home, make even more women mere workers, and so on. Mission? I would say that more than ever it can mean something. But does the Christian church know God's preference?

4. If there's mission, it mustn't be in the form of representatives who come to bring the truth to the ignorant. If that has to be the case, then it's better that there shouldn't be any. Mission isn't out for conquest; it comes into a foreign land as vulnerable as the foreigners who come into our land – with nothing to back it up other than the vulnerable truth of its own belief.

5. So preaching isn't 'We come to bring the Lord Jesus to you', but joining with those who are addressed in order to investigate what their traditions mean in a changed world. It doesn't mean, 'You aren't doing good and we know better what you need', but 'What are your traditions of faith and what are ours, and what are they worth?'

6. In this context, which relativizes not only others but also ourselves, the contribution of one's own conviction of faith has a place. Those who can't relativize themselves can't engage in mission. As long as Islam can't relativize itself, we can see from it how things shouldn't be done: it's doing things as we used to.

7. The counter-argument, that you must leave other cultures alone, is a romantic one. No one leaves them alone: the tourists descend on Bali and the Western economy descends on Black Africa. Would the Christian church be a worse disaster, or might it have something which could help people to stabilize their lives in such transitional situations? Moreover, not a single culture or religion is invulnerable or above a critical approach. Surely that's also true of Christianity?

8. So the point isn't that a church which believes in its own cause can't engage in mission. Of course it can. But the whole matter stands or falls by whether the others, those who are addressed, are taken seriously, and left free, invited to a real dialogue. Dialogue takes place on an equal footing and requires muutality, which is more than a device for catching someone's ear. First, I would find that dishonest; we would only seem to be discussing a person's truth. I also find it disrespectful, a lack of respect for others. That sort of mission is destroyed by time and deserves no better.

XVII

Church and Sacraments

'As long as the term "symbolic" is identified with "not real" (as still happens all too often in our daily usage) we can hardly speak of sacraments' (*G.van der Leeuw*)

1. Rituals in the church

Like any other venerable – if not religious – institution, the Christian church maintains rituals, actions which 1. present something that the community alone knows; 2. communicate what they represent to participants; and 3. derive their status (and power) within the community from repetition. From the beginning they have more than one function, but I shan't go too deeply into that. A community gives itself a profile through its rituals, and in so doing distinguishes itself from other communities: in other words it consolidates its identity through rituals. But its rituals also have an internal function for the community: they make its members actual participants in what holds the group together and in this way have a binding significance. Without rituals, no community lasts; that applied in earlier times and does so just as much today.

So rituals in the church aren't externals; they don't belong to it like dry leaves in the autumn. The Roman Catholic church has all kinds of them, with attractive and unattractive features. Protestant Christians, by contrast, in their zeal to internalize faith, have a tendency to look down on rituals and regard them as externals. Here they forget themselves, in more than one respect. Protestants have just as good rituals, but different ones (verbal ones); they just overlook their significance. To take just one example: in Protestant churches the appropriation and transmission of the gospel takes place by way of preaching from the pulpit, but that too is a ritual, recurring every Sunday. Not to mention preaching itself. Anyone familiar with Protestant churches knows that fixed phrases recur in the language of sermon and prayer, ritual sequences. Of course sacraments are celebrated in Protestant churches – not only with festal dress but also with prescribed formulas.

Which brings me to the theme of this chapter: the sacraments that the church maintains. Where this name comes from doesn't much matter. It's become the classical term for rituals which have taken on a special status, as opposed to lighting candles or going into the pulpit.

So there was disagreement over the number of them. To what ritual is so much importance attached that you can call it a sacrament? The Protestant version of Christianity retained two of the seven known by the Roman Catholic church: baptism and Lord's Supper (eucharist). Together they form the narrow bridge which unites the two modes of existence of the Christian church – bridgeheads (I would do better to say) of recognition and knowledge.

Why a separate chapter on the sacraments? Because as this term 'sacraments' already shows, they no longer do what they were instituted for; they no longer speak to people, bind them together and impose an obligation. What they aim to present isn't (or isn't primarily) in question. What's in question is the notion itself, the picture, the ritual that was meant to present compellingly (and attractively) what the sacrament was about. The sacrament comes from a world which is no longer ours, in any way, and therefore doesn't move us. Certainly, if we do our very best, it may well succeed, but the natural way in which the ritual pictorial language aimed at reaching the emotional level of our existence is a thing of the past.

2. Baptism and Lord's Supper

I shall try to show why the sacraments aren't attractive enough by going more closely into two of them: the administration of baptism and the celebration of the Lord's Supper (which is called the eucharist among Roman Catholic and Anglican Christians).

The answer is easiest to give over baptism. The use or administration of baptism – the official formula – comes from a time with which we are no longer familiar. In the Protestant churches that's clear from the dispute that has been carried on since the sixteenth century over whether members of the Christian church should be baptized as children or adults. What's the issue? To be a Christian presupposes a deliberate choice; only adults are in a position to make that: to baptize children means that you impose being a Christian on them against their will.

I don't deny that there's a problem here. The average Christian hasn't asked to be baptized but is usually baptized willy-nilly. But the real problem lies deeper. In origin baptism is a ritual of transition, a 'rite of passage'. Baptism means that the baptized person steps from one world to another, from the world of sin into the world of redemption. It's a step comparable to the step from death to life. That's indicated by the symbolism of immersion in water. In ancient culture water was an ambiguous medium. You could sink in it, but you could also travel on it. There are 'waters of death' which overwhelm a person, but you can be saved from these waters as Noah was saved by the ark. The reference isn't fortuitous: the church *is* Noah's ark (even in the Protestant formula of baptism), and baptism is being saved from judgment.

Therefore baptism can be administered only once; you only pass from death to life once. But the more Christian the world became, the less baptism remained a rite of passage, and the difference between the one world and the other disappeared. You were no longer a Greek or a Roman or a German who resolved to leave your tribe and go over to the Christian church. Your tribe was already a Christian tribe; there was really no more going over, and no longer any alien, foreign world to which you bid farewell at baptism.

Very much the same thing happened to the celebration of the Lord's Supper. It began as the celebration of togetherness, of belonging, on the basis of the sacrifice of the founder of the community, Jesus Christ. Bread and wine are a great bond when they stand for the body and blood that is sacrificed for the community. The community becomes something of a secret society, and the celebration becomes a secondary factor, from which others are excluded. For a long time, moreover, the celebration of the Lord's Supper was strictly secret (and Christian faith a secret doctrine and the church a secret society). In short, both baptism and eucharist presuppose a totally different world as a context, a world of incomprehension and even hostility. They therefore also presuppose a totally different church, a church which feels an alien in the world and which therefore isn't at home and doesn't want to be at home, because it's expecting the great dénouement of the drama: the coming of the kingdom of God.

This church is no longer, nor is this world. We can certainly steep ourselves in such thoughts from the past, and a detailed exposition of the significance of the sacraments could even help us here, but the very necessity of this exposition makes it clear that we've grown out of it. Against our will, certainly, but we can no longer go back to it. Not because we don't want to, but because the world in which the sacraments came into being is a world of the past. The cultural language of the time has gone; the relationship between Christianity and culture is totally different, and we no longer know the inward experience, the religious feelings, of former times. And only a fragment of the symbols has remained: a few drops of water has replaced immersion and a bit of bread with a sip of eucharistic wine the ritual meal. Those are facts.

3. Symbols

The most important presupposition of the sacraments, the need for solidarity in a hostile world, has disappeared. What's left? The pictorial language of which the sacraments make use, the symbols: water at baptism and bread and wine at the eucharist.

But having rituals is more than letting images speak; sacraments aren't a picture book displayed in the church. That's often happened in the Protesant tradition; sacraments are signs which portray what the community believes. They add the image to the Word.

But that's no longer what the classic view of sacraments meant. Even the church fathers of the Reformation didn't allow the sacraments to be exhausted in sign language but added the word 'seal' to them. Sacraments 'seal' what they present; and in this way something of the 'magical' side of the ritual was retained. Classical Roman Catholic church doctrine put all the emphasis on the magical side. What is portrayed happens, with all the controversies which that in turn provoked: does it happen automatically, or only with prayer, and if there is no prayer (no good prayer), does nothing happen?

The controversies have ebbed away. They were still the subject of deep discussions – at least among theologians – only thirty years ago, but today they're no more than topics of significance for church order: what we can accept from one another and what not. That's a significant development. I've nothing to add to it. Except the question 'Where do we go from here?'

One could say: if we add the picture aspect from the Protestants to the magical side from the Roman Catholics we are back to a rite which at least has something to convey. But we can't take this way either, quite apart from what it would result in. We can no longer deal with the symbols as previous generations did. Of course we can deepen our insight into them, through reading scientific religious literature which explains what culture maintained what symbol. We can train ourselves in the recognition of symbols, both inside and outside our personal lives. But in so doing we show that this is no longer automatic. People who have studied the subject, church authorities, can still do this easily. For us ordinary people there is something missing. What?

1. The very symbols which the Christian church uses for its sacramental rituals have taken on a value – or rather a lack of value – which makes them unsuitable for their function. Water may still be such a classic symbol of life and death, of purification and rebirth – but for us water is something to swim in. We think of sport, of competitions, of surfing and so on. I don't see how we can get back to water as a power.

2. Still less can we think 'magically' with symbols. In fact, it's as Van der Leeuw says: in symbolic actions we no longer think of something real, of something which is not only shown but also happens. It's like the national flag. Abroad it speaks to us (still, at least), but at home it says no more to us than the brand mark on a can of beans. We no longer experience its symbolic value. Therefore, for example, we no longer experience the hoisting of the flag as an event. The magic has gone out of it.

The question which remains is: is it a bad thing that we don't know what to make of the sacraments as we know them?

4. Must the sacraments remain?

Sacraments are rituals devised by ourselves (by Christianity). That doesn't conflict with the view that Jesus instituted both baptism and the Lord's Supper. Even if that's historically the case, sacraments are rituals that we ourselves have invented. Let me explain what I mean by this. The 'failure' of the sacraments in our world may be connected with it.

The believer can't dispense with an experience of God. I said in a previous chapter that belief stems from experience and depends on confirmation from experience. Confirmations are usually events: an illumination which came to you, rescue from distress, or simply a surge of joy. These are 'traces of God' in our existence. But they're fleeting; we don't encounter them every day, and yet we need them almost every day. So we make them ourselves, and those are the heavily loaded rituals that we call sacraments. They're artificially constructed points of encounter, an artificial presence of God, for faith needs encounter and presence for its confirmation. Artificial isn't the same thing as automatic. You can put out bread and wine when you want to, but the encounter with God depends on God himself. Sacraments are no automats for encounter with God.

But however attractively they're meant and however much they answer a deep need, here at the same time we have the weakness of the sacraments. Sacraments aren't 'natural' objects of experience; they are and remain artificial. They don't move at the primary and authentic level of human experience, ordinary life. That artificial character is further emphasized by the fact that in the course of time the ritual has shrunk: a meal becomes a piece of bread, or stretching out and immersing in water becomes sprinkling a few drops on a child's head.

In short, sacraments are for insiders: they're meant for insiders, and only insiders can know what they're about. That seems to me to be the great handicap for the church in our world. Our romantic feeling tells us that it would be very attractive once again to be the church as it was in the clasical world: you're in another world, and other rituals belong in this other world. There are clear differences between inside and outside. But we're no longer the church in this way, nor can we ever become so. People in our world would feel the use of the sacraments as practised in the early church to be discrimination, exclusion. Do only the baptized belong here, to God? What about the others? May only believers celebrate the eucharist? But what if you half believe and half don't? Are you then excluded?

That's the problem: we don't want to exclude, yet sacraments do exclude. Again I get back to the concept of the church. We're uncertain about that, and as long as that's the case, we don't know what to make of the classical sacraments, nor can we invent any new ones (that's not possible); we must get on with the ones we have.

I don't see this as at all senseless, but we do need to relativize. Here I find myself in good company. No less a person than the apostle Paul ventures to say in so many words that he wasn't sent by God to baptize. Foolish! For according to the Gospel of Matthew Jesus gave a specific command to instruct and to baptize all peoples.

Those who aren't baptized aren't lost because they have failed to receive the forgiveness of sins. Nor is someone lost who doesn't go to confession ('the second plank after the shipwreck'). If you live together without being married you don't live in deadly sin – and so forth. The Lord's Supper still best matches our possibilities of experience: eating and drinking together creates a bond. But what about taking into ourselves Jesus' body and blood? I don't know what to think of that. If we understand the symbols of bread and wine as Van der Leeuw would want us to, we become what Zwingli, the Swiss Reformer, described as 'cannibals'. No one can mean that. But if not, what?

It could be that we must seek God's presence, at least for the moment, not so much in artificial islands of presence, in the church sacraments, but in life itself.

The Last Things

XVIII

The Christian Expectation of the Future

'O, the laughing of the child
before the world and after its end

it tells of a little shining wind
which once sent out
shall rise above pride and pain
until Babylon and London
are forgiven and forgotten' (*A.Roland Holst*)

1. Utopia

Nowhere does the Christian tradition display such a deep reinterpretation as in the Christian expectation of the future. Certainly the theme has always been there, but it used to stand in quite a different context and was given quite a different content. The mere name under which it went speaks volumes: the Last Things. Very appropriately, for it was about what happens to a person last and therefore was also put last: death, the return of Jesus Christ, the Last Judgment and eternal life or eternal death. Since the 1960s that's changed. The expectation of the future has become much more earthy, and the warm gulf-stream of utopian longing has also spilled over into Christianity. Do only Marxist philosophers like Ernst Bloch know of hope? No, says Christianity, we also know of it, indeed we know better: in our tradition we've preserved the treasure of utopia in the form of belief in the kingdom of God, and can show what that means for human beings and the world. That, briefly, is the argument. There is no denying that we can already sense a shift, but more out of disappointment, I feel, than real insight. The move is away from future expectation, and believers are left in confusion. I shall devote this chapter to showing what's involved.

What's utopia? – let me begin there. Literally it's something like 'no place': the pre-fix 'u' stands for 'not' and 'topia' for 'place'. Utopia doesn't exist anywhere, but is what we can dream of. In itself this dream is a marvellous phenomenon. We dream of another world, other people, and in the light of that can take stock of our existing world. The dream is a criticism; the world isn't what we think it should be.

But that's not all. It also follows that we always dream on the basis of a present. Not only in the sense that the present day offers us occasion for criticism, but also that we give content to the other world, the world as it could be, with the help of the 'it's not this' experience which the present day gives us. What do we dream of? Of a world where tears are wiped from eyes, hunger and thirst are banished, injustice is done away with, and death as the last enemy is destroyed. I'm just mentioning a few things off the cuff. Everything that is included in the dream of the future 1. derives from the present, from the negative experiences of the present, so 2. we ourselves are the ones who stop the changes in this dream. Dreams of the future are often time-conditioned like this. Farmers dream of their unblemished world in a different way from city-dwellers in an industrial age; now they're experiencing yet other lacks. This also indicates the limited character of utopias. Although they're dreams of the kingdom of God, they don't come from another world and in this sense don't bring any revelation: we make them ourselves.

So to sum up, utopia is the dream of the golden age, the time when all is good. Here I must go back to something that I touched on earlier: a great current of humanity dreams of this golden age as being in the past when everything *was* still good. The stories of paradise are a good example of this; they too are utopian ideas. Although people sought the paradise of Genesis, it couldn't be found. Of course not, we say with hindsight, since paradise is utopia, 'no place'.

Another current – called by Bloch the 'warm gulf-stream' – dreams of utopia as the golden future. One day everything will be like this. At least in the Christian tradition, we're more familiar with this, thanks to passages from the Gospels and biblical books like the Revelation of John. But above all thanks to the idea of the kingdom of God.

Terminologically the two perspectives can be connected. 'Today you will be with me in paradise' is what the robber was told by Jesus on the cross. Paradise no longer indicates a past time, nor even a future age, but has become another word for heaven. 'No place' has become 'with God'.

Back to the kingdom of God. Is that the Christian utopia, the dream of *Christians*, but a dream and thus 'no place'?

In the first instance, yes (to be non-committal). I shall try to clarify that in this chapter and at the same time show that this isn't a misstatement. Except in the eyes of those people who think of the kingdom of God as something that we must realize on earth, though with God's help.

2. The kingdom of God and utopia

First an important comment. It makes a very great difference whether by utopia we mean a world which can't be found anywhere and will be never found anywhere, or something that doesn't exist now but will do so one day – soon, in the long term, or in the distant future. The utopias of philosophers usually seem to be of the first kind; they're social criticisms given substance, flesh and blood. The Christian utopia under the name of the kingdom of God has often inspired its followers to make it the second kind: the kingdom of God may not be here, but it's coming, and will be present in time in this world. Didn't Jesus teach us to pray 'Thy kingdom come', and didn't he himself bring it in, the Messiah ushering in the salvation of the endtime, the fulfiller of all expectations? The one for whose coming 'the Gentiles' themselves hoped?

It's especially this second version of the utopian dream that Christianity has got hold of in recent decades, and for many people it's made the dreaming of this dream the nucleus of Christian faith. Christian faith is the ground of hope for another world which will dawn in this world.

The question is whether that's true. Can we give the Christian tradition such a twist that hope isn't the fulfilment of faith but a substitute for it? And in addition imagine the fulfilment of hope within this world? I think that's doubtful, an over-emphasis; it can be explained as a manoeuvre for catching up which has its good points, but also its limitations.

Of course the utopia of the kingdom of God, if you make it something to be realized within the world, is very attractive. The 1960s and 1970s showed that. The Christian church knew what it was doing; it was to be the forerunner of the kingdom of God, to point the world to 'signs of the times', signs which indicate how late it is; in a word, it was concerned to make room in our world for Jesus Christ and his kingdom. The work of the church is *opus Dei*, God's work. We know this term in connection with extremely conservative Roman Catholic Christians, but I would say that the model fits Christians who have a progressive policy just as well: anyone who is concerned for a world worth living in works for God.

I agree. Isn't that so? Certainly, and I shall shortly be emphasizing it quite strongly. But what we are concerned with here is the fundamental question of the perspective in which that work of making our world worth living in is to be placed. If we put it under the heading of the kingdom of God that Jesus Christ will bring, if we make it a preoccupation with the golden future which will take place 'within the world', the whole Christian tradition goes off the rails. That's often happened. I need only recall the so-called Baptist adventure in the sixteenth century, which can also be reduced to a heroic attempt to leave behind all ambiguity and doubt and establish the kingdom of God radically, beginning in Münster. But this ended in catastrophe and did much harm to the Christian message of salvation. The Reformers (both Luther and Calvin) felt that at the time, and were extremely critical of the Baptists – and worse. That wasn't to their credit – the Baptists deserved better – but when we know the background, we can have a rather better understanding of the thunderbolts of the Reformers. Just as for us in the 1960s and 1970, among the Baptists 'in this world' took on political and social connotations. That needn't necessarily happen; we can also imagine people beginning to see the Christian church rather than 'the world' as the sphere where God's new world is being established, a realization within the church instead of within the world. I'm not saying that because I approve of the idea: the church, too, isn't the realization of the kingdom of God. But in any case there are arguments for such a view of things, and its credentials are old. That doesn't apply to a translation into political and social salvation. Christian faith isn't belief in progress. That would be to burden the ship of Christian utopia with a cargo which makes it spring a leak.

3. No 'hinterland' to the kingdom of God

The remarkable thing is that the Christian tradition says less about the kingdom of God as an expectation of the golden age than we mght expect. The Apostles' Creed has no paragraph on utopia; the apostle Paul isn't concerned with it at any stage of his thought; and the Gospel of John says nothing, because for it the future has already become present. Only certain strands of the complex work that we call the Synoptic Gospels (Matthew, Mark and Luke) and the book of Revelation mention it explicitly, and then within the framework of the catastrophic end that our world awaits. Why is that? With our ideas of the 1960s and 1970s did we go too far, or didn't the first witnesses understand properly?

I think that these first witnesses themselves went through a learning process. The utopian desires of the first generations of Christians corrected themselves. That already begins with the apostle Paul, very clearly. Not without reason, many people have accused him of having corrupted the simple Christianity of Jesus. I think that we can safely say that he didn't do that. First of all, Jesus wasn't the first Christian, and it's nonsense to speak of his 'Christianity'. As I showed in the chapter on christology, Christianity comes from Paul, who interpreted Jesus – as did the other apostles. But Paul didn't corrupt anything; he simply put forward an insight that became the axis around which the whole of Christian tradition began to turn. Jesus as Messiah brings the definitive salvation from God – certainly the apostle was familiar with that; he drank it in with his mother's milk. But in the midst of many interpretations of the Messiah current in his time Paul was very aware of, and very clearly dissociated himself from, a Messiah whose kingdom was realized 'within this world'. Paul says, as it were, 'Look out, that doesn't work', and then goes on to forgiveness, reconciliation and justification of the sinner as the necessary condition for entering the kingdom of God. The mere terminology – entering into the kingdom (Jesus also speaks of 'entering') instead of making room for the kingdom and its king – speaks volumes. Can we discover why Paul didn't follow the trail of utopia as the realization of the kingdom of God 'within this world'? Let me make a couple of points.

For Paul and for the Christian tradition which followed him, true salvation consists in the reconciliation of the sinner with God and in a new life, a life as 'new creation'. Only God can give that salvation. People can give one another (and receive!) a 'little salvation', and this is also an essential element of the Christian tradition. But the 'little salvation', social and political salvation, indispensable though it may be, doesn't make people definitively whole. We can't die for abolishing social or political rules.

I've already touched on another point: we must always win the 'little salvation' from others. Only in a perfect world would that not be necessary; but the world in which we live isn't perfect. We challenge injustice, but in so doing we create new injustice; we fight against violence, but for that we need new violence, and so on. When we intend salvation in the social and political sense, it's more of the same thing, not something different.

Even more briefly: why can't we use utopia to make a heaven on earth? Because people are sinners – this lofty statement must be made. They work for a while on an ideal, as Frederik van Eden already pointed out, and then they give it up and want to see money. For a while they're helpers of the poor, until they risk going short themselves, and then they play another tune. I'm mentioning only a few well-known features of 'us human beings'. A new world will never appear under the conditions of our 'old world'. That's what prevented Paul from pursuing utopia. Before that, something else has to happen.

That's also the reason why the first generation of Christians could express themselves so easily in the language of the book of Revelation, of catastrophes, of the Last Judgment and the disappearance of the world. Of course. First the old world had to pass away, since no new world could come out of it. These are all metaphors for the same thing. No kingdom of God will come on earth under the conditions of the present world. It's not for nothing that such passages end 'for we await a new heaven and a new earth'. Indeed, this expectation is Christian. But we don't know what the kingdom of God will look like or how it will come. It wasn't for nothing that Christianity called its dream the kingdom of *God*. The Christian tradition is utterly against what is to be expected 'in this world', let alone to be realized there.

4. *The new person: the future has already begun*

If the future remains future, if there's nothing to do but to wait for it, is the definitive salvation of God nowhere, and does the kingdom of God remain 'nowhere' in this world? 'Be still, and wait, and everything will be made new' was an enormously popular song in our churches in the 1960s: does it mean that here you see nothing but have to wait for the hereafter? Remarkably, according to the Christian tradition of faith, that again isn't the case. The new world is substantially present, as a first-fruits of God's salvation in our world of disaster. But we mustn't look to the political and social sphere for it – we won't see the new world there – but to human beings, to persons. That's precisely what the apostle Paul means by his remark 'Watch!' which I've just quoted, addressed to all who are too eager. Slow and sure wins the race: a new person must come into being before a new world will arise.

Here the Christian tradition takes a decision which has far-reaching consequences for the world of society and politics. To begin with that little word 'first': first the new person and then the new world. It's true that human beings and society presuppose each other (both socially and politically). People make a society and society in turn makes (stamps) people what they are. Hegel and Marx after him rightly emphasized that. But if we're concerned for another world, we must put the initiative somewhere. Where? Does society have the main role or do people? The presupposition of the Christian tradition is that you must begin with people. The opposite view, that society is mainly responsible, is incompatible with the Christian tradition.

So first the new person. Why? Because people have dirty hands, and you can't build a beautiful world with dirty hands. Although the attempt has been made – from Adam to Adorno – it won't succeed, and we find it difficult to keep things going. People should no longer have any egotism, should dedicate themselves to others, should lay aside their anxiety about going short: that's the way forward. But on the whole they can't do that. That calls for sacrifices, sometimes the sacrifice of life, and we aren't up to that.

To avoid a misunderstanding: of course the new world isn't a world in which sacrifice has become the sole thing. Sacrifice isn't the most splendid thing there is. It's the furthest we can go in our old world if we dedicate ourselves to others. But in the new world there is no longer need and distress, and those things for which you must be 'there for others'. We can't even begin to imagine such a new world. We can barely imagine a new person, for however we deck out this person, our imagination can't go further than a new person in the conditions of our old world.

5. How we become new persons

How does someone become a new person? That's the key question on which Christianity turns, as a religion of the way. In any case it doesn't happen as Marx imagined: social or political reconstruction doesn't produce new people, but in fact needs new people.

The Christian faith says that a new person comes into being by being recreated, reborn, justified and sanctified. It's no less than this, and therefore an act from the other side. It begins – and here I would refer to the chapter on reconciliation – with the bestowing of another status: no longer belonging to the old world which is passing away because it is condemned to death. This other status isn't an abstract truth, a kind of empty formula about which no more can be said. On the contrary, it becomes operational in the forgiveness of sins. So 'if anyone is in Christ, there is a new creation' is utterly practical: the old world is forgotten and forgiven. The forgiveness of sins is the most irrefutable way in which the new world announces itself in the old. It's the first step of renewal, the necessary first step: the old must be done away with. Well, it *is* done away. That's the forgiveness of sins.

But that's not all. The new status also – and at the same time – becomes operational through the Spirit of God which comes into a person. I'm well aware of what I'm saying; this isn't raving. The Spirit of God isn't attached to Christian faith; the Spirit seizes many people, at times which are both appropriate and inappropriate, and often we recognize that very well: in artists, in statesmen, in social renewers and so on. But that doesn't mean that they've become new persons. That happens when the Spirit of Jesus Christ comes into someone. In a spectacular way? That can be, it happens. But usually in terms of an invisible presence, only to be recognized from the outside by the fruits of someone's existence. A person becomes rather more friendly, rather less anxious, rather more ready to join in, concerned to avoid evil and slowly inclined to do good, in short on the way to the opposite of the black picture which the Protestant Heidelberg Catechism paints of the natural man (the one who isn't renewed by the Spirit of Jesus Christ): hostile to God and hating his neighbour.

And on the inside? That's hidden from outsiders and must continue to be. Jesus says that those who pray, enter into their secret room. This is converse with God and isn't intended for those outside. Except when it's practised in terms of rituals, as in church services with their liturgy. But then we always know that these are rituals.

With these few strokes I've drawn a sketch of the new person in the conditions of the old world. On the one hand that means that again it's not so totally new that anyone is bowled over by it. 'The old is past, behold the new has come' – we haven't yet got that far. But you may expect Christians to begin (quite modestly) to live not only by some but by all of God's commandments. It also means that there are things about being a Christian which you wouldn't immediately associate with the good life, and yet which have to be done. I've already talked about the sacrifice that sometimes has to be made. That's not pleasant: you didn't become a person to sacrifice yourself for others. But that's necessary under the conditions of our old world, in order to protect others. It's even unavoidable.

So what is the reconstruction of existence by the Spirit of God? To become equipped to be a human being in the creaturely sense: to be able to do what you can and in so doing develop. But also to know that there's more to it than that, that sometimes you can't develop as you want to, but have to take a step back for the sake of another or do some job that you wouldn't otherwise have done. There are limits to that – and I don't mean something exaggerated like 'Go, sell all you have and follow me.' Jesus may say that, but not I. Moreover, the world would collapse if the majority of people followed the first part of this advice. Nevertheless, such words remain an urgent summons to keep our eyes open for others as long as our old world lasts.

6. New persons in an old world: a division which cannot be healed

The Christian church preaches the saving message of the new creation and is at the same time the effect of this mesage, its product, the new creation itself under the conditions of the old world. That sounds almost like discrimination to outsiders, but it's impossible for the Christian church to say otherwise without doing away with itself, i.e. with the reason for its existence. That brings me to the division which cannot be healed, mentioned in the title of this section. Christianity is at home in this word and at the same time is not at home – moving with changing success between the two foci of this ellipse. Moreover, from the time of the apostles the Christian tradition has called Christians citizens of two kingdoms – the kingdom that is here, our earth, and the 'kingdom of heaven', above with God. The question is whether we can get away with this kind of terminology, but what it expresses is unavoidable and indispensable for the Christian tradition. I shall go on to sum it up under the heading of the two kingdoms. That, too, is only a phrase, though with credentials which go back to Augustine, but at the same time it's become suspect as a result of use and misuse, as a result of its connotations, and so on. People have even wanted to find an ideological dualism in it

221

which is said to go back to Near Eastern religious sensibilities. However, what Christianity means by this has nothing to do with that sort of thing. It owes the two kingdoms to its own faith. This is a typically Christian division, utterly steeped in the gospel itself; others have no hand in it. So as far as I'm concerned, there need be no misunderstandings. However, in what follows the terminology will take on sufficient content to make it clear why I – with the Christian tradition – think that it's indispensable.

The Christian is a citizen of two kingdoms, with a duality of existence as a consequence. The split which arises here is so great that we can't avoid the question whether the duality is really necessary. My answer would be that not only is it really necessary, but it's usual for Christians to live in a duality, as an actual fact. Christianity offers a church in which the gospel resounds, and in so doing means at the least to say that there is more to life than sport and games, the bliss of making love and being a success. But all this is also there; it even takes up the length and breadth of our daily life, and we're affected by it heart and soul. And not only *is* it there, but we ourselves can't make it anything other than it is – God's creation – any more than (in the opposite direction) you can restore creation by the forgiveness of sins that we're promised in the church. A person must also be saved for eternity.

So here is some first content to the duality. We live our daily lives in a world in from which, according to the Christian message of salvation, we must at the same time be saved. We even live them with verve! How do we combine these two focal points? It isn't easy. To withdraw is one solution: the world is of the devil. Another possibility is that something happens when you're saved; now things aren't as bad as they were. Christianity can't make this last claim without doing it away with itself, and the first gets the Christian nowhere (apart from narrow currents in the broad bed of the church, which have tried it despite everything). Only one conclusion is possible: practical action by Christians, as if the world turns out to be better than their black theory. And that's what happens. Apart from the somewhat arrogant terminology used, for example by Abraham Kuyper ('the world exceeds our expectations'), the Christian tradition leaves the world its values, speaks of the natural knowledge of God and God's will, and by that means that you don't need to be a Christian to be a human being. But human beings aren't yet Christians. At the same time the Christian church maintains its own value and independence: it hasn't come into being for nothing.

7. One God, two kingdoms

So if the actual practice of being a Christian is marked by duality, wouldn't it be a good thing if theory began to reform practice and made the two kingdoms one? That needn't be, indeed it can't be, as I've argued elsewhere. We can't turn creation into reconciliation and the enjoyment of a walk along the beach into the forgiveness of sins.

Nor should it be (in the sense of 'it better hadn't be'), for in that case you come up against the question whether creation gets lost by being bewitched into a disguised redemption or redemption gets lost by being built into creation as a kind of principle that will develop in the course of history, thanks to the church.

That brings me to another reason for not giving up this duality. As I emphasized earlier, the world must remain world and the church church. We mustn't confuse the two or mix them up. That results in a world which must be led along by the church in order to be able to be the world. It has to become 'churchly', to listen to the directives of popes and synods. History provides plenty of examples of what happens when things really get that far. The world would decline into barbarism. The church has no understanding of the world, at least no more than the world itself has.

And for the same reason, if it wanted to be able to dominate the world, it would end up in a church which became 'worldly'. History also provides instances of that – of a church which has become 'worldly' – and of that we can only say that here too the church goes to pieces: it's forced to deny what it stands for, love and sacrifice.

Things have to be done in the world which as Christians we haven't learned from Jesus, yet nevertheless have to be done. Forgiveness, not to mention the remission of debts, would be best done in business and in politics, if it were done anywhere, but that doesn't happen. So you can't do anything in this area. You betray the weak and simply support the strong, the daredevils and the tycoons. If we want to intercede for the poor and those without rights, then we need the formation of power, sometimes even violence and bloodshed. Those are the old means of the old world. And sometimes there's no alternative to acting against betrayal, deceit, injustice and lying.

An irreconcilable duality? Indeed, but not one that can't be lived with, as is clear from everyday life. It becomes unliveable with if we rob the daily world – which I've called the world of creation – of God and his commandment. The Christian tradition never did that when it called the worldly kingdom worldly. It didn't call it 'worldly' because it thought that it was without God, but because God isn't present in it as he is in the church, where the Word prevails and the Spirit seizes people. As Luther says, in the worldly kingdom God rules with the sword. We would find that rather too crude a description of God's presence there. Let's say that God rules there with his norms. In his famous Tambach lecture, Karl Barth said that we must do everything properly at the worldly level. I would prefer to say that here we work with the norms of morality and law, and these also come from God. To call the worldly kingdom autonomous is to use a term which is open to misunderstanding. The person who thought of it (Naumann) didn't mean by it no norms, but not the same norms as in personal relations. In the business world, love of neighbour, if it's possible there, works differently from interpersonal love.

There's everything to be said in one's own case and that of others for keeping to values and norms in a worldly sphere which come as close as possible to love of neighbour, and it's even worth fighting for this. But we must have no illusions. Even in the church that's very difficult to achieve, as I've already indicated. People can't very easily be moved from their egocentric existences. But that's not the only thing. Doing business doesn't work with 'I'll give you this one last chance', since that's the ruin of the all too friendly businessman; and politically 'I think you're better than me, so you be prime minister' doesn't work, for then the wrong people win; and we can't administer justice by allowing the punishment to consist in letting people off, or forgiveness, for in that case the robber has an advantage over the vicitm. It may be tried out, but we soon arrive at the limits which preserve a life worth living from chaos.

8. The Christian hope

The Christian tradition knows of faith, hope and love. So hope is very much a fundamental ingredient of the Christian tradition. But what is hope aimed at? What is its content? Not a realization of the kingdom of God 'within this world', as we've seen. Certainly it's a hope for a speedy end to the old world. The church father Origen, moreover, understood this quite literally. He said that Christians don't celebrate their birthdays; they curse the very day because it means that yet another year has passed. He exaggerated; in terms of the apocalyptic of the time the end of the world means precisely what I've just said: we shall never encounter the kingdom of God in this world. Are we then still left with a hope, with some kind of vision? Do we perhaps have to look over the horizon of time with the hope that is in us?

I think that the Christian tradition indeed means this. What happens to this world is very important to us. And rightly so. It can't be otherwise, as a living person has no alternative. But according to Christianity, there are no divine promises for the future in this sense. That doesn't mean to say that this future couldn't be, but we know nothing about it, and even the Christian tradition doesn't make us any wiser on this point. The 'great summer' is a dream, a dream which is even dreamed in the Christian tradition, but it remains a dream. We know nothing of any realization of it.

Shouldn't we then be able to say that one day the trumpets will sound, an end will come to this world, and everything will come true? My first question would be '*What* becomes true?' We've even given content to the dream ourselves, fallible people with our own, often partisan, human wishes. Must our wishes all come true? Will God satisfy our expectations? Or those of former generations who had quite different wishes?

A second question. What is 'one day'? Something like soon, later, in the distant future? Is it then that the Golden Age will begin? But if the future, at least according to the Christian tradition, doesn't come in time (won't be 'within this world'), then are we really talking about 'one day'?

What I know, and indeed know for sure, is that in time, 'within the world', as it were, one day the trumpet will sound for me and the hour will come: the hour of my death. My death isn't the end of the world; that will go on without me. I don't know how it will go on. But at all events the world will end with my death. Even if – like Calvin, for example – we begin with the idea that at their deaths people end up in a state in which, whether asleep or awake, they await the great day, the world still goes on when we ourselves stop; for me, *my* end is *the* end. Bultmann was right: H-hour isn't a vague 'sometime' for a person, somewhere in an unfathomable future, a kind of never-never, but the hour of their own death. It's there that our story ends, even if the world should go on to eternity and even if we should know that. So what is The End? Let me give a non-committal reply and say that, in Christian terms, provisionally, it's my death. What do Christians hope for? For the future which is prepared for them by God. This seems to me to be the only expectation of the future which doesn't prevaricate with its followers, in other words, which doesn't tempt people with something that they will never get.

So is this a quite personal expectation of the future? Certainly, it's typically Christian. But I grant that there's something crazy about it. People are people in and with their world. What happens to this world? Do Christians then have no hope or expectation for this world and for the people who live in it? If they did, no doubt they would then stop being Christians. In a secret place in their hearts they cherish the hope that the Creator knows something about this. But they themselves know nothing. Except that, according to their tradition, God is a God who is faithful to eternity and doesn't cease from what his hand has begun. That's the source of their courage not to abandon what they've begun either, whether out of anxiety or because they settled all too firmly somewhere, and left their concerns in the lurch.

XIX

Life and Death: The Hereafter

'Lovers and thinkers, into the earth with you.
Be one with the dull, the indiscriminate dust.
A fragment of what you felt, of what you knew,
A formula, a phrase remains – but the best is lost' (*Edna St Vincent Millay*)

1. No one comes back alive

Life, then, may be delightful, a playground or even a paradise, but it has a price tag attached to it: no one gets out of it alive. So dying isn't a choice, but a fate that hangs above everyone's head. As long as you're young and vital, you don't think about it. And why should you? Until, suddenly, a friend dies, your grandfather passes on, or you have a road accident. Then time stands still; however, fortunately it goes on, and only when you're past forty do you begin to think: 'I too will have to die one day, and how will that be?'

In all cultures this question has occupied people, and it can be read off the religions of the world. They all have an extremely important section on death and what comes afterwards. Sometimes they're even entirely inspired by it. This means that there is no people or society in which death – by which I understand, for short, having to die – isn't, and isn't seen as, the great disruption. In this respect the Christian tradition of faith is no exception. All religions are to be explained as attempts to make a discovery here in one way or another. We all have to die, but why, what happens next? Are you snatched away for good from the people where you belong? What kind of a state is death?, and so on. There's a host of questions to which people have no good answer. The dead always draw up the ladder after them, so that we can never discover what happens afterwards (if anything does).

Traditions of faith contain answers to these insoluble questions.

That makes them in a way suspicious from the start, at least in a culture which has learned to live with counting, measuring, weighing and nothing else. So there are good reasons for this suspicion; strictly speaking, we know nothing about the subject, and everything that the religious traditions go on to say is also pure faith, in other words a notion of faith with which we give content to our experience (or rather our lack of it). The only question is whether this is nonsense or whether there are at least equally good grounds for maintaining that we don't become nothing at death. I shall try to argue this last point in the present chapter, though in the limited sense that the Christian faith and being eternally safe with God are indissolubly connected. God isn't a God of the dead but of the living. The so-called hereafter – I shall come back to this unfortunate term – is a conclusion from the sketch of God that the Christian tradition offers.

2. We shall overcome?

It isn't distinctively Christian to want to survive death. As I've said, all religious traditions are attempts to come to terms with the fact that human beings must die. We can even produce a complete typology of 'solutions', arranged in accordance with the way in which people hope to transcend death.

Apart from any attempt at transcendence, I also see submission to death as a kind of solution. For example, the Portuguese poet Pessoa says:

> When the spring comes, if I am already dead by then,
> the flowers will bloom just the same,
> and the trees will be just as green as in the previous year;
> reality does not need me.
> I feel an enormous joy
> at the thought that my death is completely insignificant.

Is that sad or is it in fact joyful? Keeping to what we find here, Pessoa feels an enormous joy, or is in any case completely at ease (as he says later in the poem). For everything is as it should be. Reality doesn't need him.

That's another way of coping with 'having to die', even a very modest way. You often hear people say that we mustn't be so proud as to covet immortality. We mustn't even ask God specially to come to the defence of us human beings to save us from death. Are we so important? Surely not? Moreover, death is part of living; you have to accept it, and then it isn't a burden. If it is, then you aren't there, and if you aren't there, it isn't, so why be anxious?, said Epicurus. Only an untimely death is intolerable, but not death for someone who is old and has a pleasant life behind them.

This is a typically non-religious way of finding a place for death (or is it?). The religious traditions do it differently, because they define death differently. Not just as a biological reality (disintegration, turning to dust), as Pessoa does, but also as a social event. Death produces a gap in the clan, the family, society; we have someone less. What is the result of that for us? Above all, what happens to this 'someone'?

Let me try to provide some content. It seems that there is much to make us see death not just as a biological fact but also (and above all) in its social dimension. What do I have against Pessoa? Nothing, really; what he says is splendid, and indeed he's right. Everything will go on as usual, even if I'm no longer there. Spring will come again, and the sun rise every day as though nothing had happened.

And soon no one will know and talk
of you and me.
Other people live here,
and no one will miss us.

But that's only true – these lines were written by Ernst Jünger – when time has passed, and a new generation has come into being which has no longer known the old. For the community to which the dead person belonged it's quite incomprehensible that the sun keeps rising as though nothing had happened. So I think that we must emphasize two things, which moreover are opposite sides of the coin. To retreat to death as a biological fact is a modern way of coping with it. Dying is really a natural process and therefore you mustn't have difficulties over it. But biological death is an abstraction of death as people have experienced it all down the ages, a reduction of the experience to scientific facts. These facts (dying, passing away) are quite definite, and are even – in Christian terms – part of the good creation. Dust we are, and to dust we shall return. We shall become earth again, the same earth from which we were taken. So the Russian poet Achamatova says here that the earth is of us and we are of the earth.

But just as irrefutable is the experiential fact that people don't know how to cope with death. The know-alls among us who maintain that it isn't so bad, that death is an evolutionary piece of wisdom, can't explain why evolution hasn't taught us not to be shocked and sorry when yet another person has left us for ever:

> Do not go gentle into that good night,
> Rage, rage, against the dying of the light,

cried Dylan Thomas to his dying father.

What people experience is that through this biological disintegration a separation comes about which cannot longer be reversed. It's irrevocable and definitive. We lack someone and this 'someone' is without us. And soon we will be going the same way. Unless. At that point the religious traditions begin their story.

3. Types of transcendence

It's usual in the history of religion to distinguish four or five types of 'solutions' which disclose what really happens to those who are left behind and to the dead person. Here I shall give a short description of each of them; in part they overlap.

(a) Ancestor worship. This has become the name for an experience of death and life which separates the two sides far less. A human being is a link in the chain of an ongoing life-line of an extended and never-ending family. Parents live on in their children, even after death. Their life isn't finished. The children also see that: their dead ancestors haven't gone away, but live outside the wall of the visible world with the family. So it's good to venerate them. They represent the wisdom and the power which can support the family in times of crisis. Therefore the funeral and the reverence for the dead associated with it are important. Nothing may be neglected that needs to be done on such occasions, and vice versa, everything must be done to help the dead to the other side in the best way possible. Behind ancestor worship lies the deep-seated conviction that there is still a relationship between the dead and the living. The division isn't denied, but it's not absolute.

(b) The realm of the dead. In another approach it's imagined that the dead are gathered in a separate kingdom, in which they live on as shadows. The cultures around the Mediterranean Sea (Semitic, Greek, Roman) have this notion. The longer the dead are there, the more shadowy they become. This is very like our experience that initially, right after the death of a relative, we still have the feeling that he or she is still there. But the more time goes on, the hazier the memory becomes. Of course there are variants; the realm of the dead as a place where all the dead are kept doesn't really go with the realm of the dead as a realm of ancestors. But that isn't important. The separation is a separation which makes all contact impossible in the long run (not at the beginning). Except when you stand at the tombs of famous people. There the underworld so to speak stretches out its hand to the world above. That's why more pilgrimages are made to the tombs around the Mediterranean than anywhere else. These cultures must have had an obsession about death and burial, and often still have. It's still thought good today to pray at Peter's tomb.

(c) Death as a fiction. The denial of the great divide is known above all from Egyptian religion. The dead go on a journey, supported with food and drink, surrounded by images of the life that they led and then – as a sign that they are beyond reach – the tomb is firmly closed. This has something of a magical charming of the great divide about it (the great Dutch poet Achterberg was fascinated by this). Death isn't real death; it's a disappearing beyond the horizon, just as the sun disappears in the evening but hasn't really gone away.

(d) More magical actions are resorted to in connection with the dead, i.e. real magic. The shaman or priest sees an opportunity to bring the dead person back among the living and make his voice heard, if only for a moment. Not, of course, literally, but through the priest, who understands the signs of his presence and can communicate what he means to say. Or – another notion – the shaman is the one who knows the way to the realm of the dead and can bring back good advice for the living from there. Death is death, but through a magical ritual it's possible to cross the frontiers.

(e) Survival in the memory of the community. You can also transcend death by making a name for yourself. People of renown live on after their deaths; ancient culture knows and therefore even prizes this way to immortality. Artists make an eternal life for themselves. Only artists? According to Rikus Waskowski, even the names of the great drinkers live on.

In a more modern version we encounter this way of living on in the world of Latin American liberation theology. Fallen fighters are remembered in the group of their comrades; their names are called out, immediately followed by a 'Present'. They are there. Not truly, not in real life, since they're dead. But they're again present in the memory of their friends. For Dorothee Sölle this is the way in which

Christians talk about the resurrection. I've gone into this in the chapter about the resurrection.

(f) We survive death personally. That's perhaps the most prominent idea among developed cultures and peoples. Think first of the Indian notion of reincarnation. Human beings are caught up in a series of births; they cross over from one life to another, finally to achieve perfect purification at the source of their existence, God or even Nothingness.

The immortal soul, to which the Greek philosophers attached so much importance, is derived from this. Human beings have within them a particle that is akin to God, their thinking spirit, and so is immortal. The thinking spirit returns to God who gave it; in fact God is the great catchment area of Spirit. Aristotle thought this the best solution, and the church father Origen also approved of it. Indeed the notion of the immortal soul found much support generally among Christians of former years, just as reincarnation finds much support today. The Christian notion of the resurrection of the dead also falls under the head of 'personal survival'. In the next section I shall go into it more deeply; here I shall limit myself to a comparison with the other 'solutions'.

The scenery of the place where our dead are – the hereafter – changes in the Christian tradition. Heaven takes the place of the underworld. Heaven speaks for itself; it's the dwelling place of God, the place where God has prepared salvation. Heaven becomes the place where the dead go. Therefore sorrow is muted sorrow: the dead have simply gone before us, and we shall follow.

Where is heaven? Nowhere. In terms of our earthly relationships, heaven is beyond what we can call a place. If someone has 'gone to heaven', it is no use our searching; for us he or she is nowhere.

The Middle Ages made heaven a real parasite of fantasy. We've grown out of that, but we can't deny that people of the time reflected on it and had ideas about it. That's always better than turning your back on fables out of anxiety.

I would also like to apply that to the use of a term like the 'hereafter'. It's well-established, with all the misunderstandings and caricatures that go with it (as of course is the case with heaven). But I don't think that's a reason for dropping the term. On the contrary, to hold on to the fact that 'hereafter' and 'heaven' are metaphors for a reality seems to me to be a challenge in our culture, which doesn't know what to make of 'dying and the hereafter'.

4. Dying is inheritance and loss: the Christian solution

All these solutions, including the Christian one, don't deny that a parting takes place which is painful. Roses on the grave, splendid. Good memories? Even better. 'But the best is lost.' The Christian tradition of faith thus also presupposes that death may be a hundred times a biological fact, but it only derives its sting from the fact that people experience it as separation. Dying is falling out of a community. For the dying person, that means the loneliness of the last hour; death isolates a person. And for the community death then means a gap, an empty place. How do we cope with these two things?

'The best is lost.' That must be our starting point if we don't want to make the Christian tradition about the hereafter a mere palliative. In a sense it's naturally that: we're helpless in the face of death and mustn't give our fantasies and expectations about what comes after death more attractive colours than they can take. For Christians heaven (as their hereafter) isn't the goal of the pilgrimage, though this is how it is imagined, but rather happiness amidst unhappiness. The shipwreck of existence still has a happy ending. The coastguard finds us in time and brings us safe to eternity.

In this sense, then, dying is both inheritance and loss. The dead have a loss: they miss us; the bystanders have a loss: they have someone less. The best, the lifelike presence – which may confront us – is lost. The break already begins with aging, when we can no longer do what we want, desires and wishes fade, ending in real dying, the blowing out of the last breath. And then you can still talk of happiness that you aren't snatched away prematurely. That must be taken seriously. The Christian 'solution' isn't the denial of death (as in Egypt), nor going through life with a feeling that there will be a continuation, nor even the ongoing existence of the immortal soul (as in classical philosophy), but belief that we survive death. Personally, as I said, and by way of a gift. Dying is also an inheritance.

I shall return to that character of gift shortly. First let me say that, in its solution, the Christian tradition links up with the explicit or implicit hope of almost all humankind, that death will not be the last word. That is one of the reasons why a term like 'heaven', with its traditional connotations, doesn't wear out. There are more reasons: for example that the deficiencies in earthly life are made good there.

There's compensation. It's not just the poor Lazarus who first gets his share in heaven: the Blacks from the south of the United States have also sung of heaven as the place where all tears are wiped away and injustice will be put right. What is there against that? Why shouldn't someone who is sorrowful sing, 'O to be where no tears flow'? Must the executioner maintain his advantage over the oppressed to eternity? Heaven is the inn of eternal happiness and must remain that above all.

There's yet another way in: who renews the renewer? We may build up our world, but the builders themselves perish; they can only *believe* that they themselves will be built up 'elsewhere', in terms of an 'eternal house' not made with hands, as Paul says somewhere. People may find that a fiction, but it's meant realistically and definitely not illogically. In any case the circle within the world offers no definitive personal salvation. Thus we either exclude that salvation, or we believe that there is more than we get during our lifetime.

By way of a gift. More precisely, it consists in the continuity of the self, as I said in the chapter on the resurrection. That's really the case only in the second instance. The gift consists in friendship with the eternal God. That begins here and now, where peace with God is accepted and enjoyed. But it survives death. Friendship with the eternal God is eternal friendship. In the wake of that we survive death, according to the Christian tradition of faith, as persons, as those who say 'I'. We exchange the tent (our bodily, earthly existence) for an eternal house with God, or, as I would prefer to put it, in God. As long as we're still there, God is all in all. The separation brought by death is real, but at the same time relativized. It doesn't annihilate us.

Or perhaps we don't prize friendship with the Eternal. In that case does the Most High leave us lying along the way? The Christian church has kept that in its tradition and attached to it the label of 'eternal death', the real 'great divide'. In that case it's not only from family and relatives but also from God. That sounds logical and less fantastic than 'hell and damnation'. But we have to leave it at that. Eternal death isn't part of the message of salvation.

Anyone who has died in God's friendship is safe for eternity. Achterberg knows why:

God will easily find them
and that fellowship will be for ever.

The hereafter can easily become a way of escape, a kind of leak, out of which our responsiblity runs into nothingness. Of course no one wants that, but it happens. Moreover Christianity highly esteems Nietzsche's call to remain faithful to the earth. We shouldn't want to be regarded as 'escapists' or 'backworldsmen'. So we must be faithful to the earth.

Certainly, but how? When are you faithful to the earth? I shall do my best to clarify that by means of two statements.

To begin with, the phenomeologist Merleau Ponty's remark that Christians – on the basis of their tradition – are condemned to a 'bad faith', a kind of betrayal of the world. That's an attitude that isn't right. There is certainly 'bad faith' in our world, but this is to be found throughout humankind and not just in Christianity. Countless streams and rivulets make their life a form of escape. In their time everyone does that; they can't do otherwise if they want to survive.

But this isn't an ingredient of Christian religion. The world (our world) isn't a place of purification that we should abandon as much as possible in order to reach the goal of the journey as soon as possible. Granted, that too has been a strand in the web of Christian tradition. And what is there against someone regarding it in that way? But the mainstream was and is different. The mystical writers know of an 'eternal home' that awaits Christians, but they also know that counting on an 'eternal home' become suspect unless you begin to build it here – in terms of a certain 'this-worldly asceticism'. That means a degree of restraint. Christians don't need to have the bottom of the barrel for themselves.

The classic doctrine of the two kingdoms that I discussed in another chapter – the most used model of relations between Christians and the old world – is sufficient refutation in this respect. The life of a Christian doesn't take place in the church (although no one can be a Christian without the church), but in the secular world. Both world and church are creations of one and the same God, and Christians put themselves at the service of both. The doctrine of the two kingdoms is the guarantee that the earth is taken seriously and doesn't need secretly to be turned into the church before it can be used (and enjoyed). The earth is the LORD's – it can be and remain so.

I've been remarking *ad nauseam* that nature has been at all times stronger than doctrine, and that that will remain the case. We don't need to encourage people to remain faithful to the earth. Even the greatest 'backworldsmen' are precisely this, but their pattern differs from the usual one.

That brings me to the other statement I want to make. If for this life alone we have put our hope in Christ, then we are the most unfortunate of all people. No less than the apostle Paul says that. Note that here he's not talking of a mere trust in our present world, but of trust in Christ. Of that he says that you're unfortunate, indeed the most unfortunate person in the world, if you limit your expectations to what can be fulfilled within this world. The world made with hands, the makeable world, is too limited for what Jesus Christ has to offer.

Only for this life? That can't be. This life ends, we die, and what will be the point of what we've built?

Of course, if you dismiss the idea that it's a good thing to survive death *personally*, you face that sort of question. I see nothing wrong in that; on the contrary, why should a person think of surviving death? In our vital moments we've no need at all of a hereafter. But do things remain that way? It seems to me a colossal limitation of the comforting character of the Christian tradition. For this life alone? But here the lame remain lame and the cripples cripples. And vital? People aren't always that. What a narrow existence it would be if we were committed to keeping hidden from ourselves or others our weaknesses, the silent disintegration and dying which goes through the body – death coming nearer. For this life alone? Growing old is, if I may believe Ida Gerhardt, disintegration, but disintegration with a prospect on the other side. It's

all the time the irrefutable knowledge
that you will be renewed and recreated
when people write of you 'asleep'.
When your name on earth is forgotten.

Indeed, according to the Christian tradition of faith we can only say that the new world and the new person lie on the other side.

Prayer

XX

Communication with God

'Those who lose respect for human beings mustn't think that they can compensate for this by respect for God' (*G.T. Rothuizen*)

1. *Talking into space*

In some Shinto temples there is a great cord which believers tug sharply so that a little bell rings somewhere. In others, visitors constantly clap their hands when they stand in front of the altar. When on one such occasion I asked what was happening, I was told that the believer was addressing God, but – and this speaks for itself – he first had to attract God's attention by ringing the bell or clapping his hands. I still remember having smiled at so much childishness.

Later I thought of what our ministers and priests do at the lectern. Certainly they don't clap their hands, but they raise their voices and address God as 'O Lord', or 'O God'. Even when people 'pray softly' (a stereotyped term for inaudible prayer) they ask God to listen to them. Is that so different from what you can see in Japan?

I think back to a book by J.H. van den Berg in which he describes this ritual of praying. 'What is happening there?' a bystander asks. Someone closes their eyes, mutters or mumbles words which are addressed to someone, an invisible someone. And is there an answer? No, you hear nothing back. And yet the man or woman is content to sit there mumbling, doesn't rebel or get frustrated, and does it again the next day. Can anyone tell what is going on?

In the Christian tradition this is called 'praying'. It's like talking into space, but of course it involves more than that. Complete phenomenologies have been written which show how under a wide variety of actions there is something like praying in all religions. I argued earlier that a religious sense is part of human existence. And that religious sense evidently includes seeking contact with – shall I say – the Above and addressing that Above more or less spontaneously as though it were a Someone.

So I would prefer to use the term communication: it's broader than praying, and perhaps somewhat less loaded with ideas from our childhood. Communication with God. Is that possible, and what is it good for?

2. Getting out of the habit of praying

Many people have given up what was once a matter of course, the way of praying that they had learned at home. And once they've stopped that, they don't begin again. Just as people who have got out of the habit of going to church aren't so easy to get back again. A kind of block is put up that they don't get over. Unwillingness? Helpelssness? A mixture of both? Sometimes people are also ashamed and then it become doubly impossible: why have I got rid of what I used to have?

To answer this last question, in this section I shall make a brief list of objections to praying in terms of Christian tradition, although they don't all hold.

1. The debunker: 'Praying is a superseded form of magic, an attempt to influence the Godhead. We've grown out of that kind of idea.'

2. The 'expert' who remarks: 'Praying is wasted effort. We all know that everything is predetermined and things happen as they must.'

3. The disappointed person: 'Praying doesn't help; that's an experience that many people share. So why go on?'

4. The sceptic: 'Praying requires a certainty in faith which I don't have.' 'O God, if you're there, hear me, if you can hear.'

5. The critic: 'Praying is selfishness; people ask for a privileged action for themselves, I don't want to do that. You can even be competing with someone else.'

6. The adult: 'Praying is a bore and belongs to my childhood, and I won't and can't go back to that.'

7. The modest person: 'Who am I to be a burden on God? Praying is arrogance.'

8. The postmodern deconstructionist: 'We must manage for ourselves. Praying is a commandment of weakness, a display. Smart people don't pray.'

9. The scientist: 'Prayer is an appeal to the miraculous power of God, but there are no miracles. So I've stopped praying.'

10. The busy young person: 'I've no time for it.'

The number ten is arbitrary; besides, there are also non-arbitrary answers in our culture to the question why we should pray (in the way in which the Christian tradition speaks of it). They aren't mutually exclusive: on the contrary, some strengthen others. I shall be discussing some of them explicitly and answering others by implication.

3. Speechless before God

Being at a loss over prayer is a problem for people who have grown up with it at home. Others wouldn't find it so pressing. So this chapter is about specifically Christian problems with prayer, though I think that outsiders will also be able to make something of it.

It's not just culture that makes us speechless. I think that much more positive reasons can be given. We don't get on very well with praying because we don't know what to pray. This isn't my remark, but is a statement from Paul, who otherwise isn't usually at a loss for words. It would be a good thing if we attached just as much importance to such statements from the Christian tradition as to statements which say that we have to pray without ceasing. They aren't of course mutually exclusive.

Being speechless means that we can't find the right words. That's true; how are we to know what we must and may put forward in our appeal to God? By that I don't just mean that life is so complicated that we don't know what is good and what is not, but also that we have so little sense of God, God's power and God's purpose for us and others that the sentences we speak soon seem to us to be nonsense. This isn't a disaster; according to the Christian tradition it's foreseeable. First, it doesn't mean that communication stops when there are no longer any words. That doesn't happen with human beings, so why should it be the case in communication with God? This doesn't depend on the presence of good words in our mouth.

Which brings me to a second comment. What are we really talking about? About praying in our inner room: that's the only proper place for communication. But that mustn't be taken literally, as though you could only pray in your inner room. Rather, it means that praying is a personal matter, a solitary event, one at which no others are present.

That has a wholesome effect: we aren't controlled, we're free, and don't need to use any good or great words (though of course we may do so if we've learned them); in short, what happens is a complete secret between God and human beings who pray. The others have nothing to do with how we do it, what we do, where we do it; the only thing that counts is the One whom we have in our thoughts and to whom we address ourselves. Consciously or unconsciously, I should add. Not only are good words not a necessity, but praying can also take place unconsciously, in the sense of being not specially meant.

So to be speechless before God isn't an accusation against us. On the contrary, to be eloquent before God's face is in any case the last thing that is necessary in our inner room. Why not? That's my third comment. Because speechlessness leaves a gap open for what is really important, for God himself to make an entrance into our lives. If there are all too many words from our side, where can God get one in? So I end up with the point that being silent fits in better with praying than talking, certainly better than talking a lot. To be speechless before God amounts to having a sense of God. And doesn't communication have to begin there?

4. Need teaches us to pray

For some Christians, praying comes in last place. First you try to help yourself, and if that no longer works, there's prayer: 'You just have to pray.' Others condemn this approach. They say that it makes praying a kind of emergency exit, a back door that some people – believers as opposed to non-believers – have behind them in time of need. However, in doing this they degrade prayer, themselves and God. In this connection people then quote Dietrich Bonhoeffer to the effect that we mustn't use God for filling in those few gaps that we can't fill in ourselves. As soon as we succeed in filling that last gap, God will no longer be necessary. What about that?

I think this is a misunderstanding and dogmatic stubbornness. First of all the misunderstanding of Bonhoeffer. What he says about filling in the gaps with the help of God envisages God as the causal explanation of states of things for which at present we can't (so far) find any other explanation. In fact, if that's all you have to say about God, God becomes superfluous as soon as you're on the track of the last explanation. Bonhoeffer saw clearly that this also affects prayer. Praying then becomes something like persuading God to a supernatural intervention, to break through our scientific laws. Happily, this last doesn't happen and hold God to what we ourselves have discovered. When Bonhoeffer remarks in the same context that we must live (from God!) *with* God *without* God, he means precisely the same thing. What he's really saying is that you mustn't count on supernatural intervention from God, since in that case you have a wrong idea of God. I've explained in the chapter on God's providential order that this certainly doesn't mean that God has disappeared from the scene.

Bonhoeffer is at the same time interpreted in too callous a way if one thinks that for him praying can't be a 'back door'. It would be crazy to forbid people who are really in need – if you yourself were – to take refuge in God at such a moment. Dishonest? Shouldn't you have done it yesterday, before you were sick? Come now, that's somewhat pedantic. God is no Scrooge who keeps an account of whether we've done enough. Moreover, surely it isn't so crazy to call upon God when we face the chop and not to bother God as long as things are going along all right?

No, need teaches us to pray – there's nothing against that. Need is far too real for us to have theological squabbles about it. To God in a flash when you're in need! That has to be said.

Where there is something against it is where it's done dishonestly, when we don't mean the call honestly and break off communication when the need is past. Otherwise, the God of the Christian tradition is a God on whom people call in need. Those who do so find God's favour infinitely great. If we may believe the Christian tradition, the God of Christianity makes it a point of honour to help in need. Here I must come back to Bonhoeffer again and the way in which people have interpreted his letters.

Men go to God in their need, he says in a poem, and then notes that God is in need. That sounds rather strange, but Bonhoeffer simply means that God shares the suffering of his creatures and that you must be content with that for the moment. What is really behind this expression is opposition to the same misunderstanding that we encountered earlier. Anyone who calls on God in need mustn't expect a supernatural intervention. God doesn't work that way. If you think that, you're making things too easy for yourself. The last thing that Bonhoeffer meant was to talk away need or to forbid human beings to take refuge in God in their need.

Here I've reinstated calling on the name of the LORD, as the Old Testament can so solemnly call it. Praying is primarily and from of old turning to God with a prayer for help.

To modern ears it sounds somewhat offensive to put it like that. Indeed it's a sign of weakness, as I've already indicated. People who can cope on their own don't pray, certainly if praying is a form of asking. It's a kind of pride; you don't want to be someone who asks for help. The same kind of pride that I detect in the Dutch poet Marsman when he says, 'My sins go with me into my grave'.

Is praying in fact demeaning? Caricatures of it have certainly made it so. If people want to say how the church is running down, then they always say that there were only some old women sitting there praying, that was all. You never hear that there were old men. No, praying isn't manly, and so men don't pray.

I've mentioned this at such length because it's an attitude which not only relates to praying but also plays a role in all kinds of other relationships. People don't find it easy to ask others for help, whether out of pride, out of perplexity or for both reasons. But at present that's not the point. My point is the outcome: in this way a good deal is missed. If only someone could cry 'Help me', certainly there would be people ready to come to help. But we've learned not to do that; we've learned from one another, and the result is suffering: we can no longer ask one another, we're struck dumb.

I might say that it all hangs together. Those who no longer dare to say 'Help me' to God may not or cannot do the same to their fellow human beings.

What lies behind that? As I've said, pride: we feel prayer to be a blow to our self-respect. Perhaps that's brought about by a particular kind of piety in which we're called to pray in a childlike way. I don't like that kind of metaphor; it asks us to be childish when we're no longer children and don't want to go back to childhood, either before God or before one another.

To return to this pride which we think is owed to our self-respect: that seems to me – if I may add something else about it – a colossal mistake. At least in respect of our own situation. As if it were of such a kind that we didn't need anyone to come and support us. What an over-estimation of ourselves! Moreover, it brings us into an isolation which lies like armour-plating over our lives. 'Keep your mouth closed, don't let any one know' is the worst advice anyone can ever give anyone else.

We make a mistake at yet another point. It's an honour to communicate with God. Animals can't do that, but human beings can. Throughout the history of culture, believers, both important and unimportant, have sensed this. Those who pray have a relationship with the Most High; they put their fingers on their lips and know that they're speechless before God's greatness, but are experiencing the honour for which they're destined as human beings: to have converse with the Creator. It's worth keeping that feeling or, if it has gone, getting it back.

6. Does praying help?

Once praying is restored to honour, then the next question is whether it helps. The expression 'praying helps' is a cliché, and probably also presupposes commonplace views about prayer. What are people thinking of when they ask whether praying helps? Anyone who can only understand by 'help' that what they pray for must happen has a magical idea of praying. Praying is a means that has to work, otherwise why resort to it?

I regard that as precisely the kind of primitive thinking that the Christian tradition seeks to disabuse us of. Despite all well-intentioned prayers for healing. These bring more unhappiness than happiness. You can't ask for an arm, you can't mend a severed spinal column or cure a case of lung cancer with prayer. Is that a lack of faith? Anyone who says that is simply adding an extra burden to all the burdens that some people already have to bear, and doesn't deserve the kingdom of heaven. Praying can also make things worse.

If prayer isn't a magical way of influencing God, what is it? Does what is called intercession make sense? Does God change the course of things as it were by request? That's a crucial question, and whether or not praying is nonsense hangs on it. I shall go into this point by point.

1. Let's begin with an unambiguous saying of Jesus. 'What man among you, if his son asks him for bread, will give him a stone? Or if he asks for a fish, will give him a serpent? If you who are evil know how to give good gifts to your children, how much more shall your Father in heaven give good gifts to those who pray for them.' The question whether praying has a meaning is accentuated by such a call to trust. No stones for bread – at least not where God is

concerned, if we may believe Jesus. I might also add the parable of the unjust judge who finally gets a widow her rights because she almost wears him out with her stubborn persistence. Jesus told the parable 'that they should always pray and not sleep'. Prayer is knocking.

2. Such remarks could easily make praying an obsession, and have often done so. But that needn't happen. Over against that is the fact that God has known things all along. As I said in the chapter on the Creator, God is at least God's creature; God is so familiar with us as already to know our words before we've formulated them. So why pray? I only know one answer to that: God doesn't need it, but it's good for us, we have somewhere to turn, an ear that's open and an eye that sees. We needn't make praying a great occasion, as if God has to be brought up to date with what's happening. Prayer is knocking on the door of someone who already knows.

3. So what does prayer amount to? Let me indicate this with a story from the Old Testament. When Jerusalem was besieged by the king of Babylon and there was little prospect of salvation, King Hezekiah prostrated himself in the temple and spread the letters on which the king of Babylon announced his impending destruction of the city before God's face. He also said something; he appealed to the honour of Israel's God amidst the gods, but for me that isn't the point. That gesture of spreading out, of being open before the face of the LORD – that seems to me to be the most adequate symbol of what Christians mean by prayer. There is no bother, no compulsion; the need is laid before God. That's enough. The apostle Paul was later to say, 'Make your wishes known to God'. I read that as: 'Put it on the table, open your heart; no more is needed if God really is as Jesus described God.'

4. So there's some restraint in Christian prayer. Not because everything is already fixed, a well-known objection to praying. I've already made clear in the chapter on God's providential ordering that this idea won't do.

It will do even less because our life takes place in an unbroken chain of cause and effect. Life certainly does that, sometimes to our delight and sometimes to our sorrow. But the chain is as it were at God's service; it doesn't exclude God.

The restraint has its basis in trust. God knows all along and doesn't give stones as bread. That isn't the same thing as giving what we ask. And in any case, it causes problems. All those who pray know that. But it needn't cause any alienation: we also know that.

7. Discipline

The Christian tradition has seen prayer as converse with God, communication. I'm not exaggerating if I say that everything, the whole of the Christian tradition, is concerned simply to indicate that God is a God on whom we can and may call. We needn't know more. But of course this does tell us something more. We don't talk to an idea, we don't call on a concept. God prompts ideas and concepts (shall we say expectation, hope, love), but we don't pray to love or hope. The first presupposition of engaging in prayer is that God is a being like a someone.

The second presupposition is that God sees the individual in the midst of countless millions. How bold Christian faith is emerges only from prayer: we don't just address God, we don't just believe that God is interested in the existence of his creatures and is moved by their lot; we also make that personal. Those who pray believe that God finds them important.

The discipline of prayer is again connected with this. When they were small, my children prayed just as much for the oppressed as for Santa Claus, 'who has to ride over the roofs so dangerously'. That too is already a form of discipline; you don't just pray for everything. The Christian tradition has seen the 'Our Father' in this perspective. It's called the perfect prayer because it expresses what we lay before God. With

Hallowed be thy name,
thy kingdom come,
thy will be done,

we take account of what God finds important. That comes first, whether we're faring well or not. Then we add what we find important for ourselves.

Give us today our daily bread,
forgive us our debts as we forgive our debtors,
lead us not into temptation, but deliver us from evil.

So that includes the request to God to take into account what we think important. At the same time I read it as a firm disciplining of our packet of wishes. Jesus pares what is important to the bone.

Is it wrong to be critical of other people's prayers? I sometimes heard that said when I was a preacher, but I don't believe it. There are disordered, useless, egotistic, wily, brutal prayers, and prayers which clearly have ulterior motives.

That brings me to public prayer. 'When you pray, go into your inner room', says Jesus. In public prayer – by which I mean primarily prayer in the Sunday service – we don't stop there; we also want to pray together. That was no problem as long as the church consisted of a small group, a house community in which people knew and recognized one another. In our great church buildings public prayer can be an evil which is its own punishment. The more specific the prayers of the minister, the more people drop out, and don't join in his options which are made so publicly. I leave aside the fact that people can even use prayers for political propaganda. That seems to me not only disordered and undisciplined prayer but also exploitation of the church. Public prayer should be allowed only if it doesn't go beyond the formulas of prayer.

In turn disciplined prayer itself produces discipline in life. Being religious must include love of neighbour; the one can't take the place of the other. Nor is prayer a matter of leaving things to God, so as to get for nothing what others have to work for. On the contrary, prayer kills sloth on the lips.

'Let's not live as if we knew nothing of the suffering that others have to endure.' Such a prayer seems to me to be Christian; it wouldn't even be out of place in church.

Commandment

XXI

The Will of God

'What will survive of us
is love' (*Philip Larkin*)

1. The Christian life

The classic church catechesis ended with 'The Commandment'. The Ten Commandments were included under that heading, provided with an exposition and adaptation. In this way the church established a moral tradition in Europe which has stamped dealings of individuals and groups with one another down to the present day. So we're talking about ethics. Note well, morality or ethics has nothing specially to do with sex. That's a misunderstanding which is produced by a term like 'moral', of which 'immoral' is the reverse, and now 'immorality' stands for forbidden sexual behaviour. Older generations of Roman Catholic Christians live with that misunderstanding, but they aren't the only ones.

However, morality is an ordinary word which covers all human conduct. Our life together depends on morality; there is even honour among thieves, moral rules which must not be transgressed, at least as long as the collaboration lasts.

The Christian life also includes morality, but isn't exhausted by that. On the contrary, it's not only a much wider concept but also a concept in which and through which morality is shown its place. Morality doesn't bring blessedness; morality is rather like walking on crutches, but at the same time it's an indispensable ingredient of life, for both Christians and non-Christians.

First a contextual definition. The Christian tradition of faith doesn't abolish morality, doesn't add anything to it, but shows it its proper place. It doesn't overestimate morality: morality doesn't build the way to God, doesn't make people acceptable before God and can't take the place of belief in God's mercy. But the Christian tradition doesn't underestimate morality either: it can represent the will of God for life (or for society), with all the questions that such a formulation provokes (I deliberately said 'can'). Without morality, no community – Christian or non-Christian – can exist. Although it isn't necessary for salvation, it *is* necessary. So the Christian church has been concerned with moral upbringing at all times.

As I said, the Christian life is a wider concept than morality. Christians pray, they celebrate Christian festivals, go to church, read the Bible, reflect on the Christian tradition, in short do a large number of things that are typical of the life of a believing Christian, distinctive customs which other people don't observe. The most important and most comprehensive of these is what I have called 'communicating with God'. That finally stamps the Christian life as what it is.

But the moral side of existence also belongs there. I shall focus on it in this chapter. Faithful to tradition, the chapter will end up with the Ten Commandments. These not only form a summary of what we can call the basic moral principles, but also present them as God's will. To be precise, as God's revealed will, the term the fathers used to distinguish it from God's hidden will, God's purposes which are concealed behind God's rule over 'all things'.

2. *Doing the will of God*

There was a time when the will of God didn't cause any great problems. To know it people had to go to the church. The laws of the church were God's laws, and what the church didn't allow – and that was a lot – was sin.

For large numbers of Christians that is still the case. The church guards the treasure of (supernatural) revelation, so it can teach people the Christian virtues, and at the same time it watches over natural morality, of which it is the authorized expositor. That, in short, is the Roman Catholic view of things. Protestants held and often still hold the same view, but we have to replace 'supernatural revelation' with 'Bible': what is God's will is in the Bible, and this is expounded in the church. Someone like Karl Barth also arrives at the same point: there is only one word of God, one revelation, the revelation of God in Jesus Christ, gospel and commandment together. The Christian church proclaims this one Word. So where must you be to know God's will? In church, under the proclamation of the Word. The construction is quite different from that in the Roman Catholic version that I mentioned, and also different from that among classical Protestants, but the effect is the same: Christian life consists in obedience to God.

Is there something wrong here? Indeed. An upbringing which is concerned with obedience is not only authoritarian, but, as Dorothee Sölle has noted, produces people who are sensitive to authority, not independent. Moreover the call to be obedient to God can easily coincide with the call to be obedient to the code of society. That can reach the point where God's will is never once given any substance by the preacher: it's thought to be well known. To submit oneself to God or to commit oneself to Jesus – the Christian proclamation can sometimes end up in such 'empty' (and thus dangerous) formulae.

Now a moral code – to get back to that – needn't end up in disaster; that only happens when we can't keep the will of God and the moral code apart. Nor need the two be played off against each other; there is a connection. To make that clear, in this chapter I shall explain what morality and the moral code is. But to isolate it ends up in unparalleled disasters and catastrophes. In times of rapid social change that emerges unerringly. What our grandparents regarded as the will of God (their moral code) is a garment that no longer fits us. If we were forced to go about in it we couldn't move a step; we would even come to grief.

How is that? Because one link is neglected in the argument: the will of God doesn't come to us directly, as a voice from heaven or in terms of a special revelation, but needs assistants who convey it to us in the name of God. And assistants are fallible people, traditional people, people who want to exercise power, or quite modest people – but always human beings, and human beings aren't God. However harsh it may sound, very well meant, but forced, dedication to God or to Jesus is dedication to people who claim to come forth in the name of God. We mustn't want that.

So Christianity should reflect time and again before it identifies instructions for life (the moral code) with God's will. For I have yet to mention the mistakes, the catastrophes, the tyranny and the acts of violence that are carried out by Christians in the name of God and God's will. The history of European cultures is full of Christian violence. It would have been better to keep quiet about 'God's will' for the moment. I'm not talking about what is good and bad, but about what may or can be regarded as a commandment from God.

But in what I am saying here I don't mean to deny that there is a will of God (in the sense of instructions for life). The only question is whether we know it as well as we claim to. Nor have I said a word against moral codes – on the contrary, morality *is* always a form of code. But whether in the church or outside it, moral codes aren't to be identified with God's instructions for life.

3. The code crumbles: plurality in church and society

In the Netherlands our grandparents – suppose we put them in the 1930s – didn't go to the cinema, make ice-cream for the children on Sunday, practise birth control or live together without marrying. In other countries there will have been similar accepted patterns of behaviour. To depart from them wasn't in keeping with the code, and the code was the will of God. We think differently about that, and if we're already hesitating, our children certainly are. How has that come about?

It's because morality changes in the same way as all customs change. Partly in a way which we can't explain precisely, but partly also through factors which we can distinguish clearly and which give us an insight into that process of change. Through the development of knowledge and skill, first of all other alternatives arise to those with which our parents had to work, and the existence of other alternatives means the need to make other choices. Formerly sexual intercourse led to pregnancy, and for married people that meant twelve children or abstinence, and for unmarried people unwanted pregnancies. The pill releases us from that dilemma but confronts us with a new choice: if there is no longer any danger of pregnancy from sex, can we act more freely or have we to act just as we did before? Another example: a severely handicapped newborn child used to die of its own accord, and there was no moral problem for the doctor. Today it can be kept alive, but at the price of a heavily handicapped existence. Here again is a new alternative which requires a new choice: do we or do we not save such infants?

As well as other alternatives, new ideas appear. There is no question that we don't think in the same way as Augustine or Calvin or even our grandparents. Criminals are no longer broken on the wheel, servants aren't inferior to masters, and women are no longer thought to be subordinate to men. To sum up: a human being is a human being, whether black or white, male or female, servant or master. We even have a different view of what may and may not be. We've become more independent of the code and no longer conform so easily to what we don't think good and yet are expected to do. People have developed a drive towards freedom in our culture which isn't to be underestimated.

Moral codes, including the Christian code, change. That isn't so strange: you can compare a code with a network of tracks and paths which have come about through walking, just as a path is made in a meadow when farmers always cut off the same corner. But farmers no longer walk, since they now ride on tractors. So grass grows again on the path and new tracks have to come into being for a tractor to go along.

To complete the picture I have to add something else. Morality not only changes but also crumbles. It isn't like a gradual move from a path to a tractor-track. Some people hold on to the old as long as they can; others experience the new alternatives as a liberation. This produces the situation that in the same church community one group argues for 'termination of life on request' and the other is bitterly against it; one parental couple allows their children to live together without getting married and the other blocks them by resorting to God and his commandment. This sort of controversy runs through all church communities, and the result is that within Christianity alone there is a plurality of moralities which we didn't know earlier. I'm leaving non-church codes on one side and not even thinking of the customs of the ethnic minorities in our cultures.

For a long time Christianity thought that it could turn the tide by referring to nature (above all the Roman Catholic *magisterium* did and still does this) or to the order of creation (the Protestant preference), which was then understood as a kind of timeless criterion. But as we've already seen in the chapter about being human, 'nature' in the sense of biological nature doesn't provide any norms unless we insert them first. The possession of sexual organs doesn't oblige us to procreate, although Roman Catholic moral theologians still find that 'natural'. At most, 'natural' seems to be what people have thought 'natural' at a particular time. 'Orders of creation' are just the same: they aren't grounded in creation, but appear in history and are elevated to be orders of creation. So there's no escaping the fact that morality is a network of rules which together form a code, and this code changes, even crumbles. It can't be otherwise if we don't want to become prisoners of our grandparents' morality. But there's another side: the anxious question whether there are any fixed points at all.

4. God's will and the Bible

But surely there's still the Bible? For many Christians this question has shown the way out of the impasse. The Bible contains God's will for all times, so an appeal to scripture can solve our moral problems. I doubt that.

The Bible is indeed full of commandments, admonitions, instructions for living and dying, often given as coming from God or his prophets and apostles. But we don't observe them, or observe only a small number of them, or – even more probably – observe them in a way to which we ourselves have given content. Things can't be otherwise, for the world which was presupposed by all these commandments is no longer ours. We no longer have slaves; we no longer spike our meat to a tree with a spear; we no longer have patriarchal families (except in fundamentalist groups); and we eat anything that can be useful and nourishing, without bothering about food laws. I could go on like this for hours. In another connection I've said that if we were to do everything that is handed down in the Bible as God's commandments, we would be bad people with abhorrent deeds. And conversely, we do a whole heap of things which are directly condemned in the Bible. Yet people want to find God's will in the Bible or get it out the Bible.

That can certainly happen. The Middle Ages (Thomas Aquinas) knew this and Calvin already had precise thoughts about it. To keep to him: Calvin said that you must be careful to distinguish between ceremonial, civil and moral commandments. The first are connected with the religion of Israel and no longer have any significance for the Christian church; from a social perspective, the second group presupposes the civil, semi-agricultural, semi-nomadic society of Israel, and we no longer have such a society, so these commandments too no longer fit our situation. The third group, the moral commandments, are the commandments which are valid always and everywhere and are summed up briefly in the Ten Commandments. This is a splendid distinction, one you can live with; and at the same time you don't have to abandon the Bible. You see it in historical perspective.

But how does Calvin know what is 'civil' and thus time-conditioned, and what is 'moral' and thus valid always and everywhere? To give an example, why are the rules about extinguishing the fire of jealousy (described at length in Numbers 5) regarded as 'time-conditioned' and not the death penalty for homosexuality? He had no criteria to hand here, but simply went by society as he knew it. In this society slavery had been abolished, a year of jubilee didn't fit, and asking interest on money lent seemed to him – in contrast to Luther – to be reasonable, although it was forbidden by God. So for Calvin, the criterion for distinguishing between what was outmoded and what was always valid was drawn from the norms and values of his own society.

And that still continues to be the case. The people who are so zealous in prizing the Bible as the criterion of their teaching and life follow some instructions from the Bible and leave others aside. They must have criteria, otherwise they couldn't make a distinction.

That's remarkable for more than one reason. First of all, by definition, a criterion that put us in a position to distinguish stands above the text. I've no objection to that; on the contrary, that's how it has to be, but of course this isn't compatible with the claim that the Bible provides the norms and values. It provides us with some norms and values. However, these weren't handed down as such; we look for them. And why do we look for these particular ones and not the others? Because we recognize them, find that they fit our world, can use them or any other expression that may be suitable. At all events, the ones we can't use aren't chosen. So the criterion by which we distinguish comes 'from elsewhere'; it comes from our own culture. Ours is a culture – and I shall come back to this – steeped in Christianity, but that doesn't alter the fact that it isn't 'the Bible', nor is it 'the Christian church'.

In another section I shall explain how there's nothing wrong with this approach. Morality doesn't come from the Bible but from the light of nature. Being human comes before being Christian: people knew about good and evil long before there was a Bible, just as they had known for a long time about carpentry and building ships. Therefore morality – albeit in the context of a past time – is also in the Bible, and the Christian church down the ages was able to get it out now and then to feed to its members.

5. From moral code to discussions of morality

The well-known ways are cut off; what is left? Is there a way of getting behind what may and may not be, is proper or improper, and can we arrive at what used to be called the will of God by this way? Certainly; it has always been travelled, and Christianity, even in its orthodox garb, loses nothing by joining in. To do so we have to go over to a different kind of approach.

God wills what is good, good in the twofold sense of good-for-human-beings-and-the-world and good in the moral sense. That seems to me to be an indisputable starting-point. It leads directly to the question: then what is good? We must search that out for ourselves; there is no other answer. If we were to answer 'what God wills', then we'd be going round in a circle, since God wills what is good. Unless by 'what God wills' we mean that something (an action) is good *because* God wills it. But that's a statement with strange consequences. God and evil are then, so to speak, elevated to good or evil by God's decree. That makes good and evil purely arbitrary. Had God decreed otherwise, things would have been otherwise. Unless of course we say that God never decides arbitrarily whether something is good or bad, since because God is good, God wills the good. But then we're back at the beginning. Something (an action) isn't good because God wills it, but God wills it because it's good and we – once again – have the task and the responsibility of seeking what is good and what isn't.

We must hold to this last point: something is good, and so it's commanded, and not vice versa: because God commands it, it's good. Do we then know what good is? A little bit: we could never call God good if we had no sense of it.

We also know what mercy and faithfulness are, otherwise God could never have been praised – as tradition tells us – in Israel as the faithful and merciful God; people wouldn't have known what these words meant. Of course we can make a mistake (deliberately or by misfortune) and call something proper that is improper and vice versa, but that doesn't alter the fact that we have to work with what we regard as good and evil: there is no alternative.

This has already brought me back to discussions about morality. 'Good' is an adjective, a label that we put on people, times, actions and so on. Are we right or wrong to do that? That's what discussions of morality are about.

They don't begin nowhere; they begin with what we already had, with the moral principles with which we grew up; with an experience going back for centuries and centuries, recorded in codes, morals, customs, books and notes about what may and may not be, what is proper and what isn't.

So the discussion first of all takes place within the moral community in which we grew up. It's also easiest there, because we share much of the code with one another. Reformed Christians recognize other Reformed Christians. It already becomes rather more difficult when we come up against the plurality within Christianity, when Reformed want to discuss with Christian Reformed or with Roman Catholics: there is less recognition, because there's less of a shared code. The discussion is even harder between Christians and non-Christians, or between Christians and Muslims. But even there it must have a place, for no matter how pluralist a society may be, it must also have a moral code which is common to all. Otherwise it can't exist.

These last words already bring me to the purpose of moral discussion. In a society in which the traditional code is creaking under the weight of social changes, it serves to discover what is good. So I'm also just formulating the conditions for it. Anyone who joins in, recognizes the other as a dialogue partner with equal rights: Reformed and Reformed Covenanters, Roman Catholics and Free Church, and vice versa. People make this space for one another in such a discusssion according to the rule, 'Do to others what you would want them to do to you (give them space).' I can't think of a better rule of life for arriving at a meaningful moral discussion in a pluralist society. That isn't always very easy for convinced Christians, even less for, e.g., Muslims. However, anyone who doesn't observe this rule mustn't be in a moral discussion. It presupposes different insights, otherwise it wouldn't be neceessary. But not unchangeability, since in that case there would be nothing to talk about.

6. Searching oneself out? The light of nature

If the appeal to nature or to the revelation in creation fails, if equally there is no special revelation about what is permissible and what isn't, and nothing is left of church claims in this respect, we must look for it ourselves. Indeed that has always been the case, and will always remain so. 'We must look for it ourselves' simply means that the norms and values which dominate our society, at least as far as its basic priciples are concerned, are the fruit of human experience. Generation after generation has contributed to them, has gone through morasses of trial and error and started on paths from which it had to turn back because they were dead ends. What we now have is what finally remained, not arbitrary dictates, but rules the 'proof' of which is that it is good to observe them. So a whole world is involved in morality and its rules. Responsibility is always personal, but moral rules are 1. the product of a community and therefore 2. historically defined.

Thus morality is human work. That isn't an insight to be afraid of; it follows the whole Christian tradition. Knowledge of good and evil rests on natural light, as has long been said, in both the Roman Catholic and the Reformation traditions. Again I'm using 'natural' in the sense in which I've already used it: one doesn't need to be a Christian to know the difference between good and evil. So in this chapter I'm endorsing the classical Christian standpoint: the only thing I'm doing here is to give content to how we can understand that natural light. We mustn't see it as a special organ with which you could practise moral divination. I don't deny that there's also something mysterious about our moral sense, a spontaneous respect for others, for example, and where does that come from? Is it innate in us, as Calvin says? Does a person by nature have something like 'sympathy', as David Hume thought? Yet even if we include that in the 'natural light', it wouldn't be a moral detector that we had at our disposal, but practical wisdom which has proved effective, and does so time and again. In the eyes of its adherents there is something rational about morality, something of 'it can't be otherwise'. In this sense morality ends up in practical wisdom, so it differs notably from culture to culture, and changes its manifestation in time in order to remain precisely what it always was: practical wisdom.

Morality as human work – can morality then exist without God? Of course not, any more than the creation can exist without God. But must people know that in order to be able to live in the creation? No. Must people know of God to be moral? No. God creates the trees, but I can also recognize a tree even if I don't recognize (know) God. It's the same with our moral principles. God is the necessary condition for their existence, but not for knowing about them. That, moreover, would lead us to the absurd conclusion that non-believers don't know the difference between good and evil.

So there is something secular about morality, something of all people and not just of Christians. In their day the church fathers spoke of a heart enlightened and incorporated into the Christian tradition. Of course they saw the apostle Paul taking the same approach before them when he called on his readers to think on all that is good and excellent, and peppering his letters with the moral rules which were customary in his time. It's as though you were reading a Stoic.

And that still happens today; Christianity takes over the moral injunctions of a culture (democracy, personal freedom and so on), with all the mistakes that we can then come up against and – this is also included – with all the disagreements over what can and cannot pass for Christianity.

7. Why must that be so? Moral authority

Let me begin by noting that morality comes to us with a certain authority. Language points the way here: moral instructions are formulated with the aid of words like 'must' and 'need'. Otherwise we aren't talking about morality, but about personal preference or taste. Granted, what a moral injunction requires of us can't be compelled; morality isn't the same thing as law. But we sense a certain authority in moral rules, we feel obligated by them. Where does this authority come from, and how does it get into these rules? As long as people associated morality only with the code of the Christian church there was no problem. It had to come from God. But if we are no longer willing and able to say that, from whom must it come? A good question, but one which can't be given a simple answer. Let's begin with the question how that authority comes into the moral rules; perhaps that will help us further.

I shall start with moral upbringing. Moral rules formulate the behaviour that the group (or the person) which brings us up expects of us. We in turn assimilate these expectations; we know that things are expected of us and that we should respond to these expectations. Where there are no expectations and the expectations therefore can't be assimilated, there is no moral upbringing and people grow up faced with the gallows and the wheel. But that's an almost impossible situation. An individual always lives in a group, and however small it is, something, however little, is expected of each participant – and every participant knows that.

So we know that 'the others' lie behind the expectations. Not just others, but authorities, in fact a whole culture with a past and everything, with the accumulation of centuries and centuries of experience. That gives the moral code a colossal weight, which is further strengthened when it's also brought under the wing of the church as 'God's will'. Here too we see – I would note in passing – how easily 'the others' and 'God's will' run into each other. This is a reason for caution in dealing with the authority of the moral code.

That brings us to the most burning question: does authority (do the others) still leave us some freedom or do we face the dilemma:

away with morals or give up freedom? I don't think it's like that; moral obligations and personal freedom can very well go together. I shall demonstrate that by comparing three different interpretations of obligation.

1. One can bow before the obligations of morality as a schoolboy bows before the schoolteacher. The others are in the majority and you can't do anything about that. So you have to accept the situation. That's an almost reassuring acceptance of morality as compulsion (hence my 'schoolteacher'). The sort of obedience that corresponds to this doesn't seem to me so exalted. You don't comply out of conviction but out of fear of reprisals or a desire to please.

2. Morality is indeed something like a schoolteacher who has to be obeyed; it has authority. But it doesn't have that authority because it represents the others; I give it that authority myself. I must obey the schoolteacher, so to speak, but my obedience comes from within because I've let it in. So we obey an authority which we ourselves have recognized, but the obedience is real and not forced.

3. Morality has nothing to do with a schoolteacher. Its authority is certainly the authority of the wisdom of centuries; however, what it appeals to isn't our readiness to obey but our insight. We follow moral rules because we approve of them; what *we* think and what *morality* thinks coincide. So we have no difficulty with them and feel ourselves whole and already free.

The last possibility is certainly preferable. The first makes too much of external moral pressure; the second reduces the pressure to internal pressure; the third doesn't work with pressure but just says: if morality is the harvest of human experience then I simply *can't* have any difficulty with it, since I myself am a human being too.

If only it were always as the last view has it! But that's certainly a rose-coloured picture. What must happen if what I think and what morality thinks don't coincide? Do I just accept? We don't even do that. Why do we no longer observe the instructions of our grandparents, go to the cinema (which they were against), have children without getting married (for which you used to go to the sinners' bench), and vote for a non-Christian party (which was censored in the 1930s, but what censorship is there now for the Reformed?). With what right have we departed from this code? This question brings me to another question which is as burdensome as it's indispensable: our autonomy. I wouldn't know to what else we could appeal for our own new ways.

8. Autonomy. A suspect concept

There are plenty of Christians who have difficulty with the term 'autonomy'. I can well imagine that, in view of the past. Autonomy is a slogan which served to detach morality from the church (rightly, in my view) but was identified by both proponents and opponents with 'away from God' (wrongly). The 'autonomous person' then in turn came to be identified with those who have freed themselves from every tie and simply want to be their own lawgivers.

Literally translated, 'autonomous' in fact means being one's own lawgiver. But no one *can* set themselves up as this, however much they might want to. Human beings don't exist as individuals; they are attached to a culture by a thousand threads which are formed from the past by norms and values, and if they haven't got these from their parental home, then they've got them from work or friends. In short, everyone acts according to rules - not always the same rules, but rules. Unregulated conduct brings people to the psychiatrist's clinic.

Moreover we don't *want* anyone to be their own lawgiver; that's why we maintain a morality. 'Everyone must decide for themselves' dies on our lips, and we're right; as long as it's a matter of preference or taste, we don't bother about what another person chooses. But that no longer works with morality, since the mark of a moral injunction – which is why it is called that – is precisely that individuals may not work out at whim what to do, but have to do what the law provides. Torture is inadmissable; there's surely no question that we should say 'Everyone must work that out for themselves'.

If that were all that autonomy meant, we couldn't make anything of it; it would never work in either practice or theory. So we needn't overdo the distinction.

There's also a good, indispensable way in which autonomy can be used; it's even a sense to which we *have* to refer in morality. That emerges when we return to the society in which we live. Europe knew a time when the rule was that the religion of the prince was the religion of the people. If the prince was Roman Catholic, then the subjects were also deemed to be Catholic, and if he changed his faith (for example by becoming a Protestant), then all the subjects had to change, too. We would no longer accept that today. Why not? Because it's part of human autonomy that we may order our lives in accord with our deepest convictions.

In this sense autonomy has nothing to do with arbitrariness, with playing one's own lawgiver, but clearly indicates the social freedom in a multiple offer of convictions to opt for the conviction that we think we have good reasons for choosing. Freedom for self-determination makes such a social life possible; without it, it would disappear. I would call that autonomy as social freedom.

Its presupposition is that we trust people to choose on the basis of what they think good reasons, even if they may not choose as we would have done and perhaps we don't find their reasons very good. Autonomy as social freedom goes back to autonomy as a characteristic of our humanity: people have their reasons for acting and reasons are not to be reduced to causes. If I decide to join an assocation I do so because I'm sympathetic to its aims or have some knowledge of the institution concerned. But I don't do so because my hormones tell me to on a certain day or because I've taken charity pills. You dehumanize people if you interpret them in this way; you reject their arguments and let them continue as a product of cause and effect or – and this can be just as bad – of other people's pressure. Autonomy as 'self-determination' is opposed to such a view: the concept presupposes the presence of traditions, of norms and values (otherwise there's nothing to define); it even presupposes that I've grown up in such a network (where else would I have got my orientation from?), but expresses my freedom to do what I will with it. People can and may act differently from their grandparents; that's what they're human for.

9. The Christian view of life and morality

Doesn't insight into what may and may not be done then follow from faith? With this question I'm still moving in the sphere of the knowledge of good and evil. Moral actions need more than good insights, but first the question of knowledge must be fought out. Here the freedom of the Christian man, as Luther called it, is at stake. If, for example, only church leaders know what may and may not be done, as ordinary people we depend on them. But do they in fact have the monopoly of knowledge?

1. Morality follows from faith. Indeed, it follows from faith in so far as it's included in it. But how did it get there? Because we first put it there, and now get it out again. 'We' are not we personally; generations were also involved before us, and these said that you mustn't have sexual intercourse before marriage, that you had to go

to church twice on Sunday, that it wasn't right for Christians to go to the theatre and the cinema, and so on. I'm taking examples which make it clear that we ourselves (or our fathers) first started these rules and therefore/afterwards abolished them again. That isn't anything special in itself; that always happens with Christian faith. It takes into itself what is morally good, because by nature it calls for doing good and what doing good is is regulated by morality. Immoral Christianity is a contradiction in terms. Moreover Christianity shares that with Judaism.

2. A second relativizing comment is: whose conviction of faith? Simply in the Netherlands, we have a Roman Catholic and many different Protestant faith communities. Each of these communities has its own special moral rules which the others don't have. So from a sociological perspective you could say that there is a group morality. Of course you could claim that this was a universal Christian morality (instead of, say, an Old Reformed morality) or, even worse, was the will of God.

But at this moment my point is rather different. It seems that on the basis of faith, the Christian faith communities derive dissimilar, sometimes contradictory, moral injunctions from faith. Of course that's possible because the Christian tradition is capable of more than one interpretation. But the faith communities are opposed to precisely this conclusion. So where do the differences come from? The only solution seems to be that the faith communities maintain such special features because and to the degree that they've incorporated different moralities into their convictions, and have also pinned their identities too much to these convictions. At all events, it can't be maintained that they're derived from faith.

3. That automatically brings us to the 'Not so with you' with which the apostle Paul called on the Christianity of his day to distinguish itself from its surroundings. And indeed, if Christians were to find themselves in a society in which murder, recourse to prostitutes, the oppression of the weak or the extermination of minorities were regarded as normal, then Christians would have to live quite differently. Does our society look like that? I shall return to this point, but to begin with I would note that we must regard such an appeal with some care. In a society in which the 'different' behaviour of Christians isn't easy to see, a community can easily tend to seek that distinguishing feature in special practices: not living together before marriage, no contraception, a covering on your head in church, keeping Sunday holy, not going to the disco, and similar things. For outsiders that

then produces a bizarre picture of being a Christian. Of course every community is free to give whatever content to 'Christian' they think fit; no one needs to threaten others over that. But that's rather different from seeing that a form of group morality isn't really necessary.

10. Am I Christian enough?

The fact that it isn't so easy to indicate what makes the 'difference' gives many Christians guilt feelings nowadays. They have the feeling that they're watering down their Christianity. If they themselves aren't already doing this, there are always people around to tell them that they are.

It isn't for me to pass judgment on other people. When it comes to being a Christian, whether someone is making something of it or letting opportunities slip is a question which they have to answer for themselves in the first instance. But the Christian element certainly needn't lie in the 'difference'. That we can't point to it so clearly can also mean – and this is much simpler – that our culture is so permeated by the heritage of Christianity that 'Christian' and 'generally human' (in the sense of humanity) can be as alike as two peas. Western culture has worked over, assimilated Christian tradition in its own way. That's the reason why the actual difference in views about good and evil (views are rather different from actions) between Christians and non-Christians is difficult to bring out in the cultural, political and moral spheres. So Christians can give up all obsessions about seeking God's will. They needn't be ashamed if they can't find anything especially Christian about it.

Let me make three comments. It seems a splendid ideal for all Christians to distinguish themselves from others in every respect. But the apostle Paul was matter-of-fact enough to warn his readers against that. If you want to do that, he says, you have to leave the world. No one does that, not even the most radical Christians; no one can do it, and what I'm claiming here is that no one *need* do it either.

So can the Christian heritage remain even without a living link with the roots from which it emerged? On the basis of what I've said before about the natural light as the basis of morality, no one will be surprised if I answer yes. To the degree that Christian morality (viz. the morality inserted into faith by the church) is concerned, this morality can also continue without the Christian church to nurture

266

and cherish it. Of course other communities have taken over this task of moral upbringing.

My third comment is that the obligation to be watchful still applies to Christianity. The National Socialist ideology produced the most cruel derailment of humanity within the shortest conceivable time. That can happen again.

So isn't there something like a Christian morality and – as a form of reflection on it – a Christian ethic? It depends what content we give to these terms. There's nothing against a Christian morality, as long as everyone who use the term is aware that it's the description of the morality of a group, or rather, of one of the many Christian groups. In the same sense, Christian ethics can be a meaningful term: an ethics in which a particular group morality is made a chart by a particular Christian community. If we make more of it than that, then that's too much of a good thing. There is no Christian ethic in the real sense, any more than there is a Christian law.

Rather, what is typically Christian lies, as I wrote in the first section, in the context of the Christian tradition of faith in which morality finds its place in Christianity. This doesn't change any general rules by which people live, but gives morality its own place within faith: we aren't redeemed by it; morality doesn't bring salvation. But Christianity can't do without morality. With the help of morality – i.e. with the help of moral advice – it seeks the will of God for daily life; it has no other way. I would want to add one more thought: the Christian faith sets itself against moralism. By that I mean people who use their moral excellence as a platform to stand on. They think that this gives them a higher standpoint from which they can look down on others. That's how moralists think. I could quote Jesus' parable of the Pharisee and the publican here. It begins with the remark that Jesus told his story 'for those who thought themselves righteous and despised others'. The latter always goes with the former. Christians don't do this because they know of human sin and God's forgiveness. Morality is necessary; it's the life raft on which human society floats, but not the life raft on which we float in our relationship to God.

11. *All that God has commanded. The Ten Commandments (i)*

According to Christianity, despite everything that I've said so far, it isn't impossible to know what God's will is for human beings in the world. We can find a summary of it in the so-called Ten

Commandments. These aren't in fact commandments, but remarkably enough prohibitions, so the name doesn't fit. Moreover purists speak of the Ten Words. However, I shall keep to established terminology, though I would stress that the Ten Commandments don't say what we must do but have a negative form: they sum up 'all that is forbidden by God'. Nowadays we would call this an ethical rule formulated in the negative. Why this negative formulation? The question has led to much profound discussion, but the background seems to me to be a simple fact. The commandments are formulated in a society which is (still) at an early stage of development and they aim to protect the basic values which hold a society together: human life, property, a good name and social position. You can't make the Ten Commandments an ethics of virtue, of the kind about which the Middle Ages was so crazy (and the Roman Catholic *magisterium* still is). Significantly enough, Luther and Calvin didn't base their catechisms on the classical list of virtues, but on the Ten Commandments. There is a reason for that which is connected with their view of the Christian tradition. They were quite clear that an ethic of virtues would again lead to the self-adornment of Christians as a way to God, and that was precisely what they had dedicated their whole lives to opposing. The summons to adorn ourselves with good works appears on every page of the New Testament, but there too instructions in the form of rules predominate.

To put it somewhat crudely, the Ten Commandments formulate commonplaces. Moreover, according to the Christian tradition from Ambrose via Thomas and Calvin up to the present day, they form a summary of what is called 'natural morality'. In this context 'natural' means the same thing as in the expression 'natural light': you don't have to be a Christian for it.

Augustine coined an attractive term. God's commandments are known to people because they are *in corde scripta*, written on our hearts. Here he is repeating what he had already read in the apostle Paul. One more witness: Luther even called the Ten Commandments the '*Sachsenspiegel* of the Jews'. Just as the Saxons (of whom Luther was one), had their rules of life in the form of the so-called *Sachsenspiegel*, so the Jews had their rule of life in the form of the Ten Commandments. Is that meant as a demotion? Not at all; by it Luther wants to emphasize that the commandments contain what everyone knows or at least can know, since nowhere may you kill, steal and so on.

That doesn't prevent the Jewish and Christian traditions from presenting these rules of life as a commandment from God. According to the tradition God personally delivered them to Moses. So the natural knowledge of good and evil is brought under the protection of God.

In the next section we shall see that this claim is excessive. Not all the ten have the same weight; parts of some of the commandments go against the grain and others we feel to be totally wrong. That's often the case; in the Old Testament there are some quite direct instructions for living which are unthinkable or outmoded for us, though they were given by God. This is completely in keeping with the argument that we've already encountered in church teachers like Thomas and Calvin: ceremonial commandments (connected with Israel's worship) and civil commandments (connected with Israel's culture) are not intended for us. I mention as the most striking commandment the call to celebrate the sabbath (the only one, along with the command to honour one's parents, with a positive formulation). Christianity doesn't do that, not even by celebrating Sunday, because Sunday isn't the sabbath.

The Second Table (I shall come back to this term) contains what tradition called the moral commandments. As far as morality is concerned, these are more important to us than those of the First Table, not because God is less important than human beings, but because God can react if we make a mistake, whereas by contrast human beings can be damaged irreparably.

12. Development into a moral code. The Ten Commandments (ii)

The Ten Commandments are brief general rules in a timeless form and therefore appropriate for all times and places. That's their strength, but at the same time their weakness: how can rules which are formulated so generally give instructions for living? They can't in fact do that, and have to be developed into a moral code. I shall now discuss how that works and what we mean by it. But before that, a few pieces of information.

First, these general rules are formulated in a timeless way. That goes only for a number of the commandments, and these moreover are to be found in the so-called Second Table – the rules of a moral nature as distinct from the religious rules which together form the First Table. The terminology of this distinction goes back to the biblical account. In it mention is made of 'two tables' on which God is said to have engraved the Ten Commandments in his own hand.

What was more natural than to distribute the two sorts of commandment over these 'two tables' and to make the First Table go up to
and include the sabbath commandment, assigning the rest of the
commandments to the second? With a word-play which I've already
used before (taken from G.van der Leeuw), we could call the First
Table etiquette and the Second Table ethics.

Now a second comment on the form. The Ten Commandments
aren't numbered in the same way within the Christian tradition. The
Roman Catholic tradition combines what among Protestants are
counted as the First and Second Commandments. The Protestant
Third Commandment is the Roman Catholic Second Commandment, and so on. In the end both tradiitons again become the
same because the Roman Catholic version splits into two what for
Protestants is the Tenth Commandment.

Back to the question (now put more precisely) as to how such a
general rule as, say, 'you shall not kill' (this really means unlawful
killing) can give concrete instructions for living. That can only come
about if it's developed by additions and extensions. As a 'developed
rule' it becomes part of the moral code. The circumstances of this
development are not only interesting but also important for the
question of what today we call moral obligation. I shall indicate two
ways in which 'development' can take place.

The first and most obvious is that unlawful killing is wrong:
everyone knows that. If a person throws someone off the rocks, there
is no question that that is killing and that is impermissible. The only
way of avoiding this conclusion is to ask 'But when is killing
unlawful?' Then the discusion begins. This argument already appears
in Aristotle.

The next, more theoretical, step is for a list to be drawn up along
the lines of these practical decisions of actions which – according to
experience – may or may not come under 'killing'. That's the way in
which, for example, Calvin expounds the Ten Commandments and,
following him, the Protestant Heidelberg Catechism. This gives rise
to a moral code which is handed down as tradition – by means of
the catechism on the Ten Commandments – to countless new
generations of Christians and has for centuries left its mark on
European culture.

For despite their brevity the Ten Commandments touch on precisely the spheres of society in which a certain order must prevail if
individual and society are to be able to go on existing. Everyone
clings to life, everyone functions as a being with sexual endowments,

everyone needs property, and as individuals all are dependent on their honour and good name among others. Moreover, in some way or other, a certain order must be created in these spheres: otherwise a society will fall apart. You could almost say: as long as there is a kind of order. In this respect, given the bad name that he has, Calvin was very generous. In his view there are differences in laws and rules of a moral kind because morality must fit the situation of the time, the place and the people. So in his view you mustn't take the differences too seriously – within certain limits.

The moral code which the Christian tradition has built up around this is the culturally and historically determined content of such an order. It isn't the same as the divine commandment, but does have a function in the search for the will of God, though we aren't confined to it. The ordering of life in terms of the protection of life, the order in the sphere of sex and possessions, can be different from what we have learned; it's different in other cultures and perhaps must also be different again for us from what it was a century ago.

So this is the point at which the moral discussion begins. It presupposes what 'people' did and didn't do as Christians in former times, and at the same time except that it's impossible for us to take this over. That would be arbitrary and, to the degree that morality has an element of authority, extortionate. Not only must there be a hope derived from the moral tradition of Christianity, but a hope can be derived from it without doing damage to morality. Let me give some examples.

'You shall not kill' means protection of life against unlawful killing. A 'development' in terms of 'euthanasia is impermissible' (I define this as acceding to the request of a patient in a desperate situation to die a gentle death) thus doesn't really fit. The order that the commandment (or rather prohibition) brings doesn't mean honouring the flame of life to the last flicker but protecting it against a death which someone has not sought and doesn't want.

The same goes for the ordering of sexuality. Here, to begin with, the formulation of the Seventh Commandment (in the Protestant numbering) is already outmoded. This commandment addresses the male. He may do much in the sexual sphere; he may have several wives, he may resort to prostitutes, he may even throw out his wife, but he may not interfere with the marriage of another male, because if he did he would fertilize this man's wife unlawfully – impregnation by the male. By contrast, the woman is allowed little or nothing; she

271

may not break out of the marriage: that was so obvious that it wasn't even mentioned. These are impossible things for us today. And here the Tenth Commandment slams the door shut. In it the woman is just put in a list along with other human possessions, like houses and domestic animals. This seems to me to be sexism.

And the fence that tradition has put round this commandment also doesn't work. Masturbation would fall under it, sexual fantasies, homosexuality, and even the use of contraceptives. That seems more like 'you may not enjoy yourselves' than a command of the Creator.

I'll leave it at these examples. They clearly indicate that the code is primarily built up around the Ten Commandments with the help of yet more recent prohibitions. Not only does that not work; it's also one-sided. Fortunately the Christian tradition has another contribution to make to the discussion.

13. Love the fulfilling of the law

Christianity is regarded as the religion which is characterized by the command to love. That's true; there are passages in both the Old and the New Testaments which can only confirm that.

Loving isn't exclusively Christian, nor even exclusively religious, but a moral obligation which is to be found in almost all cultures: 'Love your neighbour as yourself' occurs not only in the New Testament but in the Old, and also appears in Buddhism and in the Stoic philosophers; Luther, Calvin and the classic Christian tradition know of it. What Christianity does is 1. to exalt love to become the supreme virtue, and 2. extend its scope to loving enemies. But it didn't 'invent' this, nor is it its sole representative. Even loving one's enemy isn't unknown to the Stoa.

If Christians are asked to do 'more than usual', that can't mean that they are precisely the ones who need to love, since we find loving everywhere. It's really a matter of doing one more thing, giving away one more shirt, walking an extra mile with someone or extending the scope of love yet further. I say this last with hesitation, since loving presupposes a concrete relationship. We don't love the whole world; needn't and shouldn't, and indeed can't, do so. That kind of exaggerated idea destroys real love, for this is directed to persons and relates to those who cross my path and need my help. I'm still not putting it sharply enough: the neighbour whom I must love as myself is the person who is dependent on my help.

I'm deliberately ending this chapter on the Ten Commandments with a section about love and loving. For Christianity of all ages, 'loving' is the positive side of God's will. 'For love is from God and God is love, Amen,' the poet Achterberg rightly says. That doesn't mean that loving is the whole story. Augustine can say that in his well-known rule, '*Ama deum et quod vis fac*': love God and then do what you like. However, he didn't mean that you can do anything as long as you love, but rather that someone who loves no longer does 'just anything', but wants what is good for another. But that's too little; love needs content, otherwise anything can be called love. 'I must kill you for love' cannot be. For mercy perhaps, or, better, so as not to become unmerciful. Or from another kind of necessity, but not for love.

Love is the fulfilling of the law, says the apostle Paul. That sounds better. The intention isn't that the disposition that we call love – love is a disposition – is enough, but that this disposition is necessary, is asked of us when we want to do the will of God in terms of the Christian tradition. What the apostle Paul calls 'the law' isn't abolished by love, and if it is already 'abolished', then it's abolished in the sense of being 'put on a higher plane'. I mean that we can test any concrete action of service and help by the question. 'Can it pass for an act of love?' For of all that we have done, only love survives.

14. *The freedom of the Christian*

The Ten Commandments have been handed down to us in a setting which has become very significant for the Christian church. They begin with the words 'I am the LORD your God who brought you up out of the land of Egypt'. None of us has been 'led out of Egypt', but according to the Christian church, this beginning has kept its significance. The one who gives the commands isn't the oppressor, but the liberator. God's commandments are indeed a yoke; any commandment is that, otherwise it wouldn't need to be given. But the yoke is easy and the burden is light, since a God who really liberates can never give commandments which lay a yoke of slavery on people.

That fact is worked out in the Christian tradition in more than one way. We can regard it as a testimony of support: the burden is light because God himself helps us to bear it. A biblical author says that God's commandments aren't heavy, and from the context that clearly means that once you've been touched by God's Spirit, they no longer feel heavy, though other people might perhaps call them heavy. I've nothing against this interpretation; on the contrary, it seems to me an authentic Christian view of fulfilling God's commandment. It's another question whether Christians succeed here, at least succeed as much as they themselves would want (and should want from God). We need to be more modest about that than earlier generations. Origen, the church father I've already quoted more than once, says to his great opponent, the philosopher Celsus: I concede that you, too, know what is well pleasing to God, but among us Christians you find the power to do it as well. That's still put relatively modestly: the *power* to do this is to be found in the Christian community; Origen doesn't say that Christians also in fact do this. That has been maintained by many Christians down the ages, to the present day. If we already have to concede that others know just as well as we do, then we're maintaining that you must be a Christian to be able to go on and do them! Certainly I want to say that for a moment, but the consequence is – inevitably – that as is well known, 'no Christians do this either'. It's just like Jesus' story about the two brothers, one of whom said yes but didn't go, and the other who said no but went after all. So it's better not to put forward this claim oneself. God determines who did what had to be done and who didn't.

No yoke of slavery – there's another development. It includes the reason why I've gone into the commandment at such length and almost demythologized the will of God: Christian freedom is at stake. For this reason Luther abolished the law of God altogether, since according to the apostle Paul believers weren't redeemed to become slaves again. I haven't gone that far; I've described morality as a means of finding God's will. But morality remains morality, a group code. If this coincides with the authority of God's will, the result is people who aren't free, who can no longer think and act independently. In the style of: it must be possible for someone, otherwise it can't be. For some people this can go so far that they think that they're doing God a service here: the heavier the pressure, the more Christian our activity. That must be a misunderstanding, even a catastrophic misunderstanding, a fundamental attack on the essence of Christian faith. Believing makes free people, not slaves of others or slaves of time, but – to quote Buber – servants of God. I recall a conversation with a woman who had become a Christian, a Reformed Christian. 'I didn't like it,' she confided: after initial joy she slowly ended up in a depression; so much had to be done! Contributions to this, works for that, sending children to this club, herself becoming a member of another and in the midst of all that a constant, slowly developing check to see that she was doing everything well and living up to the norms. I couldn't think of anything better than to read to her a sentence from an author who seemed to her to be the cause of her misery, the apostle Paul. And it is with this sentence (from Galatians 5) that I shall also end my chapter on the Ten Commandments.

For freedom Christ has made us free: stand fast and do not let anyone lay a yoke of slavery upon you again.

The Bible

XXII

The Bible and its Interpretation

'If we are likely to treat Livy and Dionysius and Polybius and Tacitus so respectfully and nobly that we do not put them on the rack for a single syllable, why not also Matthew, Mark, Luke and John?' (*G.E. Lessing*)

1. A defenceless book

To put the Bible at the end instead of at the beginning may cause surprise here and there. Have I forgotten such a thing as the Bible? No, it's something different. Part of what can be said about the Bible has already been said in the chapter about tradition. The Bible is an element of this, a link in the chain of Christian tradition. And again not just any link, but one with a special significance. That's why it is being once again discussed explicitly here.

But that isn't the only reason for this separate treatment. It also has to do with the way in which the Bible is used. At times this is so amazing that there is justification for devoting a separate chapter to it. It's also because of this that I've quoted very few biblical texts in this book. That isn't a mistake, nor is it being casual; it's deliberate. This book is full of the Bible, as anyone who reads it carefully will discover. But it always irritates me when I see the zeal with which Protestant authors above all cite a biblical reference wherever they can. I've no doubt that this zeal is well meant. Only the Bible gets split up, and this already begins to look like showing the flag. Moreover, the passages from the Bible usually aren't expounded, but simply quoted as they stand. That's a facile way of using the Bible. But above all, the whole approach gives the impression that the texts quoted have a basic purpose, that they're being used as proofs. It's as I say or write: look, it's in the Bible!

So in older Christian literature one can find that cancer is an incurable disease because it's written in the Bible of a certain evil that 'it will develop like cancer'. Childbirth can never be without pain, for 'in pain you shall bear children'. Sin is original sin, for doesn't a psalm say that we were 'conceived and born in sin'? Social welfare is useless, for didn't Jesus himself say, 'the poor you have with you always'? And still in one of the lectures to the First Christian Social Congress in 1892 we can read that an eight-hour working day cannot be in accordance with God's will, for scripture says, 'Are there not twelve hours in the day?' and when Jesus says, 'My Father works until now and I am working', that's a clear indication that workers may not slack.

Of course this is nonsense, and few Christians would recognize themselves in the statements I've quoted. But I'm afraid that this is because they would feel that the examples I've been given are used to prove the wrong things, not because they find the principle of biblical 'proof texts' wrong. That isn't enough, and still leaves the Bible too much what it has been for centuries: the most mistreated and misused book in our culture.

The Bible didn't deserve such a fate. It's the classic expression of the Christian chart for God, and generation after generation has grown up on it. It has put its stamp on European culture and offered individuals and groups the possibility of identifying themselves with biblical saints. It still does all this down to the present day. Anyone who has sat in a 'Bible School' has had the fortune not to miss any of this.

However, there is one 'but' attached to this. Precisely through its splendour, the Bible is a book which is defenceless before those who use it. Where an open approach is replaced by a dogmatic approach for the sake of orthodoxy, the blessing also becomes a curse: the source of liberation becomes a source of slavery to the letter.

2. Book is books

I said book. Strictly speaking, that isn't true. The Bible is a book made up of many smaller books, each of which is an independent unit, and all of them can be taken together only on the basis of a particular principle of reading. Moreover the whole collection falls into two main parts, the Old Testament and the New, which in turn must be read on the basis of a principle which produces unity. The Old Testament is the collection made by the Jewish people, who also give it a different name (Tenach for short), and moreover is read by Jews in a 'Jewish' way. Christianity took this over as its book (also) and gave it the name Old Testament by adding it to what it itself called the New Testament, the story of Jesus Christ (and the explanation of that story), and reading it in a 'Christian way'. Apart from what the Christian church has made of that Christian reading, it has understood one thing very well. The Christian church can get nowhere without the Old Testament (its term); the Old Testament is the unconditional presupposition for an understanding of the New. The ease with which some Christians say that every people has a holy book which can serve as their Old Testament misses the literally fundamental significance of the Old Testament. Christians needn't become Jews, needn't even say 'Tenach' when they mean the Old Testament (they don't please anyone by doing that), but they can't understand themselves without the book of the Jewish community. We're again coming to the point – to make it once again – of the relationship between Jews and Christians. Each have their own history behind them; Judaism is no longer what it was two thousand years ago and Christianity is even less so. However, the affinity is so great that the Christian churches rightly no longer dare to use the term 'mission' in connection with the Jewish community.

The Bible isn't one book but a collection of books, all of which, if we make assured history begin with Moses, cover a period of more than twelve centuries. To give some indication of the length of this period, the same interval of time would take us back to Charlemagne. Now as surely as the people who told their stories or wrote them down didn't have the ideas we do now, there is variation and even development within the books of the Bible. The Bible isn't a statue hewn out of one stone but rather a mosaic, a composition. That makes reading it extraordinarily exciting. I come from a religious community in which the father read from the Bible at all three meals of the day – from cover to cover – and the children asked him not to stop, as long as it was the Old Testament. Attractive, certainly, but what makes a mosaic a unity?

3. Looking to the Bible for certainty

The Bible is a collection of books, all of which together form a splendid mosaic. But that isn't self-evident: the mosaic calls for a view which can perceive it. For that – for the composition of such a view – a view of the Bible is necessary.

There is nothing against views of the Bible: any conversation about the Bible presupposes something of this kind. But because these views aim to provide unity in multiplicity, they play a quite dominant role. To keep to the picture of the mosaic, they say how we must look at it, but they do that by telling us what there is to see. So if this is what is suggested by views of the Bible, how can we proceed without letting the view dominate the book itself?

A view of the Bible which has gone much too far here is that of the doctrine of the inspiration of Holy Scripture, or rather the doctrine that the Bible is inspired. Through the Spirit of God, holy men (there are no women among the biblical authors) have put into writing what God gave them. So the Spirit didn't just press them to write but also saw to it that a text came into being which God found sufficient for his church. On the basis of its inspired character the Bible is God's infallible word, the guideline for doctrine and life, the arbiter in all differences, in short the supreme authority in the church. Some Protestant theologians have mentioned that with some pride. Just as the Pope ultimately represents the authority in the Roman Catholic church, so we – they say – have the Bible, and that's better, because it represents God's Word and not someone on a throne.

In the course of history there has been no lack of attempts to break down this argument, but the success has been (and is) variable. Mechanical inspiration (the writers only needed to hold the pen, and what came out was from the Spirit) is replaced by organic inspiration: the authors remain themselves, children of their time. But that is to halt between two ideas, since it's already clear that the doctrine of inspiration no longer works in this way. So out of fear other people returned very quickly to the traditional view. Here people felt that they were safest.

Indeed, for a number of orthodox Protestant Christians an abyss opens up if they cease to believe in the inspiration of the Bible. It has become the foundation of faith, and abandoning it means that your faith is already in the air. There is no longer any certainty, any basis on which you can stand. This seems to me to be a misconception. Indeed, it's a misconception in more than one respect and moreover a fundamental one. Let me sum up what I have against it.

1. This view of the Bible denatures belief, because it makes the certainty of faith rest on a theory about the Bible, namely its inspired character. If people can't cope with an aspect of Christian tradition, then they have to accept it nevertheless 'because it's in the Bible'. That's really to stand things on their heads: we don't believe because something is in the Bible but because it affects us, makes us think or

whatever. Certainty isn't rooted in a theory but in the Word that is addressed to us.

2. This theory can also be said to be a castle of sand. It has to serve as an axiom on which faith rests and as such stand outside and above the statements of faith. But it can't bear this burden, because it is itself a statement of faith. The statement 'the Bible is the word of God inspired by the Spirit' is of precisely the same order as 'Jesus is God's Son' or 'God is gracious and merciful'. It can't both be a statement of faith and at the same time a foundation for one. So this whole idea of things is impossible. The Bible isn't the firm ground on which faith is anchored: the firm ground is God.

3. It spoils our dealings with the Bible. It makes it a book of advice: what does the Bible say about sex, about war and peace, about the family, about homosexuality, and so on? Everything has to be in the Bible, or at least has to be got out of it. That is of course the problem; it gives rise to forced interpetation of texts, interpretation with the ring of other forms of cheap use of the Bible. Conversely, everything in the Bible has to be meaningful, useful, if not obligatory truth for faith.

But there, too, Christians get stuck, because there is a good deal in the Bible which doesn't address us, is impossible to accept, or can even with good reasons be condemned.

4. For large parts of orthodox Protestantism, moreover, the Bible is the Bible as they read it. Not the whole Bible, as their view of the Bible prescribes (a view with which other people's ears are deafened), but a selection, an excerpt from texts with which people are familiar or of which they are aware. Chesterton already said that Christianity would benefit considerably if everyone didn't read their own Bible but that of other people.

5. As a late echo of this view of the Bible the much-used word 'biblical' keeps cropping up. A standpoint, an attitude, is acceptable if it's 'biblical'. And again we can see that the terminology has the same guilelessness: biblical is what someone finds biblical. The card is played not with the whole Bible, but with a selection of what is offered in the Bible. The motive for this form of action is still the same: only if something is biblical does it have authority. We mustn't want the arbitrariness which is given with this terminology.

6. Away with it! – that's all I can say. To preserve the Bible, or rather to get it back, we must get rid of the classic Reformed approach. Otherwise the Bible will disappear along with this view. That's already happened in many lives. Above all for orthodox Protestant

Christians, the measures which I propose are harsh ones, but I don't see how we can do without them. I really must say as clearly as possible that it can't be otherwise. Anyone who has real respect for the Bible can't lie on the procrustean bed of this kind of view of it.

4. *The Bible as source and norm*

A view of the Bible which doesn't bind the Bible but leaves it (and thus the reader) free would seem to me to be one like this. The Bible contains what Israel thought of God and what the evangelists and apostles – by way of addition – thought about Jesus. No more and no less.

So there's nothing of 'What's in the Bible is true and therefore you must believe it.' Why should it be true? In that case we must also believe that, and so on, and so on. So discussion of this position is certainly not unimportant. Why do we attach belief to what Israel and the apostles say about God? Because it makes an impression on us, because we can make something of it, because it does something to us, makes us clear about ourselves or however you care to put it. Those who believe, believe in what they find in the Bible, in what is in it. The content of the Bible makes the book important and not vice versa; it isn't as if what is in it is important because it's in the Bible.

This last statement isn't completely true. Once you've come under the impact of the Bible, of course you don't lightly scrap whole sections or throw them on the rubbish heap. Paul may not always have been right (he didn't understand much about homosexuality), but we do listen to him with respect. However, it isn't a question of the book (from cover to cover) but of what's in it, and of the book because of that. To begin with, Christians had a whole period without a book, with oral tradition, with (shall we say) 'what's in it' before it became a text. The Christian church comes before the Bible and itself established its extent and composition. Protestantism has always had difficulty with this because it identifies the Bible with God's Word, and then you have no alternative. Then it's true, indeed the church doesn't come before the Word of God, since it is a creation of the Word. But the Bible and the creative Word of God aren't the same thing, and once we've established that, we can also do justice to the historical order: the church was there before the Bible.

I emphasize that for yet another reason. It makes it clear that the Bible isn't the 'holy book' of Christians in the same way as the Qur'an is the 'holy book' of Muslims. We haven't been given a book on the basis of which we came into being as Christianity. The book (the Bible) is the form in which the tradition of faith has provisionally come to rest. I deliberately say 'provisionally'. We shall soon see that this rest is only apparent, and that tradition never stops or solidifies in texts.

First another answer to the question what makes the Bible so important for the Christian church. It's the oldest and most wide-spread form of the Christian puzzle-picture of God. That's what its authority rests on, and on nothing else. I would compare it with the maps which someone like Vasco di Gama had at his disposal when he tried for the first time to sail round the southernmost point of South America to reach the Pacific Ocean. The maps had to show him the way; he was dependent on them. So he followed the instructions on the maps; they had authority for him. Not because of a decree of the king or emperor, but because they were an indispensable guide.

The power of the Bible lies in its content. You lose something if you don't realize that. Not only from a literary point of view, as Maarten 't Hart and Jan Wolkers, who were good Reformed boys, don't weary of telling us, but also in religious terms. Only – pioneers leave you free. You may roam, and sometimes roaming is even pleasant, you may choose to do it – all that kind of problem of authority must be kept far from the Bible. For the worst thing that can happen is that soon no one will read the stories any more. That would be a cultural and religious disaster. The Bible is second to none as a book of examples, stories, tales that people tell.

Why can't Christianity treat the Bible as a breviary? The tradition of faith stands firmly in its shoes; it's become a stream and is no longer the source (Bible) from which it emerged. That makes room for open use of the Bible: for enjoyment, for reading it for the story, not the moral.

The morality of the Bible is time-conditioned, male-centred, patri-archal morality. Polygamy is a sign of wealth – the person who can count lots of wives is blessed by God. Slaves are allowed as long as they are treated reasonably; accountability was only transferred from collective to individual at a later stage. Moral upbringing with the help of the Bible has defied the centuries, partly because the texts have been read selectively (I gave examples; no one praised Abraham because he took some women with him), partly because the Bible expresses the great principles of humanity in terms of a bygone culture. But I repeat: we needn't read the Bible for morality: we read it for the story that bit by bit shows us the face of the God to whom we can say 'You'.

6. How do we read the Bible?

For the Christian church the Bible isn't so much a book of the past which for example you read out of historical interest. Of course it can also be that. How people used to wage war, how they went on voyages at the time of the apostle Paul, how they fished at the time of Peter and his brothers – these are all interesting questions which you could put to the Bible, but they aren't the questions of the Christian church. The church reads the Bible as the saving message of God as it has been expounded by Jesus Christ, and thus asks: have we understood the message of salvation properly? There is every reason for this question. The distance between us and the authors of the time in time and culture is great; the way in which they express themselves is steeped in images and concepts which we do not know, or use quite differently. For antiquity, master and slave were a reality which lent itself well to talking of God as master. But we no longer know any master/slave relationship, so can we still say 'master, lord'? Or does lord mean something very different (or no longer anything)? I'm simply taking a well-known example of terminology which we no longer understand without such an explanation, and want to say that if the question is that of the content of the Bible as a message of salvation, exposition comes in.

Exposition means: how must we read these biblical texts and in what perspective? When have you understood what you read?

To begin with a preliminary remark. What cannot be and thus doesn't happen is for someone to leave out the exposition or interpretation of the biblical text. Even if you think that you know what is there, you've already given an interpretation. To read or to listen to a reader is the same thing as to interpret; otherwise you aren't reading or you stop reading.

Is there a rule for good exposition? The question has come up a good deal in the course of recent years. When I was at college the answer was still simple. To expound was to analyse a text from the past and extract from it a meaning for today by reconstructing what this text meant at the time. Exposition amounted to patient listening, steeping yourself in the author's argument and thus discovering the meaning of his remarks. But that involves a number of things. Do we alone do something with the text? Doesn't the text equally do something with us? At any rate, understanding is more than a historical reconstruction of the meaning of texts by, for example, Paul or John. The hearers or readers of today are also involved. Understanding means that they can join in, that the texts say something to them. Otherwise you can't speak of understanding. It is in this way – and it's the only way – that the readers or hearers of today get their legitimate place in the process of exposition. The text is there, the reader is there, and the meaning arises by the text doing something to the reader and the reader doing something to the text.

This last process can go so far that the readers – in some more recent theories – become the be-all and end-all. They aren't just presupposed by the text, but can also make what they will of it. That's what the text is for. You could say that the way of exposition which I've described went from reconstruction via origin to construction of meaning. In my view, this last goes too far.

7. Raising an echo

The point isn't that people can't make what they will of the biblical text. Exegesis is free; free exegesis is indispensable if we want to keep a 'free Bible'. But not everything can be called exegesis. The text precedes interpretation and it also precedes everything that you make of it; the text is even a necessary condition for the existence of interpretation. That's what I call the priority of the text over the reader or hearer. More rules aren't necessary, only that the priority of the text must be preserved, and that means that exegesis or reading or understanding – in whatever language one may want to use – has at all times to treat the texts responsibly. Even if you say 'We can do anything with it', that 'anything' is still bound to the text; otherwise there would be no need of the text.

A second comment: the text presupposes readers or hearers. Without readers the text remains mute. It depends on readers, it cries out for readers. That's another reason why exegesis is free, must be free and remain free. If exegesis isn't free, then the texts are bound to yesterday's readers, or the readers of the Vatican or of some synod, and we're back where we started: the reader gains priority over the text instead of the text retaining its priority over the reader.

Is there a test for adequate exposition, so that we can say, 'Now I understand what I'm reading'? Indeed, but only as a provisional conclusion. And then in the first instance still in terms of a negative statement: 'You haven't understood because the text doesn't give a point of contact for your reading.' An unassailable positive conclusion ('Now you've understood the text'), if there is one, seems to me to be much more difficult. That means that exegesis always, fortunately, keeps on. It keeps the texts in motion. A text in which ideas, concepts, meanings are expressed is only apparently at rest. That rest becomes the rest of the cemetery when there is no longer any interpretation.

The most attractive metaphor for the relationship between (biblical) text and interpretation that I have come across is that of the text as a piece of music, as a score: the piece has to sound, and for that it needs players, sometimes a whole orchestra. Reading is the same as making a score sound. But (a) it's this text, this piece. Someone who makes Bartok a kind of Schumann hasn't a very good eye, doesn't read very well. And (b) to be able to play a piece well (= to understand what you read) you need training, practice in dealing with music. That's the reason why I would prefer the Bible to be a breviary rather than a book which prescribes what we must think. The Bible is there to reflect on, not to prescribe what we must think.